If you care about the future  he
Shape of Water, Frost masterl. , ..p....s ... ...s......l journey of mission
and evangelism, which not only helps us to understand how we got here but
also offers a compelling vision for the future. This book is for those who are
passionate about mission, and for those who've given up on the whole idea of
evangelism. It is inspiring, thought-provoking, confronting, and captivating; a
call to imagine mission in the future unlike anything we have seen in the past.

CHRISTINE CAINE, founder, A21 and Propel Women

In his winsome scholarly way, Michael Frost expands our imagination for
the various shapes mission takes throughout history. With a steady hand, he
astutely guides us through the history of mission, filling us with hope for what
mission can be in our lives, our churches, our neighborhoods, our cities. I truly
loved reading *Mission Is the Shape of Water*. It made me want to sell everything,
follow Jesus, and serve his mission all over again.

DAVID FITCH, Lindner Chair of Theology, Northern Seminary; author, *Faithful Presence*

Frost has done it again! Compelling, intriguing, educating, and inspiring! A
book that shapes us as we consider mission then and now and how we can
respond to the flow of Holy Spirit.

DANIELLE STRICKLAND, founder, Boundless Communications

One of Christianity's greatest strengths is also one of its key vulnerabilities: it is
a highly transportable faith. It can find a home in twenty-first-century China just
as easily as it did in sixth-century Gaul. And this mission-flexibility can make it
vulnerable to compromise. With these thoughts in mind, Michael Frost has written
a remarkable book examining ten historical paradigms of Christian mission,
showing how the church has succeeded—and sometimes failed—to reach
radically diverse cultures with the unchanging gospel of Christ's life, teaching,
death, and resurrection. *Mission Is the Shape of Water* often inspired me, sometimes
made me uncomfortable, and taught me things in every chapter. That's how I like
my Christian books. I can see this being used as a mission textbook, a small group
study, or simply a source of personal Christian inspiration. I hope it is widely read.

JOHN DICKSON, author and historian; Jean Kvamme Distinguished Professor of
Biblical Studies and Public Christianity, Wheaton College

In this distinctive book, Michael Frost skillfully combines considerable story-telling abilities with his expertise as a leading missiologist to deliver an enlightening account of the profound testimony to Jesus that spans across history. By exploring the lives of various historical saints, heroes, and causes, Frost gleans valuable insights on how to remain faithful to the movement of the gospel passed on to us by our Lord and Savior. An inspiring read!

ALAN HIRSCH, cofounder, Movement Leaders Collective, Forge Missional Training Network, and 5Q Collective

Reading this book felt like a spring walk (a meandering even) through the garden of missional history. We are introduced to people and ideas that are at once somehow strange, beautiful, and compelling. Frost is a wonderful guide, curating stories from Christian history that seem distant but somehow close, ancient but somehow current, connecting all of us to all of them. A delightful writer, Frost's affection for his subjects is surpassed only by his obvious love for the kingdom of God that they portend. So even though it is mostly a look back, you hear a yearning on every page. And you begin to see, in the long thread of our history, the shape of mission.

BRIAN SANDERS, founder, Underground Network; author, *Underground Church*

Another extraordinary book from one of the greatest missional theologians of our day! Using a historical lens to shed light on what is needed for our time, Frost offers us an inspiring and challenging call to reimagine mission and contextualize the good news for our time and place. Read and share this essential book!

LISA RODRIGUEZ-WATSON, national director, Missio Alliance

MISSION
IS THE
SHAPE
OF
WATER

MICHAEL FROST

MISSION IS THE SHAPE OF WATER

LEARNING FROM THE PAST TO INFORM OUR ROLE IN THE WORLD TODAY

100 MOVEMENTS
PUBLISHING

First published in 2023 by 100 Movements Publishing

www.100Mpublishing.com

Copyright © 2023 by Michael Frost

Library of Congress Control Number: 2023909771

ISBN 978-1-955142-40-3 (print)
ISBN 978-1-955142-41-0 (e-book)

Cover image © Artem Sokol | iStock images
Cover design: Jude May

100 Movements Publishing
An imprint of Movement Leaders Collective
Cody, Wyoming
www.movementleaderscollective.com
www.catalysechange.org

As long as I can remember, I have been looking for footprints left by Christians who lived before me.

ROBERTA GREEN AHMANSON

CONTENTS

PROLOGUE

The Shape of Water

*Every generation makes the mistake of assuming it lives at the most
important time in history.*
ANON.

What is the shape of water?

Yeah, yeah, I know it's a 2017 romantic fantasy film, directed by Guillermo del Toro, but I don't mean that. I mean, what is the *actual* shape of water?

Initially, you might think that water is formless, so the answer would be that water has no shape. But a water droplet is spherical. And a puddle has a form. And cartographers agree on the shape of the Caspian Sea. And the water in your drink bottle is shaped like, well, your drink bottle.

The shape of water is determined by whatever container it is in. The container doesn't change the inherent properties of water. Each of its molecules still contains two hydrogen atoms and one oxygen atom. But, like all liquids, the shape of water is the same shape as its receptacle.

Which brings me to mission.

Its shape is also determined by its context.

The inherent nature of Christian mission, like the inherent nature of water, never changes. The mission of God's people has always been to alert others to the universal reign of God through Christ. In fact, even prior to the birth of Christ, God's people saw their mission as announcing his reign. That's why verses like Isaiah 52:7 declare, "How beautiful on the mountains are the feet of those who bring good news, who proclaim peace, who bring good tidings, who proclaim salvation, who say to Zion, 'Your God reigns!'" Written during Israel's Babylonian captivity, the prophet celebrates how right it is that the Jews should declare, "Yahweh reigns" right under the noses of their captors. Whether they were slaves in Babylon or ensconced in Jerusalem, Yahweh reigned, even if all the observable evidence appeared to the contrary. In fact, "Our God reigns" could be a shorthand version of the "gospel" of Israel.

Interestingly, the earliest Christians found great meaning in passages like the one in Isaiah. In fact, the New Testament use of the word *euangelizomai* ("to tell the good news") comes directly from a Hebrew word used in the book of Isaiah: *besar* ("bringer of good news").[1] In both cases the "good news" was about God's good and merciful reign. In the New Testament, that reign is embodied, revealed, and confirmed in the birth, life, teaching, death, and resurrection of Jesus.

Our mission therefore is to alert everyone everywhere to God's universal reign *through Christ*, by both speech and action, by explaining and demonstrating, by word and deed. We proclaim it with our mouths, through our joyful witness to our experience *of* God's reign, by our testimony of coming *under* God's reign, and through evangelistic preaching *about* God's reign. And we show it with our actions, by demonstrating God's reign through acts of kindness and hospitality, through healing and serving others, and by contributing to the flourishing of a just and equitable society.

These essential elements never change. Such mission is always rooted in a deep confidence in the beautiful, just, and healing reign of King Jesus. It is always focused on sharing the good news that God has revealed his kingdom and opened it up to all through the work of Jesus, who will one day return to overthrow evil and consummate that kingdom for eternity. Our message has always been, "Jesus is enthroned and is putting the world aright!" Or, as Jesus himself put it, "The kingdom of God has come near" (Mk 1:15). So, our calling is to demonstrate that truth in word and deed through seeking the redemption, reconciliation, and remediation of all. Indeed, Scripture resounds with the clarion call to "declare his glory among the nations, his marvelous deeds among all peoples" (Ps 96:3).

In his helpful article, *Evangelism in the City*, British theologian and missiologist Lesslie Newbigin said this of the mission of the church:

The congregation must be so deeply and intimately involved in the secular concerns of the neighborhood that it becomes clear to everyone that no one and nothing is outside the range of God's love in Jesus. Christ's message, the original gospel, was about the coming of the kingdom of God, that is to say God's kingly rule over the whole of his creation and the whole of humankind. That is the only authentic gospel. And that means that every part of human life is within the range of the gospel message; in respect of everything the gospel brings the necessity for choice between the rule of God and the negation of his rule. If the good news is to be authentically communicated, it must be clear that the church is concerned about the rule of God and not about itself. It must be clear, that is, that the local congregation cares for the well-being of the whole community and not just for itself.[2]

That is our mission, and it never changes. But the words we use, and how we demonstrate God's reign, are situation specific; the exact contours of the mission of God's people are fluid. Just like water. Mission is determined by the container into which it is poured. It will take different shapes, depending on the culture in which it is presented. And throughout history, our mission has been shaped differently, depending on the challenges and interests of people in each epoch.

FREEING OUR MISSIONAL IMAGINATION

I believe our imagination has been somewhat limited when it comes to thinking about the shape of mission. People tend to harken back to the early church—by which they mean the church described in the Acts of the Apostles—claiming that this is *the* shape that Christian mission should take today. "If only we could emulate the mission of the Jerusalem church," they say. But that church was peculiarly shaped by its time and place. Sure, there is much we can learn from the Jerusalem church, as there is from the churches in Antioch or Corinth or Ephesus or Rome. But we aren't doing mission in the ancient Roman world. Indeed, the very fact that the mission and composition of the churches in Corinth or Rome were so different from that of the church in Jerusalem tells us the apostles knew that context shapes mission, just as a bottle shapes water.

More recently, many have pointed to the Chinese underground church as *the* defining shape of mission. And there are certainly lessons to be learned from Chinese church leaders who took the unchanging nature of mission and shaped it to the extreme challenges of their context under the oppression and persecution of the Maoist regime. It is another *one* of the ways that context has shaped mission.

But if our only points of reference are the early church under Roman persecution and the Chinese church under Communist persecution, are we really able to discern what Christian mission looks like in a post-Christendom Western context? Don't we need our imagination enlarged somewhat?

I'm sure you've heard people (usually old-timers) say we need God to raise up another Billy Graham or D. L. Moody or some other great heroic figure of the past. I always have two reactions to comments like that.

First, if you could miraculously plonk Billy Graham or D. L Moody into twenty-first-century America, they would almost certainly *not* have the effect they had in their day. They were shaped by their contexts and responded brilliantly to the needs and interests of their times; but even those great figures—who had very lengthy ministries—saw their influence waning as they grew older. Culture was changing around them.

My second reaction to those who wish the great men of history were ministering today, has to do with the people they choose. For a start, they're nearly always *men*. I don't hear anyone crying out to God to raise up another Junia or Perpetua or St. Brigid. I can't recall anyone saying we need another Mary Slessor or Aimee Semple McPherson or Mother Teresa. But even the men who *are* proposed as being apparently so necessary for our time are from such a limited range. Why yearn for another C. H. Spurgeon but not one of the greatest evangelists of all time, Francis Xavier? Why hanker after another William Carey but not the real founder of the modern missions movement, Count Nikolaus von Zinzendorf? And why not Simon Kimbangu or Hélder Câmara or St. Boniface? I think I know the reason. Many of us only know a little bit of history—the bit we like the best.

And if the bit we like the best is all we know, we will be forever trapped in that particular historical container. You probably know Abraham Maslow's famous expression, "If the only tool you have is a hammer, it is tempting to treat everything as if it were a nail." Well, it's applicable here too. If we only have one historical container in our imaginations, every mission initiative we think of will fit that container. We don't need another C. H. Spurgeon or Francis Xavier or any other historical figure. We need Christians to be sensitive to the cultural and philosophical landscape in which they find themselves and to develop missional responses specific to that context.

One of the ways to free our imaginations and discover more "containers" is to study history. Yeah, I just said, "study history" and "free your imagination" in the same sentence! Maybe your days in history class at high school killed that possibility for you, but I'm going to try to revive it.

An excessive focus on the present leads to historical and spiritual myopia. We need Christian history to expand our horizons. For some conservative Protestants it's as if the history of the church begins with Paul, jumps fifteen hundred years to Martin Luther and John Calvin, then another two hundred years to Jonathan Edwards and then yet another two hundred years to Billy Graham. But plenty of awesome stuff happened in those big gaps in the timeline.

As historian Lord Acton wrote, "History must be our deliverer not only from the undue influence of other times, but from the undue influence of our own—from the tyranny of environment and the pressures of the air we breathe."[3]

If we're going to understand what the shape of mission looks like in our contexts, we need to understand the container into which it is being poured. To be sure, developing a deep understanding of our environment and our times is essential. But a rich awareness of our history can shed light on present trends and circumstances, helping to explain why things are the way they are today. As Edward Smither says, "Grasping the history of Christianity shapes the global church's consciousness and contributes to a healthy Christian memory."[4]

Cicero put it more bluntly: "To know nothing of what happened before you were born, is to forever remain a child."[5]

THE MANY FACES OF MISSION

Back to water again: did you know that Plato claimed that water takes the shape of the icosahedron, one of the five so-called platonic solids? It turns out that the ancients believed the physical world could be represented by these interlocking polygons—the tetrahedron (four faces), hexahedron (six faces), octahedron (eight faces), dodecahedron (twelve faces), and the icosahedron (twenty faces). Plato took it upon himself to ascribe each shape to an element. So, fire is shaped like a tetrahedron; earth like a hexahedron; air like the octahedron; ether like the dodecahedron; and water like the twenty-faced icosahedron.

I guess the idea was to illustrate the interdependence and confluence of the elements. But I like the idea of water being shaped like a twenty-faced polygon. It could mean that water has many different faces and many different meanings. If water really is shaped like an icosahedron and has twenty faces, I wonder whether we should think about Christian mission as having many faces too. I'm not suggesting Christian mission is a kind of choose-your-own-adventure. Water is water, as mission is mission. But it has taken myriad shapes throughout history and will continue to do so into the future, no doubt.

Ask a bunch of people what Christian mission looks like. They might say it looks like evangelistic preaching or church planting or hosting a feeding center. They might mention running a crisis accommodation facility or providing emergency relief after a hurricane or furnishing medical care in a poor country or advocating against sex trafficking or teaching in a Christian school.

But would they mention desecrating religious idols or establishing a city in Africa for freed slaves or starting an ashram or making beer or photographing mass murder or adopting children offered as human sacrifices or hauling a printing press through the jungle? Would they imagine that being a missionary could look like becoming an explorer or a governor or a prisoner or a student activist? All those shapes of mission are described in this book. Each shape was used by God to achieve his purposes in that time and place. Each of them is told here, not so you can emulate them, but so you can broaden your imagination on what shape God is calling you to take hold of.

Although I am not a professional historian, I am a missiologist and have taught a subject on the history of mission for the past ten years. So, even though I can't offer a comprehensive history of Christian mission, I can help us examine the various "containers" into which mission has been poured throughout the ages, from the perspective of a keen student of mission studies. Not twenty faces, as Plato suggests—but enough, I hope, to stimulate your vision for what mission could look like in your time and place.

It is also worth noting that mission rarely takes just one shape per era. We often think of the post-apostolic era of the early church being all about fierce Christians evangelizing boldly across the Roman Empire and being thrown to the lions in the Colosseum for their trouble. But there are many examples of Christians living quiet, peaceful lives in the empire, practicing hospitality, feeding the hungry, holding weekly love feasts, and sharing their faith with their neighbors. Similarly, in the colonial era of the late 1800s, we tend to imagine missionaries joining European colonizers to destroy Indigenous cultures by Westernizing them. Yet there were many examples of missionaries standing with Indigenous people, opposing colonial governments by calling out their injustices, and embedding themselves deeply in community to serve those to whom God had sent them. And the twentieth century threw up such wildly differing missionary strategies that it can make your head spin. It still astonishes me to think that Albert Schweitzer, Óscar Romero, and Billy Graham were all ministering at the same time. One was a French-German polymath—a liberal theologian, musicologist, philosopher, and physician—who gave his life to serve as a medical missionary in Africa; another was an El Salvadorian Catholic archbishop whose teachings on liberation and a preferential option for the poor saw him assassinated by right-wing forces; and the third was a conservative evangelical Baptist whose large-scale evangelistic rallies were conducted in nearly two hundred countries, attracting more than 215 million people over his lifetime. In a single era, each of them contributed to the shape of mission.

That's not to say everything done in the name of Christian mission should be affirmed or celebrated. As you'll see, many of the people mentioned in this volume made mistakes. Many other missionaries inadvertently contributed to the suffering of Indigenous people and those around them, while still others knowingly contributed to great injustices and atrocities. But, as historian Stephen Neill once wrote, "Christian missionary work is the most difficult thing in the world. It is surprising that it should ever have been attempted. It is surprising that it should have been attended by such a measure of success. And it is not at all surprising that an immense number of mistakes should have been made."[6]

Since I believe we are empowered by having an accurate understanding of history, we will examine the mistakes as well as the triumphs in our past so that we can develop a "healthy Christian memory" and find the courage to engage in mission in our own time and place. If we indiscriminately lionize old heroic figures, portraying them as flawless in their character and unparalleled in their work, we only paralyze ourselves into inaction.

In the second volume of *Church History* by John Woodbridge and Frank James, the authors sound this encouraging note:

> The history of the church reminds us that Christians can be culprits of foolishness as well as bold titans for truth. They can be egoistic and self-serving; they can be humble and generous. A single individual can embody

conflicting traits. We may find it disconcerting to discover that our heroes
are sometimes flawed ... [But] God works through sinners to accomplish
his good purposes.[7]

"BE WATER!"

There's yet another aspect to my mission-as-water analogy. It comes from
the pro-democracy protesters in Hong Kong who adopted the mantra
of local movie star Bruce Lee: "Be water."[8] This refers to the movement's
commitment to a highly mobile, agile style of protest. Rallies turned into
marches. Marches dispersed into side streets. Mass protests divided quickly
into multiple protests around the city. As one well-known protest sign read,
"We are formless, we are shapeless, we can flow, we can crash, we are like
water, we are Hongkongers."[9]

Water flows over hard surfaces and seeps into dry land. It diffuses into
cracks and crevices. It can appear like a gentle mist, or rage like a mighty torrent.
In the same way, the mission of God's people has always been like water. In
some contexts and eras, it has crashed on the shore and swept away what was
there before. At other times, it has risen slowly but inexorably. At other points,
it has had to bleed into small fissures, almost unnoticed. In yet others, it has
flowed like a babbling stream. It moves differently in contexts of persecution
and violence, poverty and fear, wealth and pride. As Bruce Lee put it, "Water
can flow or crash!" So can God's missional people.

I think mission is like water.

The key to understanding the Hongkongers' analogy of water is to know
the size of the protests they held. At one march in June 2019, it is estimated
that 1.03 million people filled the streets of the city. It became common for
protests of several hundred thousand people to suddenly cram one street,
only to retreat when the Communist regime's police arrived. Then they would
reemerge elsewhere. A mobile app was designed to allow the crowdsourcing
of the location of each action. In the streets, the protesters developed a series
of hand gestures for nonverbal communication that rippled across the crowd,
allowing them to be fluid and agile enough to confound the police. They ferried
supplies by hand through human chains. Some protesters acted as scouts,
sharing updates on police movements. As well as mass rallies and marches,
the Hongkongers engaged in hunger strikes, human chains, labor strikes,
and boycotts. They displayed protest art, set up pop-up stores to sell protest

gadgets, and they provided undercover medical clinics for those activists in need of assistance.

It is true that some of the Hong Kong protests turned violent and that some of the protesters took a more radical stance than others. But my point in using them as an illustration is that their water analogy works because there were so many peaceful protesters—close to one million people—who committed to being part of the "flow" of anti-Communist protest.

The study of Christian history reveals that mission is the same. The world is rarely changed by single heroic figures. The shape of mission is never epitomized by the life of one famous missionary, no matter how impressive their ministry was. Mission is like water, in that it flows most effectively when hundreds or thousands of nameless, faceless Christians humbly submit to the task of contributing their bucket to the torrent.

I remember having this idea surprisingly reinforced for me in a park in the American northeast. Tucked into the northwest corner of Massachusetts in the stunning Berkshires lies Williamstown, a small college town best known for being the home of the exclusive Williams College. I was passing through the area when my host told me Williams was famous in the world of American missions because it was where the 1806 "Haystack Prayer Meeting" had occurred. I was embarrassed to admit that I was unaware of what that was, so he took the opportunity to turn off the freeway and detour through the town. There, on the fringe of the Williams College campus, in a rather unimpressive park, is one of those metal historical markers that you find across the US. This one read: "On this site in the shelter of a haystack during a summer storm in 1806 five Williams College students dedicated their lives to the service of the church around the globe. Out of their decision grew the American Foreign Mission movement."

I had questions. First, how do you take shelter in a haystack? Aren't they just big round balls of cut grass? Well, it turns out that back in the nineteenth century, farmers used wooden frames, like a teepee, to stack newly harvested hay into a cone-shaped mound. They would leave the inside hollow to prevent it from fermenting and catching fire. The five Williams students had been meeting in a nearby grove of trees to discuss William Carey's book on foreign missions when a wild summer thunderstorm whipped up. Seeing the hollowed-out haystack in the nearby field, they made a break for it.

Makes sense. But how could something as prosaic as five young men waiting out a rainstorm in a haystack ignite the American foreign mission movement? In their hiding place, the five men continued their conversation and then prayed, asking God to reveal his will for them regarding overseas mission. Afterward, they sang a hymn. It was then that one of them, Samuel J. Mills, the twenty-three-year-old son of a Connecticut clergyman, announced loudly over the wind and rain, "We can do this, if we will!" The moment must have sent chills through the students. In his history of Williams College, Arthur Latham Perry wrote, "The brevity of the shower, the strangeness of the place of refuge, and the peculiarity of their topic of prayer and conference all took hold of their imaginations and their memories."[10]

Flushed with enthusiasm, they decided to form a permanent prayer group on campus and called it the Haystack Prayer Meeting. I assume they chose a bigger venue than the cramped haystack because within a couple of years it had become a large student group called "The Brethren" (Williams was an all-male school at the time), whose purpose was to promote and mobilize students to foreign mission service. Two years later, The Brethren morphed into the American Board of Commissioners for Foreign Missions (ABCFM). In 1812, they sent their first missionaries to India.

I share that story because that nondescript park in Williamstown felt to me like the site of a modest fissure from which leaked a small spring, which would eventually turn into a torrent of mission. The names of those five devoted students, who met together near the Hoosic River in Sloan's Meadow, were recorded, but they are largely forgotten today.[11] But from that small spring flowed a river of mission work. On the 150th anniversary of its formation, the ABCFM announced that they had sent out nearly five thousand missionaries to thirty-four different countries.

Some of us will be called by God to be at the headwaters of a new flow. Others of us will be called, like droplets in a mighty river, to play our small part in contributing to the surge of love and grace throughout the world. If only we are willing.

LEARNING TO BE LESS AMBITIOUS

Recently, a pastor named Joey Cochrane wrote a *Christianity Today* story about how studying church history made him less ambitious.[12] He examined the personal lives of some of his favorite evangelical leaders from history—people like the seventeenth-century pietist August Hermann Francke and the early twentieth-century Dutch theologian and politician Abraham Kuyper. And he discovered that their family lives were a mess. They were often so overworked, or in Kuyper's case wracked by depression, that they neglected their wives and children.

We could easily compile a lengthy list of the famous Christian men throughout history who were disinterested husbands and fathers, some of whom were out-and-out delinquent in their responsibilities. My wife, Caz, says she wishes church history, dominated as it is by men, was written by the wives of famous men rather than their male biographers. But Cochrane's point isn't that we necessarily need more exposés; instead he says we need to celebrate the less impressive achievements of women and men who prioritized their families as part of their commitment to mission.

Cochrane wrote, "I think what evangelicals actually need is *less* fascination with the dark sides of our fallen heroes and more appreciation for the quiet, daily faithfulness of pastors, professors, revivalists, and activists who managed to swim against the powerful social and cultural currents of their times that often placed an unrealistic demand on their output and performance."[13]

Maybe our fascination with the heroic figures of the past comes down to our lack of faith that God can accomplish great things by a torrent of unnamed, faceless everybodies. We think God needs heroes. But the stories you'll read about in this book—while dotted with some impressive women and men—are the narrative of mission being shaped like water, flowing inexorably toward the end God intended from the beginning. It is the story of the "less ambitious" souls who submitted themselves to God's purposes and quietly went about that work in every corner of the globe.

After young Sam Mills zealously exclaimed, "We can do it, if we will," his haystack companions took the line as their motto. It's a somewhat ambiguous sentence. It suggests that, although they felt they had the capacity to do what God was calling them to, up until that point they had lacked the *will*. It sounds like he was saying, "If we set our minds to this, we can do it!" There's nothing like the naivety of youth, is there? But God in his grace can work with our overconfidence as much as he can with our lack of confidence. However, God chooses not to work contrary to our wills.

My purpose in this book is to expand your imagination, to help you develop a healthier Christian memory, and to inspire you to action; to lessen your ambition to become a hero and increase your belief that God wants to partner with you in his mission. God won't necessarily make you famous or do extraordinary things through you, but God will marshal your contribution to his unstoppable mission—whether it is large or small, decisive, or insignificant—to rescue, restore, and reconcile all things through his son, Jesus.

We only need to be willing to explore what questions God is asking of us in our time and to ask what we can draw from the historical examples we'll look at to help us discern what our shape of mission should be.

So, let us start at the beginning ...

The First Shape

GOD SLAYING

I am a Christian. No need to wring the confession by torture. I avow it.
Your gods? I do destroy them–not in remote and secret places–but openly,
publicly, where magistrates and governors can hear.

CYPRIAN OF CARTHAGE

In *Damascus*, a fictionalized account of the life of St. Paul, novelist Christos Tsiolkas imagines the brutality of life in the first century AD. Cruel sacrifices are made in temples. Men get drunk and find crude pleasure in brothels and with their slave girls. There is violence, death, and misery. The atmosphere is foul and tragic, and the narrative is littered with slaves and refugees, the starving and the helpless.

An Ephesian woman named Lydia finds life just as brutish. Aside from the normal travails of a loveless marriage and the threat of starvation, she suffers a terrible grief at having a daughter born without an arm and being forced to leave her to die on a hillside—a second-rate offering to the gods. Her anguish gives way to fury, and she secretly comes to loathe the gods that appear so indifferent to her situation and the suffering of her child.

Eventually she finds her way to the Christian evangelist Paul, who offers comfort in her grief and speaks to her guilt at having abandoned her disabled child to the wolves. Initially, Lydia is furious with him, and rages at the stupidity of his belief in one God and one Lord named "Jesus"—a mere criminal executed by the Romans. But Paul persists, "Don't you understand, Lydia? This Jesus whom you believe scandalous and base, he knows what your daughter suffered. He knows because he understands what it is to be the most despised. Don't you see, sister? Our Lord is not only the Lord of justice. He is also the Lord of love."

When Lydia calms herself, Paul asks, "What other gods would weep for your child?"

At that moment, in the humble home of a Christian family, surrounded by other believers, Lydia is changed. She says, "I looked around the decrepit hut. No incense, no altars, no idols. I did not understand, but at that moment I pledged myself to their world and not the world of the gods. I dried my eyes and I said, 'I believe.'"[1]

Christos Tsiolkas's novel skillfully portrays the horrors of the ancient religious world: the constant sacrifice; the bowing and scraping to a pantheon of gods who at best are unmoved by their worshiper's circumstances; the fertility gods and the lower gods who must be satisfied; and the higher gods who could send floods, droughts, famine, or pestilence. Every misfortune set off a horrible rhythm of guessing and second-guessing as to which god was offended and why. No wonder the Christian message offered strange relief to those victimized by paganism. Such religious neuroticism is soul-crushing.

We catch a glimpse of this in the Acts of the Apostles, where the Lystrans have mistaken Paul and Barnabas for the Greek gods Zeus and Hermes (Acts 14:8–18). At that time, there was a well-known regional folk tale that the gods had once visited earth, looking for a bed and a meal. Only one poor, elderly woman took the gods in, unaware of who they were, and shared her meager portions with them. Everyone else turned their back on the strangers, closing their doors on them. In retaliation, Zeus and Hermes slew everyone except for the woman, upon whom they lavished a great bounty. So, when Paul and Barnabas arrive in town, miraculously healing a man who had been lame since birth, the Lystrans aren't about to make the same mistake twice. Terrified that this could be a second incarnation of the gods, they scream in terror, "The gods have come down to us in human form!" (Acts 14:11) and send word to the priest of Zeus—who arrives with a sacrificial bull.

The Lystrans' immediate attempt to appease the gods shows how deep their fear ran. The gods were capricious and untrustworthy. People were merely pawns in their hands, like mice being toyed with by a cat.

Paul is aghast at the Lystran's misunderstanding and tells them, "We are bringing you good news, telling you to turn from these worthless things to the living God, who made the heavens and the earth and the sea and everything in them" (Acts 14:15).

In the deathly morass of polytheism, the news that there is only one God—who made the heavens and the earth, and who loves us—is indeed good news.

This was the cultural container into which Christian mission was poured in the first few centuries of the church's existence. The shape of mission for the early church necessarily involved the destruction of idols, the debunking of myths, the offer of freedom, and the message of hope. And the first followers of Jesus had their work cut out for them. If it wasn't enough to address the terror caused by the belief in the erratic Greco-Roman gods, Christians also faced a spate of new religions that sprouted up across the Middle East and Asia Minor at that time. These "mystery religions"—which we now group under the general heading of Gnosticism—brought scores of new, esoteric gods. There were literally gods everywhere!

"God slaying" was therefore an essential component of Christian mission. Today, god slaying sounds like a somewhat disrespectful way to undertake mission. We blanch at the thought of missionaries going to foreign lands and attacking the beliefs of those who live there. And rightly so. In the twenty-first century—where the West has dominated the global economy, politics, and the religious landscape—it is indeed disrespectful for wealthy, powerful Westerners to do violence to Indigenous faith practices. But in first-century Asia Minor, polytheism had created a pitiless world, especially for women and children and the poor. And the earliest Christians came to them, not from a position of cultural superiority but as fellow commoners set free by Christ. Slaying gods brought freedom to oppressed people.

So, let us now look at how those early god-slayers engaged their culture in order to understand the shape of their mission.

A SENT PEOPLE

Christians living in the years 50 to 450 were profoundly aware of their responsibility as a *sent people*. Pastors and missional practitioners Kim Hammond and Darren Cronshaw refer to this concept as "sentness"—the way that being sent by God into the world shapes one's identity and practice.[2] And the early church had buckets of sentness. They believed they had been dispatched to poor, frightened people to set them free from the bullying, capricious gods who were crushing them.

Here is the ancient historian Eusebius describing the sentness of the church in this period:

> And they, as being distinguished disciples of such great men, went on, in every place of the churches, building the foundation which had been laid by the Apostles, further extending the preaching, and sowing the saving seed of the kingdom of heaven widely throughout the whole world. For indeed most of those who were then disciples, soul-struck with a love, more violent than desire for wisdom, towards the divine Word, had fulfilled the former exhortation concerning salvation, dividing their goods among the needy. And then setting out on journeys abroad, they were fulfilling the work of evangelists, making it their aim to preach Christ to those who had not yet heard the word of the Faith and to pass on the scripture of the divine Gospels. And all that these did was to lay foundations of the Faith in certain foreign parts. Then they appointed others as pastors, and put in their hands the nurture of those newly brought in, and themselves went on to other countries again, and other nations, God giving them grace and working with them. For then still a great many wonderful powers of the divine Spirit were working in and through them, so that from the first hearing, multitudes together as one man accepted in their souls reverence toward the Creator of the universe. It is impossible for us to enumerate by name all who, from the first succession to the Apostles, have become pastors and evangelists in the churches throughout the world.[3]

Eusebius was clearly impressed.

Notice how this description mirrors the way Jesus commissioned his twelve disciples, giving them "authority to drive out impure spirits and to heal every disease and sickness" (Mt 10:1), and sending them out to proclaim the kingdom (Mt 10:16–42). As they went, preaching the good news of the kingdom, the early Christians accompanied their preaching with "a great many wonderful powers of the divine Spirit."

In a time when most people didn't travel far from their hometown or region unless they were traders, it's remarkable that the early Christians considered themselves sent people. They were profoundly aware of their responsibility to share the good news of the kingdom with every tribe, nation, and tongue. And share the good news they did! But how did they do it?

ARTLESS EVANGELISM

In the book of Acts, the only specifically evangelistic sermons we have are from Peter and Paul. They give us a glimpse into the content of the early church's witness—whether by preaching or by more relational means, such as conversational faith sharing. Trying to figure out what evangelism looked like after Peter and Paul is an interesting challenge. One useful source for this comes in the form of a series of third-century documents called the *Clementine Literature*, two of which (the *Clementine Recognitions* and the *Clementine Homilies*) purport to be the recollections of a man named Clement, telling the story of his conversion by Barnabas and his missionary travels with Peter. There is much conjecture about who wrote these documents and whether Clement really was a convert of Barnabas or a friend of Peter, but even if they are fictitious, they still provide a fascinating snapshot into ancient evangelistic practice.

Clement (or pseudo-Clement, as historians refer to him) begins by detailing his religious searching, his doubts about the afterlife, his love of celibacy, and other background material, before focusing on his encounter with an evangelist preaching in Rome. The *Homilies* state that this man was Barnabas, although the *Recognitions* say Clement didn't meet Barnabas until later in Alexandria. In any case, the depiction of the preaching of this evangelist gives us a helpful insight into what mission was like then—particularly the role of public proclamation.

Wandering through Rome, Clement sees a crowd in an open marketplace or square and hears a commotion. Intrigued, he draws closer and sees it is a preacher contending with a fractious audience. Clement writes, "Then I went with them. And I came, and stood with a crowd which was standing around, and listened to his words."[4]

Even if this is a novel, rather than a historical report, it reveals what the author understood early Christian evangelism to look like. He continues:

> I came to the conclusion that he was speaking truth, not with dialectic skill, but setting forth in an artless way and without preparation, what he had both heard and seen ... And even from the crowd standing around he produced

many witnesses in support of what he was saying. But while the crowds welcomed what he was guilelessly saying, the philosophers, whose motives were from secular culture, fell to laughing and scoffing at him, making jokes and pulling to pieces with immoderate assurance, bringing to bear, like great armaments, their syllogisms.

But he thrust aside their trifling, and was not for accepting combat with their artful questioning, but undaunted, did not break off from what he had to say.[5]

What stands out to you from this picture of evangelism? I'm drawn to the author's several references to the detractors' "art*ful* questioning" and the evangelist's "art*less*" preaching.

The philosophers' "artful" communication would have been sophisticated, well prepared, and self-conscious. To refer to someone as "artful" is to compliment them as clever or skillful, especially in a crafty or cunning way. In other words, the evangelist's detractors had turned up with pre-prepared objections. They had practiced their interjections to make themselves look intelligent and to make the evangelist look foolish.

In contrast, referring to the preaching as "artless" indicates that the preacher spoke extemporaneously, and, as Clement says, "without preparation." What is implied here is that it was raw, personal, passionate communication. Today, this is the kind of public discourse we are often drawn to. It seems more authentic than an overly rehearsed speech or a series of memorized talking points. But in ancient times, emotional, heart-felt speech was considered unsophisticated, precisely because it was unprepared. This might have been what Paul was referring to when he told the Corinthians he had preached the gospel to them "not with wisdom and eloquence, lest the cross of Christ be emptied of its power" (1 Cor 1:17). Nonetheless, the writer of the *Clementine Homilies* is impressed by the "guileless" nature—the sincerity—of the preacher.

The *Clementine Homilies* gives us this precious glimpse of early evangelistic mission: the preaching was from the heart. It was sincere, innocent, and without deception, even in the face of cynically concocted heckling.

Also, note that "from the crowd standing around he produced many witnesses in support of what he was saying." In other words, this wasn't a single evangelist at work. There was a group of them, working together, one taking the lead, while the others provided support from the audience.

SLAYING FALSE GODS

Today, we tend to share our faith by commending the beauty of the gospel and the benefits of God's grace. That might be because, in the increasingly secular West, we assume most people either have a distant memory of their church-going upbringing or they have no faith at all. The early Christians couldn't make either assumption. Because of the explosion of "mystery religions"—each with its own esoteric take on spirituality—if the early Christians had *just* preached Christ, their hearers might have simply added Jesus to the smorgasbord of gods already on offer. The early Christians didn't want to add Jesus to the polytheistic buffet. They wanted to wipe the buffet clear, shattering all other religions on the floor and presenting Jesus as the only God on the table. They believed they had to kill these false gods. And the Christian's playbook on that had been written by a fellow named Lactantius—a Christian adviser to Emperor Constantine I. Historian Kenneth Scott Latourette describes him this way:

> Lactantius, a teacher of rhetoric and a pupil of Arnobius, who, like the latter, did not come into the church until mature life, but who was later entrusted with the education of one of the sons of Constantine, wrote a book which he addressed to Constantine and whose title may be translated as *The Divine Institutes.*[6]

That book was a classically styled, philosophical refutation of the anti-Christian tracts that had begun circulating from Gnostic and Roman scholars. In it, Lactantius prescribed the following approach:

> Now the first step is to understand religions which are false, and to cast aside the impious worship of gods made with hands. The second step is to perceive with the mind the fact that God is one, most high, whose power and providence made the world from the beginning, and direct it towards a future ... The third step is to know His Servant and Messenger, whom he sent on embassy to earth.[7]

Lactantius's approach can be summarized as (1) attacking polytheism and (2) presenting Christ. Let's look at each of those tactics.

THE ATTACK ON POLYTHEISM

Trying to refute belief in multiple gods didn't start with Lactantius. As already mentioned, Paul attacked polytheism in his ministry at Lystra. And in Athens, at a meeting of the Areopagus, he berates idol worship this way:

> "The God who made the world and everything in it is the Lord of heaven and earth and does not live in temples built by human hands … Therefore, since we are God's offspring, we should not think that the divine being is like gold or silver or stone—an image made by human design and skill."
>
> ACTS 17:24, 29

Lactantius continues this tradition, but the post-apostolic Christians tend to be less tactful than Paul in Lystra or Athens. To our modern ears, their assaults on polytheism are almost offensive. Latourette says Lactantius "pilloried … the absurdities of the prevailing polytheism and the immoralities of the gods."[8]

Their argument was twofold.

First, the early Christians would ridicule the uselessness of inanimate objects. And I mean *ridicule.* Evangelists would mock idols, showing them to be merely wood or metal, saying they had no power or effectiveness. Listen to how one early church apologist makes this argument. There's no gentleness here:

> With what discernment indeed to dumb animals judge by light of nature concerning your gods! Mice, swallows, kites, know they have no feelings. They gnaw them, trample them, sit on them. Unless you drive them off they would nest in the god's mouth. Spiders spin over his face, hang their webs from his very head. You wipe and clean and scrape, and those whom you make and protect—you fear! It never occurs to you that you ought to know God before you worship Him … That which supports the general madness is the multitude of mad people.[9]

If anyone in their audience claimed they had prayed to their god, making appropriate sacrifices and supplications, and that the god had heard them and answered their prayer, the Christians had a common response: any efficacy derived from praying to this piece of wood or stone was in fact the deception of an evil spirit. This was the *second* plank of their attack on polytheism—evil forces manifest themselves in idols to prevent individuals from seeing the truth.

Second-century church father Justin Martyr, in his *First Apology*, makes this point:

> In time past, low-down demons contrived manifestations of themselves. They seduced women, and defiled boys, and showed themselves as terrors to men, so that those who did not judge of this behavior by reason were thunderstruck. Carried away by fear, and not recognizing them for low-down demons, they styled them "gods" and hailed each demon by the name that each had chosen for himself.[10]

The basic message was, "Your god is just a useless lump of wood, and if it has afforded you any value, it's the power of a deceiving demon, not a god." Note the commonality with Paul's argument to the Corinthians, where, after explaining that he has presented the gospel with plain speech and without guile, he writes, "The god of this age has blinded the minds of unbelievers, so that they cannot see the light of the gospel that displays the glory of Christ, who is the image of God" (2 Cor 4:4).

PRESENTING CHRIST

Having cleared the buffet of all other gods, the earliest evangelists would then present Christ as the only God and Savior. And here there is much we could emulate today. Historian and missionary John Foster notes the variety of ways they do this:[11]

By appealing to the Hebrew Scriptures. You might think that Gentile audiences wouldn't care much about the Hebrew Scriptures, but the early Christians nonetheless explicitly anchored their teaching about Jesus in Old Testament prophecy. For example, Justin quotes the Old Testament 114 times in his *First Apology*. In this the early Christians were following the example of Peter and Paul, who did so in their preaching.[12]

It seems the early church was anxious not to appear to be presenting a brand-new religion to the empire. As Gnostic religions were popping up everywhere around this time, the church felt it was important to show the historical depth of their faith in Christ, and that his birth, teaching, death, and resurrection had been foretold for generations.

By using the concept of the Logos. Pagan Romans didn't hold the Hebrew

Scriptures as authoritative. Why should they believe what Israel's prophets had said? John Foster explains:

> It was soon evident that a preacher to the heathen who would get his message home, must think not only of the scriptures which he might bring, but of a point of contact with all that his hearers brought. For a missionary of the second century, what could compare, as a point of contact, with the widespread philosophic conception of the *Logos*?[13]

According to learned Greeks and some Hellenized Jews, the *Logos* (Word) was "the Way"—a pre-existing force by which all things were made, the energizing force that sustained the world, and the moral order that maintained stability and tranquility. Hellenized Jews seized upon this idea and claimed that force was in fact Yahweh.

But the early Christians went further, claiming the *Logos* was not just a stabilizing force but had become personified in human form. In other words, they would preach, "The *Logos* of which you speak—the all-pervasive, creative, sustaining power that holds all things together—that power became a man named Jesus."

This is evident in John 1:1–4:

> In the beginning was the Word, and the Word was with God, and the Word was God. He was with God in the beginning. Through him all things were made; without him nothing was made that has been made. In him was life, and that life was the light of all mankind. The light shines in the darkness, and the darkness has not overcome it.

It can also be seen in Paul's letter to the Colossians. Although he doesn't directly refer to the *Logos*, the idea of Christ as the all-pervasive force that holds the universe together is clear when he writes,

> The Son is the image of the invisible God, the firstborn over all creation. For in him all things were created: things in heaven and on earth, visible and invisible, whether thrones or powers or rulers or authorities; all things have been created through him and for him. He is before all things, and in him all things hold together.
>
> COLOSSIANS 1:15–17

Similarly, in *The Epistle of Mathetes to Diognetus*, the writer says, "Truly God Himself, almighty, all-creating, and invisible, Himself from heaven has sent the Truth and the Logos, holy and incomprehensible," after which he explains, "In gentleness and meekness as a King He sent His kingly Son."[14] The *Logos* is not only the unifying power of the universe, but it has also been sent to us as the man, Jesus. This was a primitive form of contextualization and theology, and it had a powerful effect.

In his book on the early church, John Foster, a former missionary to China, explains how this same approach worked there:

> During my fifteen years in China I knew what it was to stand in a similar situation with regard to pre-Christian thought there. Tao is "the Way"—the Way all things were made, Itself before all things; the Moral Order, the Way men should live, Itself the incomparable Good.[15]

Foster goes on to explain that John's Gospel was translated into Chinese as, "In the beginning was the Tao, and the Tao was with Shang-ti [Lord of Heaven], and the Tao was Shang-ti. All things were made by Him ... And the Tao became flesh and dwelt among us."[16]

For the early Christians, presenting Christ as such a pervasive life-giving force showed the redundancy of polytheism. There was no longer a need for fertility gods or earth spirits or any heavenly pantheon of capricious deities because Christ is before all things and in him all things hold together. He is loving and trustworthy. This message was heard with great relief by those terrorized by the fear of the gods.

By witnessing to their own conversion. Just as Saul's conversion is told three times in the New Testament, the early church Fathers were more than willing to share their own conversion stories, attesting to the power of the gospel in their personal experience. Tatian the Assyrian, a second-century Christian theologian, had spent some of his early life studying Greek philosophy, and had even been initiated into a Gnostic cult. His study of the Hebrew scriptures and his disgust with pagan Roman religion led to his conversion to Christianity:

> With my thoughts bent upon these weighty themes, I chanced to come across certain barbarian scriptures, too old to compare with the teachings of Greeks, too divine to compare with their error. I came to put my trust in

these, because there was no conceit about their style, nor anything artificial
about the speakers, the composition of it all was easy to understand, things
to come were foretold, the messages given beyond expectation, and the
universe had one guiding principle. And, my soul taught of God, I understood that there are some things which tend toward condemnation, but
others which set free from the bondage of the world, and snatch us from
rulers many, aye from ten thousand tyrants.[17]

Note Tatian's emphasis on the liberation from bondage that resulted from the
slaying of oppressive gods in his life.

Another writer, the third-century bishop Gregory Thaumaturgus (also
known as the Miracle Worker; a student of Origen) describes his conversion
more emotionally: "Like some spark it came dropping into my inmost soul,
and there, being kindled and catching fire, was love: Love towards the Word
(Logos) Himself ... the most lovely, and towards this man, His friend and
representative."[18]

By demonstrating the Christian life. The early Christians devoted
themselves to sacrificial acts of kindness, loved their enemies, and forgave their
persecutors. They cared for the poor and fed the hungry. Amid the brutality of
life under Roman rule, they were the most stunningly different people anyone
had ever seen. Indeed, their influence was so surprising that even the fourth-
century Emperor Julian (331–363) feared they might take over the empire.
Referring to Christians as "atheists" (because they denied the existence
of pagan gods), and believing their religion to be a sickness, he penned this
directive to his officials:

We must pay special attention to this point, and by this means effect a cure
[for the "sickness" of Christianity]. For when it came about that the poor
were neglected and overlooked by the [pagan] priests, then I think the
impious Galileans [Christians] observed this fact and devoted themselves
to philanthropy. And they have gained ascendancy in the worst of the deeds
through the credit they win for such practices. For just as those who entice
children with a cake, and by throwing it to them two or three times induce
them to follow them, and then, when they are far away from their friends
cast them on board a ship and sell them as slaves ... by the same method,
I say, the Galileans also begin with their so-called love-feast, or hospitality,

or service of tables—for they have many ways of carrying it out and hence call it by many names—and the result is that they have led very many into atheism [i.e., Christianity]. Why do we not observe that it is their benevolence to strangers, their care for the graves of the dead and the pretended holiness of their lives that have done most to increase atheism? I believe that we ought really and truly to practice every one of those virtues ... For it is disgraceful that when the impious Galileans support not only their own poor but ours as well, all men see that our people lack aid from us.[19]

By the attraction of Christian community. Diognetus, Aristides, and Origen all commend the beauty and power of Christian community as "proof" of the truth of the gospel. Here is how Aristides puts it: "He who has, provides extra without reproach for him who has not. If they see a stranger, they bring him in to shelter, and rejoice over him as a very brother, for they call one another 'brothers' ... And they are ready to lay down their lives for the sake of Christ."[20]

By the contagiousness of their triumphalism. All the aforementioned techniques—preaching the Bible, appealing to commonly held ideas, sharing personal testimonies, demonstrating the values of the kingdom, and living out Christian community—are still things we might do today, but the sixth thing that characterized the shape of the early church's mission of god slaying was their incredible confidence in the triumph of Christ. They genuinely believed Christianity was taking over the empire, and nothing could stop it. Read this lengthy but interesting passage from the early Christian author Tertullian, written around the year 200:

> We have filled everything of yours, cities, tenements, fortresses, towns, markets, the very camps, divisions, companies, palace, senate, forum. We have left you only the temples. We can estimate your armies; in a single province they might be more. Despite inequality as to troops for what war should we not both be capable and ready, we who so willingly face slaughter, if it were not preferred, according to this discipline of ours, to let us be slain rather than let us slay? We could, both unarmed and without insurrection, join battle with you by just going on strike, by ill-will leading to a mere walk-out. For if we, so great a force of men, were to break off from you for some shore at the world's end, it would surely covert your empire with shame for loss of so many citizens, of whatever kind, yes, and the very

desertion would prove your punishment. Doubtless you would be terrified
at your loneliness, at everything gone silent, at a certain stillness as of a
world that is dead. You would search about, whom you could govern. You
would be left with more enemies than citizens.[21]

The picture is one of a declining Roman Empire, propped up entirely by the
goodwill of Christians who have permeated every aspect of society. Indeed,
later Tertullian says, "Humankind has always deserved nought of good from
God's hands ... Yet, if we compare calamities of former times, they fall more
lightly now, since God gave Christians to the world."[22]

GOD SLAYING IS A DANGEROUS BUSINESS

When you start dismantling the ancient religious structures of a whole empire,
you can be sure you will be met with resistance. The violent persecution of the
Christians as a consequence of their missional work was swift and vicious. The
reasons for that oppression are varied. Of course, there were religious motivations; some Romans were genuinely fearful that the gods would retaliate if they
discovered that humans were turning from their belief in them and abandoning
their sacrifices. But there were nationalistic motivations as well. To be Roman
was to be in the thrall of the *Roman* gods, not a Jewish-style monotheism or an
Israelite savior. And the tip of that spear was the belief in the divinity of Caesar
himself. The mission of the Christians was seen as a treasonous activity.

But naturally, economics played a part too. Threatening a whole religious
system that is maintained by priests and temples—with whole industries
committed to the manufacture of idols and amulets—is likely to incur the
wrath of those that perpetuate such a system. We get a glimpse of this in Acts
19, when Paul and his friends are engulfed in a riot in Ephesus, started by the
disgruntled silversmiths whose work had been disrupted by the Christians'
preaching.

A businessman named Demetrius, who made silver shrines of Artemis,
stirred his fellow silversmiths into chanting, "Great is Artemis of the Ephesians!"
(Acts 19:28). This might sound like religious devotion, except we've already
heard Demetrius' earlier speech to his colleagues, in which he announced,
"There is danger not only that our trade will lose its good name, but also that
the temple of the great goddess Artemis will be discredited" (19:27). Their
motivation is hardly devotional. It is mercantile.

Persecution usually began with lies to discredit the Christians and alienate them from their potential converts. In Minucius Felix's story of the conversion of the Roman lawyer Octavius Januarius, around the year 200, he describes what he and other Roman intellectuals had thought of the early Christians:

> Accept it from us, as from people who remember with sorrow their own attitude, how unfair it is to pass judgment without knowledge and examination of the facts. We once fancied that Christians worshipped monsters, devoured infants, and joined in incestuous banquets ... [and accepted] slanderous stories about Christians adoring the genitals of a priest.[23]

Christians not only had to endure arrest, torture, and execution for their faith, but they were also the subjects of this kind of gross attack on their beliefs and behavior. When it became known that Christians referred to their spouses as "sister" or "brother" (in Christ), their detractors charged them with incest. Having heard they drank "blood" and ate "flesh" as part of their weekly ritual, the Roman authorities claimed they practiced cannibalism.

Even after the strange conversion of Emperor Constantine I and the end of imperial persecution, Christians were maligned by many. As we noted earlier, when the church became known for all the good they were doing in the empire, Emperor Julian the Apostate (331–363) dismissed it as "pretended holiness" and declared that their mission was to "increase atheism," by which he meant to turn people away from belief in the classic gods. He was wrong on the former—their holiness was no pretense—but he was right about the latter. The Christians were indeed promoting atheism: an unbelief in pagan gods. Julian attempted to steer the Roman Empire back toward a belief in the pantheon of gods—hence his title "the Apostate"—but to no avail.

And so, after the slander failed, the early Christians became the objects of the most horrific forms of torture and death. Tales of their martyrdom are well known, if not sometimes overstated. In her book *The Myth of Persecution*, Candida Moss, professor of theology at the University of Birmingham, UK, challenges some of the assumptions we often make about the nature of Roman persecution. Though it's often held that attacks were widespread and organized, Moss believes they were scattered and haphazard, concluding "Christians were never the victims of sustained, targeted persecution."[24] But when incidents did occur, they were shocking, as was the case with Polycarp of Smyrna, who was burned to death when he refused to renounce Christianity; and Ignatius of Antioch, who was thrown to the wild beasts in the arena. In his book on the impact of Christianity on European society, historian Tom Holland says,

> The willingness of Christians to embrace excruciating tortures—which to those who sentenced them could only appear as lunacy—was founded on an awesome conviction: that their Savior was by their side. More than the temples and the fields for which the antique heroes of Rome had been willing to sacrifice themselves, Christ's presence was something real. He was there in the arena, as once he had been nailed to the cross.[25]

The effect of this behavior cannot be overstated. The suffering of Christian martyrs was a testament to their conviction that there was only one God, and he was with them in their humiliation and suffering. Martyrdom was a supreme act of subversion and a significant part of the mission of god slaying. By willingly facing their accusers, the martyrs were proclaiming that Christ had disarmed the powers and authorities by his cross and was their advocate, standing with them in the face of those who claimed to rule them.

Although the stories of male martyrs were inspiring, it was often the accounts of women that carried an even greater sense of Christ's triumph for the early church. This might have been because women were seen as weaker and in need of greater protection. And yet there seemed to be no accounting for how these Christian women stood before their accusers and willingly bore the sentence of death.

Two celebrated stories of this time are worth noting: the executions of Blandina of Lyon in 177 and Perpetua of Carthage around 200.

Blandina, a slave girl, was horribly tortured and thrown to the wild beasts of the Lyon amphitheater. Her status as a female and an enslaved person was highlighted by Eusebius who wrote of her, "A small, weak, despised woman, who had put on Christ, the great invincible champion, and in bout after bout had defeated her adversary and through conflict had won the crown of immortality."[26] You can hear the tone of god slaying in that description.

In *Dominion*, Tom Holland also writes about Blandina, saying,

> Every torture inflicted on her, every torment, she had fearlessly endured. The radiance of her heroism had put even her fellow martyrs in the shade ...

That a slave, "a slight, frail, despised woman," might be set among the elite of heaven, seated directly within the splendor of God's radiant palace, ahead of those who in the fallen world had been her immeasurable superiors, was a potent illustration of the mystery that lay at the heart of the Christian faith.[27]

The other noted female martyr of this time was Perpetua, who was trampled by bulls in the arena before her throat was cut by a gladiator. She had kept a diary of her imprisonment, sections of which were incorporated into Tertullian's description of the martyrdom of early Christians. In it, Perpetua describes a vision she received in which she appeared as a gladiator sent to fight a fearsome Egyptian in the amphitheater. In her dream, Christ was her "lanista"—the man who purchased, trained, and looked after gladiators. Taking her cues from Christ, her trainer, she defeated her opponent and strode through the Porta Sanavivaria, the gate through which victorious gladiators left the ring.

That a woman would dare to see herself this way demonstrated how the Christian faith differed from the gods of the day, where physical strength and might equated to the divine strength of their gods. Only in the Christian faith could one so visibly and obviously weak be considered strong and victorious.

GOD SLAYING TODAY

The shape of mission during this period was evangelistic, confrontational, and triumphalist. It was concerned with sweeping away that which impeded the advance of the gospel—especially the entrenched system of polytheism and idol worship. Living in a post-Christian Western context today, we might imagine there isn't much we can learn from their example because we don't live in a culture that fears the gods and serves idols in order to appease capricious deities.

But I disagree.

Contemporary Western culture is just as awash with idolatry as the third-century Roman Empire—we are just more circumspect with our idols. They aren't made of wood or stone, but instead are fashioned in our hearts and minds.

The COVID-19 pandemic and its subsequent economic repercussions have cast a harsh new light on what we worship and where our hope lies. Careers have stalled. People's savings, marriages, and retirement plans have disappeared. We are discovering that many of us have made idols of these things. People feel lost, alone, disenchanted, and resentful.

John Calvin famously said, "The human heart is a perpetual idol factory."[28] We make gods of even good things—like sex, work, our creativity, and our influence. They shape us. They determine our actions. They guide our futures. They demand our allegiance. In *Counterfeit Gods*, Timothy Keller shows how a proper understanding of the Bible reveals the unvarnished truth about societal ideals and our own hearts. As he defines it, "An idol is something that we look to for things that only God can give."[29]

Giving a more tangible description, American theologian and pastor Gregory Boyd says this about contemporary idol worship:

> There are an endless variety of idols people use to satisfy their hunger. Secular Western people today typically try to get life from what they achieve, what they possess, or whom they impress. The misdirected homing device of some leads them to work eighty hours a week, sometimes sacrificing family and friends in the process of climbing the ladder of success to achieve "the American dream." Others strive to gain the applause of the crowd, performing or achieving their way to fame. And then there are the multitudes that tend to experience the inner void as a gnawing boredom with life. They chase after peak experiences, believing that the next risk-taking adventure, the next experience of falling in love, the next lurid sexual experience, or the next drug-induced high will make them feel fully alive. At best, however, these merely provide a momentary diversion from their emptiness.[30]

Today, we ought to be ready to not only destroy idols but to also debunk myths, offer freedom, and bring a message of hope in a very noisy and overwhelming world, where we are bombarded with the promises of numerous idols. That hope lies in the simplicity of one God, Lord of all, who saves us and who can be trusted to care for our needs. That ancient message is as needed today as ever. We must learn to slay the secular gods of our age—such as consumerism, materialism, systemic racism, and sexism. And just as the Roman Empire unleashed its fury on the early Christians for slaying their gods, we must be ready for modern society to react with unbridled anger when confronted by the uselessness of their idols. As Keller explains,

> When anything in life is an absolute requirement for your happiness and self-worth, it is essentially an "idol," something you are actually worshiping.

When such a thing is threatened, your anger is absolute. Your anger is actually the way the idol keeps you in its service, in its chains. Therefore, if you find that, despite all the efforts to forgive, your anger and bitterness cannot subside, you may need to look deeper and ask, "What am I defending? What is so important that I cannot live without?" It may be that, until some inordinate desire is identified and confronted, you will not be able to master your anger.[31]

We won't be tortured and thrown to the wild beasts of the amphitheater like Blandina or Perpetua, but we will be mocked and marginalized. Nonetheless, if we wish to learn from the shape of early mission, we need to recover greater boldness in evangelism. Not just the kind of evangelism that tells people they are sinners, but the kind that unmasks counterfeit deities, destroys idols, and slays the secular gods of our day.

Having said all that, I want to re-sound the note of caution I made earlier. The first Christians were a marginal, culturally powerless group, notwithstanding Tertullian's confidence that they were taking over the empire. They were fringe-dwellers in society, and their "attacks" on polytheism would have been heard by their contemporaries as novel, not threatening. Clearing the decks of *all* gods and presenting this new Savior as one who reveals power through meekness, strength through gentleness, life through death ... well, that was certainly innovative. I suspect their message was heard as both uncompromising and well-meaning. As Paul wrote to the Corinthians, when it came to any claims about God, the Jews would always demand an impressive sign before they would believe; but the Greeks looked for wisdom (1 Cor 1:22). They wanted a sophisticated cosmology, a clever new way of understanding the world. But as Paul says, "We preach Christ crucified: a stumbling block to Jews and foolishness to Gentiles" (v. 23).

When a "foolish" new sect (as they would have been seen) came condemning the wisdom of the world, it would have been heard and received entirely differently from how Christians in the West are heard and received today. We are not a fringe clique, no matter what those bemoaning the marginalization of the church say. We come with the wind of a thousand years of cultural power at our backs. Our religion has dominated Western society, and we have exercised phenomenal influence because of our preferred-religion status. You might feel that most of that power and influence has ebbed in recent decades, and I would agree, but that's beside the point when people hear us condemning their idols and demanding loyalty to our God.

It is one thing for a powerless, young African woman from Carthage to condemn the Romans' gods as useless; it is a very different thing for an ordained minister from a wealthy institution with a checkered history on racial and gender equality to condemn Western culture today.

I think god slaying is still necessary, but it must take a very different shape today. Perhaps our biggest challenge, in our selfie-saturated world, is to slay the idol of self. We are so obsessed with our own needs—for comfort, for safety, for security—that we often fail to see the gods at work in our own lives, let alone the gods at work in those around us. We can learn from the earliest Christians how to invest great confidence in the faithfulness of God and the uniqueness of Christ. We can admire their uncompromising stance on condemning the oppression of religious neuroticism caused by polytheism. But now is the time for greater circumspection. We bear the burden of the inconsistent history of the church and need to learn ways to free people from the domination of their idols without resorting to coercion and control.

As Timothy Keller says, this will mean being willing to "antagonize a society's idols while showing respect for its peoples and many of its hopes and aspirations. It means expressing the gospel in a way that is not only comprehensible but also convincing."[32]

We could also recover a form of mission that is rooted in a deep sense of confidence in the unfurling of God's kingdom. The early Christians believed their God reigned, and that his reign was total, utter, and complete. They brooked no challengers to God's rule. And they declared that Christ was the only way to know this God and be freed from all that led us astray. We too can rightly be triumphal about God's hand on the future, but we need to be cautious about ever appearing triumphalist. It doesn't play well for a powerful institution, albeit a fading one, to appear haughty or self-confident.

The Second Shape

PEACEMAKING

*To love means loving the unlovable. To forgive means pardoning the
unpardonable. Faith means believing the unbelievable. Hope means
hoping when everything seems hopeless.*

G. K. CHESTERTON

Early in the eighth century, a British missionary named Boniface strode ashore in Frisia, in the coastal area of northern Germany. He had come as part of a wave of missionaries sailing across the North Sea from Scotland and northern England.

Frisia was a scary place. It had been plagued by tribal fighting and pagan superstition; and Boniface—a solid, no-nonsense kind of guy—went straight to work. He began hosting rousing debates with the pagan priests, dismissing their fears and mocking their gods, much to the amusement of onlookers who were impressed with his garrulous good nature. But when he heard that the local community lived in fear of upsetting the god Thor, he went full god-slayer on them.

According to a local tradition, Jupiter had once visited earth, and in the very place where his feet first touched land—in Frisia—a massive oak tree had sprouted. It was known as Thor's Oak, or Donar's Oak, and the care of the sacred site had fallen to the Frisians who worshiped under its branches and offered sacrifices at its trunk. Nobody dared touch the sacred tree for fear of being instantly struck dead.

But Boniface wasn't having any of that. He was filled with the kind of robust, fearless faith that characterized the missionaries from the British Isles, and he happily took it upon himself to desecrate Donar's Oak to show the Frisians their god of thunder was no god at all. Boniface produced his handy axe and with much fanfare proceeded to the tree, followed by a terrified crowd who expected him to be fried by one of Jupiter's thunderbolts at any minute. Then, just as Boniface started to chop at the base, a great wind blew up and toppled the ancient tree. Not only had Jupiter not struck Boniface down, but his God had also finished the job of destroying Donar's Oak for him. The people were amazed and converted to Christianity.

Adding insult to injury, Boniface used the wood from the tree to build a chapel, which he dedicated to St. Peter with these words:

> This humble tree's wood is used to build your homes: let Christ be at the center of your households. Its leaves remain evergreen in the darkest days: let Christ be your constant light. Its boughs reach out to embrace and its top points to heaven: let Christ be your Comfort and Guide.[1]

We'll return to Boniface's story later, but it illustrates the fact that god slaying didn't come to a complete end in the fourth century.

EUROPE DESCENDS INTO DARKNESS

Some Christians seem to think that once Emperor Constantine was converted in 312, Europe became a Christian empire. But it wasn't that simple. Certainly, the persecution of Christians ended by the late fourth century; and Constantine's son, Constantius II, enacted legislation forbidding pagan sacrifices and the worship of images, and ordering the closure and deconsecration of all pagan temples. According to the Roman Christian poet Prudentius, all that was required for a pagan temple to be repurposed by Christians as a church building was the removal of the cultic statue and altar.[2]

You can understand why the early Christians thought the kingdom had come, and Christ was about to return. The continent was theirs. But their joy was short lived. Trouble was brewing beyond the empire. In the north, the Goths and Visigoths—nomadic Germanic people—were rising up against Roman rule. Meanwhile in the east (Central Asia, the Caucasus, and Eastern Europe), another nomadic people, the Huns, were doing the same.

The story of the fall of Rome is a long and complicated one, involving political corruption, military incompetence, civil war, and marauding pagan armies. It goes far beyond the Goths and the Huns attacking the city. Indeed, the Goths and the Huns were also at war with each other. But the upshot is that, in 408, the Gothic commander, Alaric, besieged Rome, causing a dreadful famine within its walls before being paid by the Romans to withdraw. He returned in 410, breaching the walls and sacking the city for three days.

Europe descended into darkness. The Goths and Huns continued to attack villages and cities through the West (and each other) until the *pax Romana*— the order imposed by the Romans—unraveled into complete chaos. Likewise, the influence of the church receded during these difficult times. European society fell back under the spell of polytheism, and people found themselves overcome by superstition and fear.

This was the situation that faced Boniface when he strode ashore in Frisia. Try to imagine living in an isolated village in northern Germany, Denmark, or the Netherlands in, say, the fifth or sixth centuries. Frozen winds whipped up from the North Sea. Winter days were short and dark. Thick, gloomy woods held who-knows-what horrors. Plagues intermittently swept through the land. If crops failed and sufficient food wasn't stored, winters brought privation or even starvation. Small villages often felt beleaguered by dark forces beyond their control, which led them to embrace a variant of Germanic paganism that was a mash-up of old religious beliefs and new cultic practices. Sickness, famine, long winters, and floods were attributed to supernatural entities that inhabited the landscape—including elves, dragons, and shape-shifting water spirits. To appease these dark forces, cultic practices arose—including the sacrifice of inanimate objects and animals to these deities, particularly at certain religious festivals during the year. Many of these practices involved trees and megaliths … hence Donar's Oak.

When a loud, confident, joyous outsider like Boniface turned up, unafraid of goblins or ghouls, unconcerned by threats from the priests of Jupiter, wielding his axe and proclaiming freedom in Christ—everyone listened!

While Boniface's act of desecration could be viewed as an example of the god slaying we looked at in the previous chapter, it also needs to be understood in the broader context of the Celtic missionaries' work of *peacemaking*.[3]

Peacemaking has always been important to God's people. In the Old Testament, the Hebrew word *shalom* is usually translated "peace" and refers to

Israel's hope for all things to be set right again. It can include a personal sense of wellbeing, but it also has social and political dimensions. Shalom involves being right with God and with past enemies. It means community, justice, and the end of all divisions and hatreds. True shalom includes peace with God, with others, with the world, and even with the earth itself. As Israel struggled with internal discord, while surrounded by enemies and threatened by drought and famine, its prophets spoke of a coming shalom—a day of the Lord when peace and righteousness would be established.

When Western Europe found itself in a similarly dark and frightening time in their history, God sent his emissaries from small islands to the north to proclaim true peace for the nations and justice for the oppressed. For them, shalom was central to the teachings of Christ and made possible through the empowering work of the Holy Spirit. In Christ, we find peace with God and the strength to reconcile with our enemies. As Paul writes in Romans 14:17, "For the kingdom of God is … of righteousness, peace and joy in the Holy Spirit."

Indeed, this link between justice and peacemaking is essential in the mission of the church. Theologian Sebastian Kim explains it this way:

> The meaning of shalom needs to be understood not only as the existential state of being in peace and being "without war" (peacekeeping) but also in the transformative sense of actively making righteous and just relationships with others, or peacemaking. For this reason, the relatively unknown biblical text "righteousness (justice) and peace will kiss each other" (Ps 85:10) is one of the most pertinent in the Old Testament when we try to understand and implement the biblical teaching of shalom. There are ample discussions on righteousness (justice) and peace in isolation from each other, but the psalmist particularly emphasizes their integral relationship.[4]

Similarly, in their Cape Town Commitment, the Lausanne Movement affirms the missional endeavor of working for both peace and righteousness when it declares: "We are to be peacemakers, as sons of God," and "We give ourselves afresh to the promotion of justice, including solidarity and advocacy on behalf of the marginalized and oppressed."[5]

For Boniface and the other Celtic missionaries, and for us today, the way of Jesus is good news—news that liberates us from fear within and without and brings us into the shalom ("peace") of the life of God. This peace comes to us primarily through his very presence with us—by the Holy Spirit—who is our ever-present companion and guide. And the Spirit brings the surprising smile of God to peacemakers in the world, as Jesus announced: "Blessed are the peacemakers, for they will be called children of God" (Mt 5:9).

And not only did the Celts bring the good news of peace with God in Christ, but they also brokered peace across Western Europe, uniting what had been a dangerous place of seething unrest. By dispelling superstition, converting kings and warlords, and overseeing the signing of peace deals, they changed the face of Western Europe. As historian John Dickson writes, "The major campaigns into pagan Europe in the 600s and 700s were waged with the old Christian weapons of persuasion, service, prayer and suffering."[6] They walked onto the soil of the mainland with feet fitted with the readiness of the gospel of peace (Eph 6:15), helping guide people out of the chaos of a corrosive empire filled with fear, oppression, and worship of false gods.

CAN ANYTHING GOOD COME OUT OF BRITAIN?

The idea that the hope of Europe would come from the British church would have been considered laughable at the time. Britannia (as Britain was then known) was not the center of the empire by any means. It was situated at its far edge. But more than that, the British church had been under a cloud since the 400s, owing mainly to what is called today "the Pelagian controversy"—a theological disagreement between British bishop Pelagius and two giants of the European church, St. Augustine and St. Jerome. Pelagius's views on original sin were ultimately condemned as heretical, but not before his opponents heaped scorn upon him—sadly casting a pall over the whole British church. By the mid-fifth century, many people would have scoffed, "Can anything good come out of Britannia?"

Well, plenty of good did indeed come out of Britain, including one of the most famous Christian missionaries of all time—St. Patrick. Today, we think of him as the patron saint of Ireland, but St. Patrick was a supreme peacemaker, and his example established the method of subsequent Celtic missionaries.

Despite his fame, there is surprisingly little we can be sure about when it comes to Patrick. Much of what passes for his history is really mythology or hagiography. He was a slave boy of uncertain origin, born around 378. He may have been from Britain or France, but possibly from Spain. In his autobiographical sketch, the *Confessio*, Patrick mentions being abducted from his homeland and then serving as a slave in Ireland. While there, he had some sort of religious epiphany about which little is known. He then fled east to Britannia and devoted himself to religion full time before traveling to Rome. While in England or Rome he had a vision he described this way:

> I saw a man coming, as it were from Ireland. His name was Victoricus, and he carried many letters, and he gave me one of them. I read the heading: The Voice of the Irish. As I began the letter, I imagined in that moment that I heard the voice of those very people who were near the wood of Foclut, which is beside the western sea—and they cried out, as with one voice: "We appeal to you, holy servant boy, to come and walk among us."[7]

Some years into his mission, someone revealed a long-held secret about Patrick to his fellow bishops. Patrick wrote, "They brought up against me after thirty years something I had already confessed … some things I had done one day— rather, in one hour, when I was young."

Patrick does not tell us what he did. There's no point in imagining what it was, but Patrician scholars have wondered whether Patrick thought of his zealous Irish mission as penance for his youthful sins. His contrition clearly proven, Patrick was commissioned to return to Ireland as a missionary with a papal blessing in 432–33.

A powerful and commanding figure, Patrick didn't shy away from disputing with the Druids over their hold over common people through their witchcraft. (More on this later.) This might cast him as a divisive person, but in fact Patrick was always motivated by a desire to bring peace. In *Confessio*, he writes:

> There were many who tried to prevent my mission, saying behind my back, "What is this fellow up to, talking to God's enemies?" … I have done my best always to be honest and peaceful with Christians and pagans alike … I have spent whatever money I possessed for the benefit of the poor … I have given presents to kings and persuaded them to release slaves … I and my companions have at times been arrested and put in irons, our captors ready to kill us, yet the Lord has always set us free (without violence) … Every day I expect to be killed or reduced to slavery, yet I am frightened by none of these things, because my heart is set (at peace) with God.[8]

Patrick's approach to peacemaking had various dimensions. First, and most obviously, he was concerned to broker peace between people. In this respect he acted like a mediator between warring tribes or factions. But Patrick's vision of peace wasn't limited to simply ending open conflict. He knew true peace would only hold if justice was dispensed and things were set right. And he believed these things were only possible if people experienced an inner (or existential) peace that came from God alone. Second, therefore, he preached making peace with God. Third, he insisted people make peace with themselves (dealing with the competing impulses of the heart). And fourth, he insisted on peacemaking between people and creation.

The heart of his ethic of peacemaking is expressed in St. Patrick's hymn *The Lorica* (or "Breastplate"), in which he asks for protection from the various dangers of life, as well as all the malevolent forces in the world. It begins, "For my shield this day, I call: A mighty power: The Holy Trinity! Affirming threeness, confessing oneness, in the making of all through love," and concludes with the well-known entreaty,

> Christ beside me, Christ before me; Christ behind me, Christ within me, Christ beneath me, Christ above me; Christ to right of me, Christ to left of me; Christ in my lying, my sitting, my rising; Christ in heart of all who know me, Christ on tongue of all who meet me, Christ in eye of all who see me, Christ in ear of all who hear me.

For Patrick, trinitarian theology was the framework for all peacemaking, and the omnipresence of Christ was the source of its power.

In his book *The Celtic Way of Evangelism*, George Hunter says Patrick's Irish heritage was invaluable to his success as a missionary and as a peacemaker:

> The fact that Patrick understood the people and their language, their issues, and their ways, serves as the most strategically significant single insight that was to drive the wider expansion of Celtic Christianity, and stands as perhaps our greatest single learning from this movement. There is no shortcut to understanding the people. When you understand the people, you will often know what to say and do, and how. When the people know that the Christians understand them, they infer that maybe the High God understands them too.[9]

28   MISSION IS THE SHAPE OF WATER

The British church of the time wasn't highly regarded by European Christians, especially after the Pelagian controversy. They were cut off from the centers of Christianity—Rome, Alexandria, and Jerusalem. The Scots and Irish were regarded by European Christians as passionate, unsophisticated, uneducated people whose heroic leader, Patrick, was a former slave who had committed some shameful, unnamed sin in his youth.

In other words, can anything good come from Britannia?

As you might know, this question mirrors the comment Nathanael made when first told about Jesus of Nazareth: "Nazareth! Can anything good come from there?" (Jn 1:46). To those in Israel, especially the religious elite, Nazareth was an uncouth place from which godly leaders did not emerge. Likewise, no one expected the conversion of Asia Minor, Greece, and Macedonia—which in turn led to the conversion of Europe—to be initiated by the church in Antioch. But it was. In other words, the first conversion of Europe came from the far southeastern edge of the empire (Antioch), while the second conversion of Europe after 400 began in the far northwestern edge (Armagh in Northern Ireland). It is interesting that God uses the overlooked and unimportant to accomplish his purposes. And, when it comes to peacemaking, it is rare that those in the position of power are able to truly bring peace—peace cannot be imposed on those in need of it. The best brokering of peace comes from the ones who are caught in the conflict themselves, which is why, today, the United Nations often uses those involved in a conflict—soldiers, women, and others—as an essential, and more successful, part of its peacekeeping work.

It is no surprise then that the leading light of the Antioch church was Paul, a man with a shameful past as a persecutor of Christians; and the leading light of the Irish church was a former slave boy, also with a shameful past. God's willingness to work with such people is entirely consistent with Paul's message to the Corinthians:

> Brothers and sisters, think of what you were when you were called. Not many of you were wise by human standards; not many were influential; not many were of noble birth. But God chose the foolish things of the world to shame the wise; God chose the weak things of the world to shame the strong. God chose the lowly things of this world and the despised things—and the things that are not—to nullify the things that are, so that no one may boast before him.
>
> 1 CORINTHIANS 1:26–29

THE HIBERNO-CALEDONIAN MISSIONS

But something was brewing in Britannia! The followers of Patrick, inspired by his example and disciplined by his rule, began spreading out across the British Isles, preaching the gospel, and establishing monastic communities. And although Patrick's exploits were sometimes shrouded in mystery, the facts about the Irish (Hibernian) and Scottish (Caledonian) missionaries from the fifth and sixth centuries are far better known. These days, they are often referred to as Celtic, but technically they were Hiberno-Caledonian missionaries. They began by evangelizing the Scots and the Celtic-speaking Picts in the north and soon found themselves sailing across the North Sea to modern-day Norway, France, Germany, Denmark, and the Netherlands. Historian Diarmaid MacCulloch refers to "the restless energy of Celtic Christians, for whom the sea was a series of trackways to their neighbors and cultures far beyond."[10] Throughout the seventh and eighth centuries they would unleash one of the most influential missional movements in history.

Two of the prominent figures of this era were Columba and Columbanus.

Columba (c. 521–597) was a fiery young Irish nobleman who had caused the deaths of many of his soldiers in a bungled military campaign. Racked with remorse, at the age of thirty-two he vowed to win for Christ as many pagans as Christians whose death he had caused. He disciplined his passionate temper and became a gentle soul with such a devotion to peace-making that he earned the nickname "the Dove." The former warrior now became known everywhere for his love of nature and for his love of God and people. Like Patrick, his commitment to peace arose from the ashes of his shameful past. As a nobleman and military man, he possessed strong organizational skills and set about planning a campaign to evangelize the Picts. He chose Iona, a remote island off the west coast of Scotland, as his base; and there he established a monastery for training missionaries and praying for the conversion of Britannia.

At this time, as we noted earlier, the Picts were under the influence of Druids—members of the learned class among the ancient Celts. They behaved like priests, teachers, judges, and kings, lording it over the Picts, ruling with great superstition, based on what they claimed was the lore of the gods. The Druids were said to believe that the soul was immortal and passed at death from one person into another. Their name may have come from a Celtic word meaning "knower of the oak tree," which gives us an insight into why, much later, Boniface was so quick to take his axe to Donar's Oak in Frisia. He'd seen how powerless and yet destructive this stuff was.

Columba and his band of missionaries preached the peace of God to the Picts and, while initially the going was tough, they saw a great breakthrough when Brude, king of the Picts, was converted and Christianity became established in the north. Columba's influence was enormous. Iona and her daughter monasteries nurtured hundreds of missionary-evangelists who fanned out throughout Britain and were credited for the end of Druidism and the conversion of the kings of the Picts and of the Scots.

A disciple of Columba, Columbanus (543–615) gathered twelve companions, and together they set sail for the continent. They crossed the channel and landed in Brittany in 585, where Columbanus spent twenty years in mission work. Like his mentor, Columbanus could be impetuous and headstrong; but unlike Columba, he had difficulty reigning himself in and was known for being eager, passionate, and dauntless. It was this wildness in Columbanus that many on the continent came to associate with all Celtic missionaries, seeing them as impassioned hotheads from the north. These qualities were both the source of Columbanus's success and the cause of his mistakes. As he and his disciples pushed further south into Italy, some suspected the Celts wanted to overthrow the Italian church and that Columbanus wanted to claim the bishopric of Rome for himself. Firebrands like Columbanus can be easily misunderstood. As a result, he was forced to publicly dispel any assumptions about his ambitions and declare his allegiance to the bishop of Rome, saying,

> We Irish, though dwelling at the far ends of the earth, are all disciples of Saint Peter and Saint Paul ... we are bound to the Chair of Peter, and although Rome is great and renowned, through that Chair alone is she looked on as great and illustrious among us ... On account of the two Apostles of Christ, you are almost celestial, and Rome is the head of the whole world, and of the Churches.[11]

One of the key aspects of the Hiberno-Caledonian missions was their commitment to peacemaking. This was partly a matter of simple practicality—it was hard to conduct evangelistic mission when tribes were warring with each other. But, at a deeper level, bringing peace was intrinsic to their mission. They believed that a personal sense of peace with God needed to be expressed in peace with others. They delivered the message of the gospel not as a foreboding or frightening warning, but as a promise of new life and human flourishing.

Another significant figure in this period is one we've already met: the redoubtable Boniface (672–754). A former British nobleman turned Benedictine monk, he was trained for a time at Columba's monastery on the island of Iona before being consecrated by Pope Gregory II in 722 and embarking on his missionary journey to Frisia.

It's debatable whether to group him with the Hiberno-Caledonian missionaries because he took a vow of allegiance to the pope and was committed to spreading a Roman form of Christianity among the Germanic peoples. But in temperament and missionary style, Boniface was a true Celt. Like Columbanus, he was known as a fiery and uncompromising missionary, but this was tempered by his effusive good nature. His confrontational display at Donar's Oak might give the impression that he was a rabble-rouser, but, as Edward Smither says, "Boniface's mission work relied more on building relationships with local people and preaching."[12]

Today, he is venerated as the patron saint of Germania and is known as the "Apostle of the Germans." Historian Norman Cantor called him "one of the truly outstanding creators of the first Europe, as the apostle of Germania, the reformer of the Frankish church, and the chief fomenter of the alliance between the papacy and the Carolingian family."[13]

That last point—the negotiation of a treaty between the Vatican and the Carolingians—was extremely important for peacemaking. I will introduce you to the Carolingians in the next chapter, but now it's enough to say that the treaty Boniface oversaw would ensure some level of political stability in Western Europe, while also guaranteeing the freedoms of the Christian missionaries in Germania and the Frankish territories.

THE CELTIC PEACEMAKING METHOD

So, how did they do it? What was unique about the Celtic missionaries that led to their great success in evangelizing Northern and Western Europe when the European church had failed to do so? And what part did peacemaking play in their approach? Let's look at the distinctive aspects of Celtic mission.

Monastic preparation. As I've written about places like Iona, perhaps you've imagined the classic, stone castle-like monasteries of the Benedictines in the twelfth century. But Celtic monasteries were more like villages than castles. And they were not just places of retreat and contemplation as we often think of monasteries. They were missionary training centers, established with the intention of equipping people to save other people's souls. The centers housed not only monks and nuns but also a range of other people, including craftsmen, teachers, scholars, and families with children. This diversity contributed to the missionaries' understanding of Christian community and peacemaking. The leader was a lay abbot or lay abbess. In contrast with the culture of the day, the role of women was perceived differently in Celtic communities, and therefore a female leader was quite common.

In the center of these monasteries there was a square, and in the middle of the square stood a tall Celtic cross, usually in stone, with the vertical arm much longer than the horizontal. The presence of the Celtic cross symbolized that Christ was at the center of the community's life, contributing to their collective flourishing.

The Hiberno-Caledonian monks always built their monasteries on islands, coastlines, or at the mouths of rivers. There were various reasons for this, but one was so that their missionaries could easily access the ocean and set off to distant lands. Part of their traditional commissioning ceremony was to take those missionaries deemed ready for service to the river's edge and pray certain prayers of commissioning over them, charging them to the task of evangelism, before pushing them off in coracles (circular fishing boats).

Most coracles included at least two missionaries. The monks would float out to sea and be caught by the winds and the tides and propelled to wherever God chose to send them. Sailing from Scotland or northern England meant they would usually land in modern-day Denmark (due east), Holland and Germany (due southeast), or Brussels and France (due south).

St. Brendan is said to have undertaken a mammoth journey by sea from 512–530. The story of that voyage was retold in 900 as *The Voyage of Saint Brendan the Abbot*, and included references to sea monsters, volcanic islands, and various exciting adventures. More mythic than history, it nonetheless shows how the Celtic missionaries were known for their hardiness, their love of action, their spirit of adventure, and their supreme confidence in the providence of God.

Communal life. Life in a Celtic monastic village was rich, and the monks who trained there built deep bonds of friendship around their common mission. Each of them knew the day would come when they would leave the community and travel to distant lands in need of peace and hope. But they would not travel alone. Using an approach rooted in trinitarian theology, they traveled as small communities. Their understanding of the triune God shaped their devotion to unity in diversity and equipped them as expert peacemakers. When up to a dozen missionaries arrived in a new area, they would approach the settlement's leadership and seek permission to set up camp nearby. The team "would meet the people, engage them in conversation and in ministry, and look for people who appeared receptive."[14] In due course, "one band member or another would probably join with each responsive person to reach out to relatives and friends."[15] They would minister for weeks and months among them, eventually pursuing baptisms and the founding of a church. They would leave behind a team member or two to provide leadership for the fledgling church and move, with a convert or two, to the next area. As Hunter says, "The church that emerged ... would have been astonishingly indigenous."[16]

Deep providential spirituality. The missionaries' spirituality was rooted in a deep and profound sense of peace and trust in God's protection and direction. Thus, they were freed from fear. Celtic missionaries were noted for their sense of confidence and serenity. While the Frisians and the Franks lived in fear and superstition, the Celts' experience of God's providence gave them victory over terror and other destructive emotions.

When they arrived in villages beset by fear of ghouls and goblins and terrorizing Roman gods, their supreme confidence in Christ's power and authority made their message appealing and brought peace to those they met. We see this in Boniface's act of chopping down Donar's Oak. Another example of this was Columbanus's missionary journey to Bregnez in Austria, where he encountered a group of devotees preparing a huge barrel of beer to honor their deity— the fierce god, Wotan. Like all good Celts, Columbanus had no problem with imbibing alcohol, but he didn't want good Germanic beer wasted on a false god. According to the story, the missionary condemned the worship of Wotan and then simply blew on the barrel, and it exploded, leaching the offertory beer into the ground. This illustrates the missionaries' unshakable confidence in God's presence with them and the rightness of their peacemaking mission.

Impassioned disposition. Confidence in Christ aside, the Celts were emotional people—volatile personalities known for openly expressing the full range of human emotions. Serving God gave them outlets for expressing their constructive emotions through indigenous oratory, storytelling, poetry, music, dance, and so forth. They also found ways to connect their message to the deepest concerns of their listeners. They helped Europeans see how their feelings mattered to the Triune God, and this in turn contributed to an internal sense of peace with God.

EVERYONE WANTED TO BE ROMAN

So, whatever happened to Celtic spirituality? And why did it not survive in Europe, especially when it was established by such impressive founders? In a way, these missionaries were victims of their own success. Within eighty years, they had been so good at uniting the Germanic, Frankish, and Gallic tribes, and reintroducing Christianity, that the church in Rome began to fear that Celtic practices would become the norm. The Hiberno-Caledonians wanted to honor their traditional allegiance to the Bishop of Rome, but they had a different way of doing Christianity. And so, in 664, at the Synod of Whitby, the Roman church and the Celtic missions came together to decide which approach to doing church should become the official one.

The synod had been called by King Oswy of Bernicia—an Anglo-Saxon kingdom in what is now southeastern Scotland and northeast England—who was trying to settle a marital dispute as much as an ecclesial one. While Oswy followed the Celtic traditions, his wife, Queen Eanfled, held to the traditions of the Romans. And they wanted certain matters settled.

The big issue on the table was the dating of Easter. The Celts used an older way to calculate the date and thus celebrated Easter on different days than the Romans. The Roman church had already had this out with the Eastern church and failed to reach an agreement, so they fought tooth-and-nail to keep the Celtic church from undermining them. But this issue was personal to Oswy and Eanfled. Each Easter, while the queen was feasting, her king was still undertaking the Lenten fast. The royal couple wanted things sorted out in order to avoid embarrassing calendar clashes.

But then there was the issue of hairstyles. Yes, *hairstyles.*

Monks at this time cut their hair in what was referred to as a "tonsure." The Roman monks traditionally shaved the crown of their heads, so that their remaining hair imitated a crown of thorns. The Celtic tonsure consisted of a straight line shaved between the ears, with all the hair forward of the line shaved and the hair grown free to the back.

It's heartbreaking to think that in the midst of the revival of Christianity in Europe, Christians were fighting about calendars and hairstyles.

Ultimately, the Romans won out. Despite being a Celtic ruler, Oswy decided in Rome's favor, because, as the Benedictine monk Bede recorded it, "Peter was the guardian of the gates of heaven and Columba of Iona was not."[17] But according to historian Diarmaid MacCulloch, there was a deeper cultural explanation. He says that around this time, after all the chaos and bloodshed of recent years, Europeans had become obsessed with the ancient power of imperial Rome. He writes, "Everyone wanted to be Roman: the memory of the empire stood for wealth, wine, central heating and filing systems, and its two languages, Latin and Greek, could link Armagh [in the northwest] to Alexandria [in the southeast]."[18] The peace established by the Hiberno-Caledonian missionaries prompted a nostalgic yearning for the old *pax Romana* without any realization that the peace offered by God far exceeded the sense of order imposed by the old empire. Sensing this, Oswy decided Rome should rule on matters of religion.

Irish writer Brendan Lehane confirms that the Whitby council shifted the scales in favor of Rome:

> From now on the city of Peter was to be the center of civilization and the arbiter of religion. Those "few men in a corner of a remote island" were to wield their colossal and disproportionate influence now in infinitely diluted form ... In their way the Irish had restored the faith in Britain and in larger parts of the continent. Their dramatic, awesome reputations had spread far from the trails that individuals carved. And now they were reversed, banished for the felonies of tonsure and calendar by men who were newer to religion than they.[19]

In the following decades, more and more monastic communities were instructed to adopt the Roman forms. The more they lost their Celtic habits, the less they engaged in missionary activities. In the end, most of the monastic communities turned into closed monasteries with monks being concerned about saving their own souls. By the end of the first millennium, the Celtic

Church as such had become history on the European mainland and was maintained only in pockets in northern Britain.

In his magnum opus *The Ecclesiastical History of the English People*, Bede, a monk from northeast England, tells the rather touching story of the conversion of Queen Eanfled's father, King Edwin. One of his court advisers, himself a convert to Celtic Christianity, was trying to convince Edwin to consider his eternal destiny, reminding him of the fleeting nature of our time on earth. The adviser asked Edwin to imagine a small brown sparrow flying through an open window into the warm, brightly lit, lavishly appointed royal hall … and then straight out a window on the other side of the room, back into the cold darkness outside. Like that bird, the adviser said, we pass through this earthly existence for but a few seconds compared with eternity. The image was enough to move the king to convert to Christianity.

I've always liked that story. But Diarmaid MacCulloch suspects Bede made it up because he thought it would appeal to his readers. It was an image for all Europeans, not just old King Edwin. MacCulloch writes,

> The troubled people of Europe sought not only good drains and elegant tableware, but a glimpse of the light which could make sense of their own brief flights out of the darkness. The missionaries of Christianity talked to them of love and forgiveness shaping the purposes of God, and there is no reason to believe that ordinary folk were too obtuse to perceive this could be good news.[20]

Good news, indeed. The Celts were peace-bringers, and their mission was shaped by the darkness and fear that pervaded Europe at that time.

PEACEMAKING TODAY

Our world is in turmoil. Over the past few years, we've lived through a global pandemic, leaving the poorest nations in the world facing dire economic repercussions for a generation. Even in nations more economically insulated from the worst effects, we are hearing reports of a general sense of malaise and anxiety among the populations. This is aside from the millions of people who have lost loved ones to the disease itself.

Wars and conflicts in long-term hot spots such as Palestine, Yemen, Syria, and Afghanistan continue to flare up, and the world has been rocked by the conflict initiated by Russia's 2022 invasion of their neighbor, Ukraine. In recent years, freedom movements have kicked off in Iran, Myanmar, and Hong Kong, and political instability has shaken nations such as Peru, Haiti, Pakistan, and Sri Lanka. Even more stable nations such as France, UK, and the US have experienced widespread protest movements—and, in the cases of the latter two, unsettling transitions of political power.

We also live at a time when the planet is experiencing the horrific effects of climate change. Uncontrollable wildfires have devastated Australia, California, Canada, and Greece. Flash flooding has wreaked havoc in Turkey, Germany and Indonesia; earthquakes have impacted China, India, Iran, the Philippines, Russia, Turkey and the Caribbean; and locust plagues have destroyed crops in Asia, East Africa, India, and the Middle East.

And in case you missed it, rain recently fell on the peak of the Greenland ice cap for the first time in history. That might not seem concerning, but it was so unexpected that local scientists had no gauges to measure it. Rain on the ice cap is one of the starkest signs of a climate crisis.

Again, those experiencing the brunt of all this turmoil are the poorest nations in the world. According to the World Bank, global economic growth is slowing sharply in the face of elevated inflation, higher interest rates, reduced investment, and disruptions caused by the war in Ukraine. The World Bank warns,

> Given fragile economic conditions, any new adverse development—such as higher-than-expected inflation, abrupt rises in interest rates to contain it, a resurgence of the COVID-19 pandemic, or escalating geopolitical tensions—could push the global economy into recession. This would mark the first time in more than 80 years that two global recessions have occurred within the same decade.[21]

Even in a wealthy nation such as the United States, 10.5 percent of the population, or thirty-four million people, live in poverty. The poverty line for an individual American is $12,880 per year, which is $35.28 per day.[22]

Upon learning of his wife's death, Macbeth exclaimed, "[Life] is a tale told by an idiot, full of sound and fury, signifying nothing," and it feels as though Shakespeare speaks for many people today.[23] The depth of the world's problems appears too great. Making meaning out of tragedy is too difficult. What hope is there?

Do you think the world needs peace?

Do you think the world needs to unite to solve the challenges of pandemics, plagues, wars, and climate change?

As never before in recent memory, the world needs peacemakers. It needs people whose hope is set on higher things and whose confidence in the sovereignty and grace of God overrules any anxiety about the future.

Christians today need to work as peace-brokers, bringing together opposing sides, soothing fears, and developing lasting solutions to the world's problems. This isn't to suggest that we can heal the world in our own strength. We know our only hope is in Christ. But as the Celtic missionaries understood, we must show people that our eternal hope shapes us into hope-filled people in the here and now. The Celts feared no Druid, nor any king. They refused to quake before fearsome Germanic gods. They dismissed stories about goblins and ghouls. They smashed idols. They brokered peace treaties. They ended wars.

Today, we often see the church taking sides in the issues that vex and divide society. Rather than being peace-bringers, as Christians we can often contribute to division by aligning ourselves with certain political agendas, shadowboxing with unseen enemies. Immersed as we are in a culture of left-right polarization, we give into the temptation to champion one side or the other, unable to see the limitations of our side or the positives of the other. It can be incredibly difficult for some of us to admit that white Christian progressive-liberalism is as much a modern creation as white conservative Christian fundamentalism. Genuine peace-bringers don't merely call for an end to the conflict between the left and the right; they also invite people to something more—something beyond both camps.

In saying this, I am suggesting that we should be committed to something more than a live-and-let-live kind of peacemaking. Proponents of peace studies call this "negative peace"—the cessation of open conflict without any sense of justice or deeper reconciliation. Peacemaking—"positive peace"—on the other hand, must include reconciliation, justice, and new life. It is akin to what the psalmist dreams of when he speaks of righteousness (justice) and peace kissing each other (Ps 85:10). As mentioned earlier, the Old Testament notion of shalom includes an integral relationship between justice and peace. Positive peace is a call for us to rise above our simplistic categories and find reconciliation, restitution, and renewal together.

The shape of Celtic mission should inspire us to consider how we might bravely disentangle ourselves from other agendas and find our vocations as peacemakers.

In 2018, the British magazine *New Internationalist* published an article titled "10 Steps to World Peace." Those steps included such things as eliminating exclusion, developing equality between men and women, sharing wealth more equitably, tackling climate change, controlling the sale of arms, and strengthening democracy. These are big, challenging tasks, but the writer, Hazel Healy, showed how success in each of these endeavors would have direct impact on fostering a more peaceful world.

It was Healy's tenth step that especially caught my eye. Healy said we need to look *within* in order to achieve world peace. She wrote,

> Peace starts with you. Ordinary citizens can make a difference. When's the last time you said sorry? Think about who loses when you win. Are the people around you heard and respected or marginalized, ignored and left out? Make a decision to care about what happens to them. Start a constructive conversation with someone you disagree with. Challenge "them-and-us" thinking in yourself as well as in others. Every one of us can choose to make society more just and peaceful, or more unjust and warlike.[24]

This is exactly what the Celtic missionaries were doing—changing their world by changing lives. They believed that breaking cycles of violence and vengeance was only possible by bringing about a whole new outlook in the people they reached. That's true peacemaking.

3

The Third Shape

FLAME BEARING

Go forth and set the world on fire.
IGNATIUS OF LOYOLA

In the late 1950s, when the great biblical scholar F. F. Bruce came to write the early history of Christianity, he found himself torn between focusing on the church as an institution or retelling the story of the Holy Spirit's work among his people. Bruce was haunted by the words of William Inge, the dean of St Paul's Cathedral, London, who said, "The real history of Christianity is the history of a great spiritual tradition." By this, Inge was referring to the pattern of the Spirit's unceasing witness, even if, at times, it is only through a small remnant of the faithful. In response, Bruce wrote, "The difficulty of the would-be historian is this: it is relatively easy to trace the fortunes of a visible institution, whereas the course of a great spiritual tradition is much more elusive. And yet, the two are so closely interwoven that it is impossible to treat of the one without constant reference to the other."[1]

Bruce decided to title his book *The Spreading Flame* because, as he saw it, the advancement of Christianity was like that of a growing wildfire. He writes, "The redeeming message of Christianity burst as a great light on the people that walked in darkness."[2]

Bruce's book only covers the spread of the church until the eighth century, but the idea of the faithfulness of the Holy Spirit's witness even in the darkest periods of history is an apt consideration as we move into the Medieval period. By then, god slaying and peacemaking were no longer the primary shapes for Christian mission. Polytheism had been (largely) eliminated, and large swathes of Western Europeans were living in peace. The region was still being threatened by enemies from beyond and by the ambition of its local rulers, but the Hiberno-Caledonian missionaries had changed the whole socio-spiritual outlook of Europeans, especially in the north. However, waves of darkness would sweep over European society in the subsequent centuries, and the church's fortunes would wax and wane during that time. Still, the Spirit always ensured that the flame of gospel truth burned on. During this period, the shape of Christian mission became that of *flame bearing* in the darkness.

While things in the north of Europe had stabilized, all wasn't well in the south. In the mid-eighth century, Rome was particularly vulnerable to attack, leading Pope Stephen II to look for Christian allies to protect the city. At this very time, a nobleman named Pippin the Short illegitimately seized the Frankish throne from the last Merovingian king, Childeric III. Pippin's authority wasn't universally accepted, and, needing allies to acknowledge his right to rule, Pippin met Pope Stephen II in 751 and promised to protect Rome in return for a papal blessing on his monarchy. The pope eagerly agreed.

We can only guess why a king called Pippin the Short felt he needed affirmation from others. Nonetheless, to repay the pope's endorsement, he expanded his rule into Italy by subduing the state of Lombardy and granting the papacy a swathe of territory stretching across central Italy. This area eventually became known as the Papal States, a region over which future popes would rule. So, it turned out that this sweet deal between the Frankish king and the Bishop of Rome was working out nicely for them both.

Normally, the basis of a monarch's rule was either heredity or military— he was either born a king or he seized the throne by force. But, as a result of his deal with Pope Stephen, Pippin now complicated the traditional role of Frankish kingship by relying on ecclesiastical authority to rule "by the grace of God." This deal had enormous and long-ranging effects on the very shape of European society. I suspect not even Pippin and Stephen could have guessed where these new, but not yet clearly defined, powers and responsibilities would lead. The pact they signed would ultimately create what we now call European Christendom. Some Christians think the establishment of Christendom occurred under the rule of the first Christian emperor, Constantine, in the fourth century; but technically, the reciprocal legal agreement between church and state happened here at the royal palace of Ponthion, when Pippin and Stephen promised to look out for each other.

Historian Owen Chadwick explains the gravity of that moment:

> The long drawn-out consequence of this realignment for both the unity and disunity of Christendom were enormous. For the first time in history the pope had acted as a supreme political authority in authorizing the transfer of power in the Frankish kingdom ... These were steps of the highest importance for the future. They were moreover highly treasonable. The pope had passed from mere neglect of his duty of political obedience to the Greek emperor to the downright seizure of political power.[3]

Pippin the Short died in 768, leaving his throne to his two sons, Charles and Carloman. The brothers had a pretty fractious relationship but managed to rule jointly until the death of Carloman in 771. Charles then eagerly took control of the Frankish realm, disregarding any claims to the throne by Carloman's heirs. Today, we know him as Charles the Great or Charles Magnus—or, more commonly, Charlemagne.

THE RISE OF CHARLEMAGNE

By all accounts, Charlemagne was a man of genuine Christian conviction—but kings will be kings, and his family arrangements weren't exactly traditionally Christian. He had five wives (only one at a time, mind you), several concubines, and fathered at least eighteen children.

But aside from all this, he was the first man to ascend to a "Christian throne" to rule "by the grace of God." All this might have been a footnote in history had it not been for Charlemagne's extraordinary skill as a ruler and his insatiable ambition to extend his kingdom. Not content with the Frankish throne, he conquered Lombard in 774 and declared himself king of the Italians. After that he forced the Frisians along the North Sea into submission, defended Gaul against Muslim attack, annexed Bavaria, became the ruler of Asturias in northwestern Spain, and was even granted a vague role as protector of the Christian establishment in Jerusalem.

Uniting all this territory under his rule made him incredibly powerful, and so in 800, when a new pope, Leo III, was under threat from a faction of Romans who charged him with serious personal misconduct, he sought refuge with Charlemagne. Like his father before him, the Frankish king saw an opportunity to further legitimize his rule and demanded that Leo acknowledge his newly expanded kingdom. Leo obliged and crowned him "Emperor of the Holy Roman Empire." Charlemagne was now the king of Christian Europe. Later he would be called *Europae pater* ("father of Europe").

THE RISE OF EUROPEAN CHRISTENDOM

As I mentioned earlier, this alliance between the church and state that came to epitomize European history, almost to our current time, is referred to as Christendom; and is often characterized as a Faustian deal. When a pope who had been charged with misconduct crowned a king with a harem of concubines the ruler of Christian Europe, he signed a deal that seemed to favor civil interests over religious ones. As G. K. Chesterton once quipped, "The coziness between church and state is good for the state and bad for the church."[4]

Christendom is that era of European history that lasted until the twentieth century and was typified by a theocratic understanding of society and a close partnership between church and state as the two main pillars of that society. This partnership can be seen in the institution of the following:

- the coronation of monarchs by leaders of the state church
- baptism as official form of birth registration
- compulsory attendance at mass
- tithing as a state-imposed tax (which partly funded the Crusades)
- forced baptisms of immigrants
- the "Christianizing" of some pagan practices and the banning of others

The acquisition of the enormous power and influence conferred on it by the state always appears to lead toward the corruption of the church. By the eighth century, the empire was broken into a patchwork system of parishes—territorial units under the clerical jurisdiction of one priest. In this way, priests became responsible not only for their sacred duties but also for secular duties such as the collection of tithes (church taxes) and the registration of births, deaths, and marriages. The legal marriage between the church and state turned the clergy into secure, well-compensated bureaucrats. And rot began to set in.

THE CHURCH'S FLAME DWINDLES

It was necessary to outline all that background to explain how, after all the excitement and effectiveness of the Celtic missions, Europe could fall back into darkness. The "spreading flame" F. F. Bruce spoke of had dwindled to a barely flickering light. A heartbreaking example of this can be seen in the decline of the Benedictines. Once a flame-bearing movement, the Benedictine order was formed in the mid-sixth century, long before Charlemagne and Pope Leo III. But even the Benedictines became corrupted by the privileges of Christendom after 800. Allow me to take a big jump back in time to show you how they once shone brightly and how their decline came about.

The Benedictines emerged from the ministry of St. Benedict, whose life is as difficult to reconstruct as St. Patrick's (see the previous chapter). We do know he was the son of a Roman nobleman from Nursia in the Italian province of Perugia and was sent to study in Rome, possibly around 500. However, Benedict found the city a hotbed of licentiousness, drunkenness, and violence. A devout man of deep spirituality, he was disgusted by the breakdown of civil society and retreated to a cave beside the lake near the ruins of Nero's palace above Subiaco. There is no evidence he intended to establish a monastic order. He was effectively a hermit, living in his cave for three years, provided with food and robes by Romanus, a monk of one of the nearby monasteries.

But these were frightening and confusing times for committed Christians. The papacy behaved more like a small state than a church, offering little spiritual guidance to the people. Christians felt as though the world was ending. When news spread of a saintly, flame-bearing hermit living in a cave about forty miles east of Rome, people began making pilgrimages to the site to learn from and be blessed by Benedict.

Eventually, Benedict was persuaded to become an abbot of a more tradi-tional monastery; but—not one to do things by halves—he founded twelve monasteries, each with twelve monks, each reporting to him. More people flocked to him. Wealthy Roman families offered their sons to become monks under his care. It seemed as though Benedict was the only light in the midst of the dark chaos caused by the final fall of Rome.

Later still, Benedict traveled south, followed by a few disciples, to a pagan district about halfway between Rome and Naples. There, on a steep hill above Cassino, he preached the gospel and saw many people converted. Eventually, this would become the site of the Benedictine motherhouse at Monte Cassino, where he would formalize the rhythm of life for his monastic communities: the Rule of St. Benedict.

Around this time, the Hiberno-Caledonian missions were under way in the north. But Italian Christians in the south might well have been unaware of their work. They were under the yoke of the Lombards (a Germanic people), and hanging onto faith at that time mainly meant keeping the Rule of St. Benedict—the only light they had.

The Rule makes for interesting reading. It's certainly very thorough. It specifies the rhythms, principles, and practices of a Benedictine monastery, including explanations of the roles of monks, nuns, abbots, and brothers. It contains a list of seventy-two spiritual tools, based on various biblical and traditional sources—such as the Lord's two great commandments, the Ten Commandments, the Corporal and Spiritual Works of Mercy, the Golden Rule, the Cardinal (Deadly) Sins, and the Theological Virtues—as well as other guiding principles, such as humility, suffering for the kingdom, and loving one's enemy. It also outlines the day-to-day life of the community, including the Divine Office, prayer times, sleep times, meals, and clothing.

In the Rule, Benedict describes the monastery as the monks' "workshop" and presents twelve steps for the monks to climb in order to attain holiness— including "the acceptance of suffering ... silence except when answering questions ... restraint in laughter and frivolity" and "constant awareness and sorrow for sin."[5]

It's hard to imagine, but it appears that life in southern Italy was so chaotic, so licentious, so immoral, that a rule like this was seen as a flame that provided light, warmth, and guidance in the midst of the darkness of the times.

Benedict died around 550, but the community at Monte Cassino continued to submit to the Rule. However, when the monastery was sacked by the Lombards around 580, the monks fled to Rome. It is believed they took their devotion to the Rule with them, which led to its later diffusion throughout Southern Europe.

What began with a pious hermit living frugally in a cave became a comprehensive religious system for monastic living throughout Europe.

A hundred years after Benedict, many of the monasteries bearing his name and purporting to follow his Rule were affected by the worst excesses of Christendom. They became wealthy from rents, tithes, feudal rights, and pilgrims who passed through their houses on their pilgrimages. The massive endowments, powers, and responsibilities of the Benedictine abbots drew them into the affairs of the secular world, and monks abandoned manual labor to serve as scholars and court priests. The Benedictines came to so epitomize Christendom in all its forms that in 1964, in view of how the Benedictine Rule contributed to the evangelization and civilization of the empire in the Middle Ages, Pope Paul VI proclaimed Benedict the patron saint of all Europe.

I suspect Benedict would have turned in his grave.

THE CISTERCIANS REKINDLE THE BENEDICTINE FLAME

But we're not done with the Benedictines yet. Even though they present a sad case study for the corruption of the church under Christendom, they would eventually burst into flame again, taking back Western Europe and bringing revival and restoration to society. And for that we can thank the formidable Benedictine monk, Bernard of Clairvaux.

By the turn of the first millennium, the corruption of Benedictine monasteries was well advanced. In 1098, a Benedictine abbot, Robert of Molesme, could stand it no longer. His monastery in Burgundy had fallen into spiritual decline, with most monks abandoning the Benedictine Rule. Robert, along with about twenty supporters, left his monastery and moved to a plot of marshland just south of Dijon called Cîteaux, intending to establish a truly Benedictine community. Cîteaux means "reed" in Old French. Robert chose to use the Latin version of this term, *cistercium*, naming his new community the Cistercians.

Embracing a severe form of asceticism, these bearers of the flame sought to be purified and strengthened for a lifelong labor of prayer. They refused to accept any feudal revenues, believing them to be sullied by the church's collusion with the state.

We're talking about some hardcore monks here.

Initially, the Cistercians regarded themselves as regular Benedictines, albeit more "perfect" (reformed) ones. But they soon came to distinguish themselves from the monks of unreformed Benedictine communities by wearing white tunics instead of black. A white Benedictine or Cistercian was considered the holiest of all monks.

In 1111, the new abbot of the Cistercians, Stephen Harding (an extraordinary man in his own right), embarked on an expansion program to start

Cistercian monasteries across Europe. That year, Harding commissioned a group of monks, led by Bernard de Fontaine—a nobleman who had taken holy orders at the age of twenty-two, just four years earlier—to start a new monastery in Clairvaux.

A supremely eloquent and strong-willed mystic, Bernard of Clairvaux was to become the most admired churchman of his age.[6] As with Benedict before him, the flame of Bernard's passion drew young people—particularly those who were seeking a better way than the church was offering them at the time. The Clairvaux abbey soon attracted a strong flow of zealous young men. As Bernard's fame grew, the Cistercian movement grew with it. Daughter houses and monasteries were founded across France, into England and beyond.

The Cistercians under Bernard took seriously Benedict's words in the forty-eighth chapter of the Rule, which states: "For then are they monks in truth, if they live by the work of their hands." The work of their hands? Monks were meant to be known for being devoted to prayer and study, not work. Nonetheless, taking Benedict at his word, the Cistercians introduced manual labor for monks as a principal feature of their common life and the primary means of their financial support (since they refused to accept any filthy lucre from the state). They came to embody the Benedictine motto, *ora et labora*—"pray and work." For the Clairvaux community, the working part wasn't simply about funding the monastery; they worked in their fields for God! You might not think it, but this simple idea—that a monk should express piety through work—would change European society forever.

For a zealous monk, prayer is an offering to the divine; the primary expression of devotion to God. Monks were taught to pray from before dawn until after sunset. But now, the Cistercians added work as a true mark of godly devotion. And if they were to embrace manual labor as a way to express their love for God, they would inevitably work as devoutly as they prayed. And if work was part of religious vocation, then—also inevitably—they'd work extremely hard and for long hours.

The idea of manual labor as an act of consecration turned the Cistercians into lean, hardworking men. They worked as tirelessly as they prayed. A monk's life consisted of about three hours in church at the Divine Office; five hours devoted to manual labor; and two or three hours given over to biblical study. The exact number of hours changed according to the seasons of the year, both natural and liturgical, but the three-part rhythm of worship-work-study was maintained throughout the year.

The Cistercians reclaimed unwanted or marginal land and worked it constantly, turning fallow, useless dirt paddocks into productive fields. In the process, they created a large, disciplined, unpaid labor force. And, as a monastic order, they were free from the tariffs and taxes imposed by feudal lords, so their business enterprises—whether wheat, wool, or beer—were remarkably profitable. They didn't pay conventional wages to their monks (workers), and they weren't taxed by the state. Nearly every cent they made was profit; and this in turn helped finance the founding of even more monasteries. With the proceeds from their agricultural ventures, and a steady stream of young men now signing up to the order, Bernard rolled out Cistercian monasteries across Europe. No other religious body had grown so large so quickly. By the time of his death in 1153, Bernard had directly founded sixty-eight monasteries and overseen the establishment of another 270 monasteries from Sweden to Portugal and from Scotland to the eastern Mediterranean.

The monks, often drawn from the educated families of Europe, began experimenting with new and innovative farming techniques, hydraulic engineering, and metallurgy. They developed the use of large waterwheels for power and an elaborate water circulation system for central heating. They instigated new approaches to transportation, fermentation, and harvesting crops. These techniques were adopted by other farmers in central Italy, southern France, Spain, and the Netherlands. As a result, all of Europe experienced a massive economic boom in the twelfth century. Some of these techniques are still in practice today.

Five hundred years after Benedict's death, and three hundred after the decline of his order, the Cistercians had not only revitalized Benedictine monastic life but had also altered the world as many Europeans experienced it. They truly lit a flame that spread into the far reaches of the Western world, bringing dramatic change to society.

SETTING THE WORLD AFLAME

While the Cistercians changed European society from within, three hundred years later another missionary order would change the way Europeans saw the rest of the world. They were the Society of Jesus, better known as the Jesuits.

Just as the shape of Cistercian mission was formed by the decline of European society, Jesuit mission would be shaped by what would become known as the "Age of Discovery"—a period in European history, from the fifteenth to the eighteenth centuries, of extraordinary overseas travel. Bear in mind that although the term "discovery' was used, European explorers weren't in fact "discovering" anything. The lands they claimed to have found were already inhabited. Indeed, for non-Europeans, this period would be characterized more as an age of invasion than discovery, culminating eventually in the rush by European nations to colonize almost every corner of the planet.

It was the Portuguese who kicked things off with their highly lucrative travels to the Atlantic archipelagos of Madeira and the Azores. Soon they were exploring the coast of Africa—and, in 1498, forging a sea route to India.

Not to be outdone, in 1492, the Spanish king commissioned Christopher Columbus to cross the Atlantic. And we all know how that worked out. Then, in 1519–1522, Ferdinand Magellan's crew completed the first circumnavigation of the globe. These discoveries led to numerous naval expeditions across the Atlantic, Indian, and Pacific oceans, and land expeditions in the Americas, Asia, Africa, and Australia that continued into the late nineteenth century.

At this very time in history, just as the world was opening up to Europeans, God was preparing a group of men to be flame-bearers of the gospel to the ends of the earth.

The first of these was a raffish Spanish courtier and soldier, Iñigo López de Oñaz y Loyola. By his own account, Iñigo wasn't a particularly likeable young man. In 1521, while defending the fortress town of Pamplona, a French cannonball shattered his leg. The army doctors didn't set the leg properly, and the protruding bone created an ugly lump under the skin. So, he insisted on having the leg rebroken and reset. Without anesthetic, of course. The consequence was that his injured leg ended up shorter than the other, leaving the once-dashing Iñigo with a limp for the rest of his life.

He had grown up in the castle of Loyola, the thirteenth child of Don Beltrán Yañez de Oñaz y Loyola—a brash, free-spirited womanizer who had fathered several children by other women. Iñigo's grandfather was an even more shadowy character, regularly in conflict with the crown. But as landed gentry, society let them get away with bad behavior. Iñigo figured that being a courtier of Loyola allowed him to flout convention and behave any way he liked. And he did. He paid more attention at dancing and fencing classes than academic ones. Like his father, he became a dandy, a womanizer, and sensitive to insult.

But things changed after the siege of Pamplona. While recovering in his castle after his broken leg was reset, Iñigo began to experience visions and moments of spiritual euphoria. This was extremely out of character; normally he fantasized about beautiful women or personal glory. Now St. Francis of Assisi and St. Dominic visited him in his dreams. He started reading John Fleetwood's illustrated *Life of Christ* and a book of saints' legends.

Everyone agreed that something very strange was happening. At thirty years of age, having shown no prior interest in spiritual matters, Iñigo began to devote himself to serving Christ—a process that took nearly two decades and included intense study, pilgrimages, and submission to a rigorous system of what he called "spiritual exercises."

This was a vocation to which he felt himself eminently unqualified. Due to his disinterest in formal education as a child, he was barely literate. He was forced to start his education all over, sitting in classes with people much younger than himself. Iñigo was a plodder. The dashing, arrogant courtier had turned into a humble, limping monk. He joked that he had turned from a beautiful butterfly into an ugly caterpillar.

While a student at the University of Paris, though he was then in his forties, Iñigo developed a close bond with several other devout younger men— including Francis Xavier (a fellow Spanish nobleman) and Peter Faber. It was at this time that Iñigo began calling himself by the Latin, *Ignatius*.

THE SPREAD OF THE JESUITS AND IGNATIAN SPIRITUALITY

The group acknowledged Ignatius as their leader and embraced his spiritual exercises as their collective rule. Together they were to form the nucleus of what would later become a religious order known as the Society of Jesus—or, more popularly, the Jesuits.

Approved as an official religious order by Pope Paul III in 1540, the Jesuits wanted to elect Ignatius as their first leader. He declined after the first vote, believing his vanity and the licentiousness of his earlier life disqualified him. He also knew most of his companions were far more theologically knowledgeable. However, they insisted, and eventually he accepted the position and served until his death sixteen years later.

Ignatian spirituality is based on the Gospels and on St. Ignatius' Spiritual Exercises, whose purpose is "to conquer oneself and to regulate one's life in such a way that no decision is made under the influence of any inordinate attachment."[7] The Exercises culminate in a contemplation whereby one develops a facility to "find God in all things."[8] The Jesuits' motto is *ad majorem Dei gloriam* ("for the greater glory of God").

I can't begin to recount the enormous influence the Jesuits have had on global Christianity. Theologians such as Karl Rahner and Hans Urs von Balthasar; philosophers, including Pierre Teilhard de Chardin; writers such as Gerard Manley Hopkins; and martyrs, missionaries, and even Pope Francis, have all been influenced by the Jesuit flame, which has illuminated far-flung peoples and places of the church. Today, the Ignatian Exercises still offer many a means of finding freedom through the recognition that God loves us, wherever we are and whatever we have done. Ignatian spirituality aims to help people overcome preoccupation with self and turn their energies to serving others.

Their commitment to flame bearing has made the Jesuits an extraordinary missionary force throughout the world. St. Francis Xavier, one of the seven founders of the order, is thought to be one of the most effective evangelists of Christian history; and the Roman Catholic Church asserts he has converted more people to Christianity than anyone since St. Paul.

Francis was born Francisco de Jasso y Azpilicueta in 1506 in Javier (Xavier in Navarro-Aragonese), in the Kingdom of Navarre (present-day Spain). He was the third son of the president of the council of the king of Navarre. Ignatius provided the order's central leadership, but Francis went on to be its most effective evangelist. Historian Stephen Neill said of him, "To a passionate but disciplined nature, profound devotion, and an eager longing for the salvation of souls, Xavier added the wide outlook of the statesman and the capacity of the strategist for organization on a large scale."[9]

The Jesuits quickly became so successful in their ministry of preaching and care of the sick throughout central Italy, that they were approached by King John III of Portugal, who commissioned Francis Xavier to evangelize the peoples in his new Asian dominions. In 1542, Francis set out for Goa in West India, the center of Portuguese activity in the East. He spent three years evangelizing pearl-fishing communities along the coast, baptizing around ten thousand of them. While in India, Francis turned the Jesuit creed into poetry for recital by the Goans. Out of this sprang a vibrant indigenous tradition of music and dance in Indian churches.

Francis moved his center of operations to Malacca on the Malay Archipelago, preaching to tribal people in the Spice Islands (Moluccas). During this time, Francis met a Japanese man named Anjirō, a samurai warrior who had been charged with murder and fled his homeland. Anjirō had heard of Francis and traveled from Kagoshima to Malacca specially to meet him. He told Francis extensively about his former life and the customs and culture of his homeland. Anjirō became the first Japanese Christian and adopted the name of Paulo de Santa Fe.

As a result of meeting Anjirō, Francis's eyes were now fixed on taking the flame of the gospel to Japan. And so, in 1549, Francis, Anjirō, and several companions arrived in the Japanese port of Kagoshima.

Francis was deeply impressed with the Japanese people, but he had to adapt his missionary methods to reach them. When evangelizing the Paravas (the Goan pearl fishers) and the Malays, his vow of poverty impressed them greatly. But the Japanese were repelled by such humility, thinking him unworthy of their attention. So, Francis pivoted. He abandoned any outward expression of poverty for a kind of asceticism more attractive to the Japanese.

THE JESUITS ADOPT A NEW MISSIONAL APPROACH

In 1551, when the Japanese church had grown to two thousand converts, Francis returned temporarily to India, leaving the church in the care of his companions. After a decade of mission in Asia, a new attitude was emerging among the Jesuits. As Diarmaid MacCulloch describes it, it was the belief that "other world faiths might have something of value and reflect God's purpose, and it was worth making an effort to understand Indian culture, language and literature."[10]

No one embodied this more than the Italian Jesuit missionary, Robert de Nobili (1577–1656), who took the unprecedented step of living in southern India as if he were a high-caste Indian holy man. To help more effectively spread the flame of the gospel, he adopted Indian dress, became fluent in the local language, and pointed out to people he was not Portuguese like the other missionaries. The difference between Italians and the Portuguese might have been lost on the Indians, but that didn't stop many of them from embracing him as a kind of guru, following his teaching and accepting Christianity. For a time, this put de Nobili out of sorts with the Jesuit hierarchy; but eventually they were won over by his effectiveness in evangelism and his detailed knowledge of Hinduism and Buddhism.

Meanwhile, Francis was struggling in India, burdened by administrative affairs that frustrated him no end. He had come to believe that the most effective way to see the conversion of Japan was via the Chinese. At that time, the Japanese looked to China for wisdom. The only problem was that China wasn't Christianized. Or even close to being Christianized. But that was no obstacle to Francis, who decided he needed to convert the Chinese in order to reach the Japanese. So, in 1552, Francis set off to launch a mission in China, even though China was closed to foreigners. However, on December 3, 1552, Francis died of fever on the island of Sancian (Shangchuan, off the Chinese coast) while attempting to secure entrance to the mainland. He was just forty-six years old.

If you look at a map of Francis's world journeys, you will be astonished by his extensive itinerary. While many of us struggle to share Christ with our neighbors, Francis was instrumental in the growing wildfire of Christianity, taking the gospel to India, Japan, the Malay Peninsula, and the Moluccan Islands (Indonesia). Owen Chadwick wrote of Francis,

> He was a man of sudden decisions or insights or enthusiasms, always eager to be penetrating new ground and converting unknown tribes and undergoing danger for his faith. He mastered none of the numerous languages which he encountered, he settled nowhere, he wandered onward with sudden half-chivalrous resolutions.[11]

Francis came to embody the spirit of Jesuit mission, but it was Ignatius of Loyola who carefully articulated the primary characteristics of their approach: "Whoever desires to serve as a soldier of God beneath the banner of the Cross in our Society ... founded chiefly for this purpose: to strive especially for the defense and propagation of the faith and for the progress of souls in Christian life and doctrine."[12]

Monks bore the flame of the gospel either alone or in pairs to villages where no white man had ever been, dethroning idols, challenging shamans to contests of holiness, and planting churches in their place. Ignatius outlined the various ways this could be achieved: "public preaching, other ministries of the Word of God, spiritual exercises, education in Christianity, hearing confessions, and administering other sacraments, works of charity, reconciling the estranged, ministering to persons in prisons and hospitals and similar services."[13]

The flame-bearing mission of the Jesuits was rooted in a deep dedication to the glory of God and an intense personal love for Jesus. They were completely at the disposal of the universal church, willing to serve anyone anywhere, and totally devoted to each other as fellow companions. In both their visible activity and their contemplative life, they were hardworking, adaptable, learned, and joyful. But it should be admitted that not all Jesuits were so exemplary in their conduct. Sadly, they were products of their own time, both for good and for ill. For example, by the mid-seventeen century, they had established dozens of missions to Africans, but they also kept Black slaves. Slaves worked on more than twenty Jesuit plantations in South America, making wine and growing sugar and other crops to support Jesuit colleges on the continent. All the while, the missionaries sincerely worked to "save the souls" of their slaves. In this way the Jesuits found themselves somehow able to live with the dreadful contradiction of exploiting the physical bodies of the souls they were seeking to save.

As shameful as this example is, there were also some beautiful examples of selfless Jesuit mission. Allow me to introduce you to two remarkable flame bearers: Mme. Marie Martin and Mme. Marie-Madeleine de la Peltrie. Both were aristocratic French widows who, aided by the Jesuits, founded a frontier mission work among the Algonquin and Iroquois people of Quebec, Canada. Both women had been trapped in unsatisfactory arranged marriages but yearned to serve God in a remote corner of the world. When each of their husbands died, they seized their opportunity. Even though Marie-Madeleine was only twenty-two and Marie nineteen, they escaped their aristocratic families (who had other plans for them) with the covert help of Jesuit authorities. In Canada they launched an educational mission to the first-nations population of Quebec, learning local languages and writing dictionaries and devotional literature. In the 1640s, Marie-Madeleine managed to move her considerable fortune out of France, much to her family's displeasure, and used her wealth to start the Order of Ursulines of Quebec and to support the frontier work of Jesuit missionaries in the province. MacCulloch writes of them, "They shared at one remove the early struggles of the Jesuits and acted as a reservoir of strength and encouragement for them in the Society's frequently harrowing sufferings at the hands of hostile native peoples."[14]

FLAME BEARING TODAY

I am not the only one who has drawn inspiration from the flame bearing of the Benedictines, and from St. Benedict himself—although, some Christian commentators have come to very different conclusions about what we can learn from them. They claim that the West today is experiencing the same kind of moral decay that Benedict found in his time, and that rather than seeking to influence the center of a rotten system, we should instead follow Benedict's example and disengage.

Chief among them is Rod Dreher, who—in his book *The Benedict Option*—argues that the continuation of civility and Christian morality within Western culture is a lost cause. Instead, he posits, Christians should withdraw from engagement with contemporary secular culture and establish local forms of community as loci of Christian resistance against the prevailing culture—just as Benedict had done. He writes,

> The reality of our situation is indeed alarming, but we do not have the luxury of doom-and-gloom hysteria. There is a hidden blessing in this crisis, if we will open our eyes to it. Just as God used chastisement in the Old Testament to call His people back to Himself, so He may be delivering a like judgment onto a church and a people grown cold from selfishness, hedonism, and materialism. The coming storm may be the means through which God delivers us.[15]

Dreher's prescription for taking the "Benedict option" is that we should modernize the essential elements of monastic life in the Middle Ages. I probably won't do justice to his approach, but it involves the following:

- embracing basic Benedictine principles as tools for living the Christian life, such as the recovery of the idea of the church being an alternative society of believers
- embracing the church's function as a "school for the service of the Lord" (as Benedict described the monastery)
- a commitment to the dual spiritual rhythms of prayer and work
- the welcoming of outsiders who wish to learn our peculiar way of living

Dreher says that this kind of community must be joyful and confident, not dour and fearful, as it prepares for a time when it can emerge and reestablish its influence over society.

Agreeing with Dreher is Scottish philosopher Alasdair MacIntyre, who writes,

> What matters at this stage is the construction of local forms of community within which civility and the intellectual and moral life can be sustained through the new dark ages which are already upon us. And if the tradition of the virtues was able to survive the horrors of the last dark ages, we are not entirely without grounds for hope. This time however the barbarians are not waiting beyond the frontiers; they have already been governing us for quite some time. And it is our lack of consciousness of this that constitutes part of our predicament. We are waiting not for a Godot, but for another— doubtless very different—St Benedict.[16]

Personally, I'd rather we take the "Cistercian option" and brew delicious beer, revolutionize industry, feed the poor, patronize the arts, and preach Christ. Or go for the "Jesuit option" and mobilize a movement of young people, under orders, ready to serve anywhere, do anything, with no thought to their own wellbeing or personal reputation. And I'm not the only one to think this way. Whatever they choose to call it, many Christians are seeking to do these things and mobilize young people in this way.

What the Benedictines and the Jesuits had in common, and what many Christians hold to today, is the belief that the world is in darkness. For St. Benedict, Roman society was in disarray, and all sense of order and morality had broken down. He believed he was carrying a small flickering candle of faith in the encroaching night of the European soul. In a similar way, Francis Xavier saw the world beyond Europe in utter darkness—culturally, religiously, economically—and sought to bear the flame of the gospel to them.

Neither order achieved their aims without compromise and corruption, but they have also provided beautiful examples as flame-bearers for Christ.

How much we can learn from them hinges on how much darkness we see in the world around us. Dreher and McIntyre clearly see our time as immoral— similar to Benedict's Rome. Dreher, in particular, seems to view the Supreme Court's 2015 Obergefell v. Hodges ruling on same-sex marriage as the last straw. For him, that was the final confirmation that the US had abandoned all Christian morality and had fallen into complete darkness. This is similar to the Religious Right's perception of the court's 1973 Roe v. Wade ruling on abortion.

It's clear that Western societies are no longer paragons of Christian virtue (not that they ever were). But is it all dark out there?

In 2018, the Our World in Data group released a trove of information that appeared to suggest that overall, things aren't as bleak as is often suggested. Among other things, they showed that levels of extreme poverty have fallen significantly, child labor is on the decline, life expectancy is rising, and child mortality is down. More people live in democracies than ever before. Globally, education rates are up, literacy is up, and access to the Internet is up. In the US, teen births have dropped, as has the violent crime rate. Americans are spending a much smaller share of their income on food. And they're smoking less.[17]

Furthermore, movements like #MeToo, Black Lives Matter (BLM), and the Global Climate Strike—though some Christians find their strategies distasteful—are in fact part of a global effort to stamp out misogyny, sexism, racism, and inaction on climate change. The outing of hundreds of previously admired, powerful men who have been accused of sexual misconduct or assault is an indication that things are getting better. The truth will come out, and injustice will be addressed. Overt racism has become more publicly visible, precisely because people are more willing to uncover it.

In his book *Dominion*, historian Tom Holland reveals that many of these socially conscious movements owe their vision to foundational Christian teachings, whether their proponents accept those teachings or not. He points out that belief in the sanctity of human dignity is rooted in the creation story in Genesis 1, and that we need to face the fact that virtually everything considered "woke"—from BLM to #MeToo to gay rights to civil rights to workers' rights— finds their roots in fundamentally Jewish and Christian assumptions.[18] The flame continues to burn, even if it feels like just a flicker at times.

But in saying all this, we need to also recognize the world still needs flame-bearers. Yes, there are some areas where culture is becoming less dark, but there is still so much work to be done. The COVID-19 pandemic not only took a colossal toll in human life, but it also contributed to an increase in human trafficking.[19] Indeed, thirty-five million people are victims of sex trafficking every single day.[20] And as for poverty and disease, we should know that 4.3 percent of all children in the world die before they are fifteen years old. That amounts to 5.9 million children dying every year, or sixteen thousand every day, or eleven children every minute. And how can any Christian relax or withdraw from the world when, in the US, 25 percent of Native Americans and 20 percent of Black Americans live in poverty.[21] As Max Roser from Our World in Data summarizes:

> The world is awful. The world is much better. The world can be much better. It is wrong to think that these three statements contradict each other. We need to see that they are all true to see that a better world is possible.[22]

I'm not suggesting everything is all sweetness and light. But I am suggesting that measuring a society's morality based *solely* on its views of marriage and reproductive health is a narrow matrix. A society is not all dark when it fights for the planet and for the rights and freedoms of women and people of color.

Keeping the flame of faith burning is still our work. How brightly it burns depends on how dark the world around it is.

The Fourth Shape

SPIRIT SEEKING

Our Lamb has conquered: let us follow him.
MORAVIAN MOTTO

In 1968, the patriarch of the Eastern Orthodox Church, Ignatius IV, gave an address to the World Council of Churches Assembly in Uppsala, Sweden. In it, he urged the church not to over-rely on ecclesial strategy and technique but instead to draw on the power and guidance of the Holy Spirit. He said,

> Without [the Spirit] God is far away, Christ belongs to the past, the Gospel is a dead letter, the church is merely an organization, authority is domination, mission is propaganda, worship is an evocation, and Christian action is a slave-morality.
>
> But in him, in an indissoluble synergy, the universe is lifted up and groans and travails to bring forth the kingdom, the human being is struggling against "the flesh," the Risen Christ is here, the Gospel is a life-giving force, the church means communion with the Trinity, authority is a liberating service, mission is like Pentecost, the liturgy is both a commemoration and an anticipation, and human action becomes more godlike.[1]

Little did Patriarch Ignatius know that charismatic movement of the 1960s would usher in the Jesus movement of the 1970s—with thousands of converts flooding into churches and parachurch organizations. Some of the fastest-growing US denominations trace their roots back to that time, which in turn released a new era in church planting and radical discipleship. And when churches experience a new move of the Holy Spirit, it brings with it a renewed commitment to mission.

Our survey of church history now brings us to the Reformation, which many Protestants see as a move of the Holy Spirit in opening the eyes of a church that had become mired in selling indulgences and demanding penances. But what's perhaps surprising to learn is that, after Martin Luther's famous break with Rome, it took a century before Protestants discovered their duty to Christian mission and for Protestant groups like the Pietists and the Moravians to emerge as leaders in world mission. While still devoted to the Scriptures and committed to the message of the gospel, like all good Protestants they were also deeply intuitive people, compelled to seek the Spirit and go wherever they were led.

Let's look at the Spirit-seekers.

THE SLEEPY PROTESTANTS

In 1510, Martin Luther undertook a pilgrimage to Rome. A devout Augustinian monk, he embarked on his visit to the so-called Holy City with the utmost earnestness. He claimed that when he arrived, he fell on the ground, raised his hands, and exclaimed, "Hail to thee, holy Rome! Thrice holy for the blood of the martyrs shed here."[2] While there, he visited the graves of forty-six popes and cemeteries containing the bones of eighty thousand martyrs. He was an intense guy!

And like all zealous monks, Luther readied himself to crawl up the Scala Pilati, a marble stairway in the papal palace, known later as the Scala Sancta (Holy Stairs). They were said to be the very steps that Christ used to enter the praetorium of Pontius Pilate in Jerusalem. According to Roman Catholic tradition, Saint Helena, mother of Emperor Constantine the Great, had the stairs shipped from Jerusalem to Rome so the devout could walk in the very footsteps of Christ.

By the sixteenth century, the tradition had developed that the penitent would walk up the twenty-eight steps on their knees, reciting the "Our Father" on each step, in order to release a soul from purgatory. Luther wanted to free his grandfather—Lindemann Luther—from the cleansing fires of the afterlife. But the whole exercise turned out to be a huge bust for Luther, who found the ritual demeaning and pointless. Later, he said that he sensed the phrase, "The just shall live by faith" resounding in his heart as he labored up each step. But he pressed on and dutifully completed the rite. It was only when he reached the top that the emptiness of the ceremony truly struck him. He couldn't contain his doubts about the efficacy of his prayers for those in purgatory, and breathed, "Who knows whether this is true?"[3]

More than three hundred years later, the British novelist Charles Dickens would visit the Scala Sancta and be stunned by the indignity of the practice, writing, "I never, in my life, saw anything at once so ridiculous and so unpleasant as this sight."[4]

Luther would have agreed. After his experience in Rome, he wrote,

Although I was a holy and irreproachable monk, my conscience was full of trouble and anguish. I could not bear the words, "Justice of God." I loved not the just and holy God who punishes sinners. I was filled with secret rage against him, and hated him, because, not satisfied with terrifying his miserable creatures, already lost by original sin, with his law and the miseries of life, he still further increased our torment by the gospel ... But when, *by the Spirit of God*, I comprehended these words; when I learned how the sinner's justification proceeds from the pure mercy of the Lord by means of faith, then I felt myself revived like a new man, and entered at open doors into the very paradise of God [italics added].[5]

In this passage, Luther describes a profoundly spiritual experience—a release from fear and doubt and a sense of deep, abiding comfort in the grace of God. (The Reformation was as much a spiritual revolution as a movement of ideas.)

It would take another seven years before Luther would nail his protest to the Wittenberg church door and, in doing so, launch one of the most tumultuous eras in European history: the Reformation. Thousands would give their lives to be part of bringing change that led to far greater diversity of thought in Christian faith and would profoundly affect the cultures of those nations and provinces that embraced it. It would also spark various conflicts, beginning in 1523 and ending in 1648 with the Peace of Westphalia. Estimates of the death toll from these European religious wars between Protestants and Catholics exceed five million.

It would seem inevitable that a theological revolution based on a redis-covery of grace, freedom, and the individual's access to God would stimulate a great wave of evangelistic ministry … as well as a great revival in mission. But that wasn't the case. In fact, as we saw in the previous chapter, the great mission movement of the sixteenth century wasn't initiated by the Protestants but by the Jesuits, who were founded in 1540. By 1550, Francis Xavier was single-handedly evangelizing half the world. The Protestants had their hands full just surviving the counter Reformation, so global mission wasn't on their radar yet.

During this period, there was an absence of Protestant missionary orders. Catholic missionary orders were more plentiful and comprised of single men and women without children or property. Their vocation required them to swear vows of chastity and poverty. And they were well educated. Of the Jesuit movement, it was said: "The qualities that fitted it for this work were especially in its cosmopolitan character, its faculty of accommodation and mobility, its military organization and centralization, its absolute obedience and the complete submerging of the individual in the common cause."[6] In other words, a Jesuit missionary could go anywhere at any time, as long as they were commis-sioned by a superior. But the early Protestant missionaries were described this way: "They were unlettered men with more zeal than knowledge, artisans and farmers, married men, with ground to till, houses to build, and families to support."[7] Mobilizing family men with farms and businesses, no matter how godly they might have been, was far more difficult than getting a Jesuit to Japan.

Despite their sluggish start, some Protestant missions were launched. Sadly, they were not terribly successful.

In 1555, French theologian and reformer John Calvin sent a mission team from Geneva to Rio de Janeiro. Canadian pastor and author Tim Challies describes what happened:

> The leader was a wealthy merchant from Geneva, and a professing follower
> of Calvin, Villeaignon (alternatively spelled "Villegagnon"). Along with him
> were dozens of other Genevans, who landed in the bay of Rio de Janeiro and
> settled on a small island off the coast. Things went well for a while. However,
> the leader had—along the way—flipped back to Roman Catholicism, and
> he grew jealous and suspicious of the other Calvinists. He had the disciples

of Calvin arrested, charged with treason, and sought to punish them under Catholic law.[8]

Despite torture and promises of release if they recanted and became Catholics, the missionaries held to their faith. Their three leaders were hanged, and the rest were sent back to Geneva. Then in 1622, the Dutch East India Company, although unenthusiastic about mission, allowed chaplains to work in Dutch colonies in the East Indies (modern-day Indonesia), but with few results.

Other Protestants also joined in the missionary efforts. In 1662, George Fox, the founder of the Society of Friends (Quakers), sent three missionaries to China as evangelists in search of Prester John, reputed to be a Christian king of the Mongols (and descendant of the Magi). They never made it and were never heard of again. Fox himself traveled extensively, and many early Quakers joined him in this work, becoming known as the "Valiant Sixty." At first, their work was extending the Society of Friends across Britain and Ireland, but they were soon spreading the gospel in mainland Europe, as well as in colonial North America and the Caribbean.

But these were isolated efforts and, as you can see, less than successful ventures. It would take around a hundred years for Protestants to find their missional mojo. And when they did, it emerged from a somewhat unlikely corner of the church.

THE PIETISTS WAKE UP

Despite the passions unleashed in the Reformation, by the 1600s the state churches of Germany, Denmark, and Holland had declined into cold intellectualism. Rationalist philosophers like Christian Wolff and Gottfried Leibniz wielded enormous influence. Instead of faith in God and trust in the promises of the Bible and Christian doctrine, people were taught to trust their own reason and senses. The flame of the Holy Spirit dwindled to a flicker. We will look at the effects of the Enlightenment in more detail in chapter five, but for now it is enough to say that rationalism replaced belief in a vague supernaturalism. Traditional Christian morality and church attendance were increasingly considered quaint and old fashioned.

Yet—as we've seen again and again in times of religious decline—God raises up fresh renewal movements. He places in the hearts of his people a yearning to seek fresh experiences of the Spirit. In the seventeenth century, those people were the Pietists.

Pietism was a renewal movement within the Lutheran Church that called for spiritual transformation in the lives of Christians via prayer and Bible study. It was a call for spiritually dead Lutherans to seek the Spirit with all their might. Today, we use the term "piety" to refer to the quality of being religious or reverent. But originally a Pietist was someone who had experienced a deep sense of the indwelling presence of God (sometimes also referred to as "religious enthusiasm"). At a time when most Lutherans were Christian in name only, the Pietists were impassioned and energetic about their faith.

Consequently, Pietism had a long-lasting effect on the European church and eventually give rise to the flowering of the Protestant missions movement. But the Pietists didn't break away from the state church as the Anabaptists did. They were willing to remain Lutherans but sought to be a renewing force within the church.

Pietists embraced the following values:

- the disciplined life (frugality, humility, restraint, sense of duty and order)
- subjective experience of the individual (indwelling of the spirit, a sense of conviction)
- practice rather than theory (though committed to study, they were suspicious of a doctrinaire knowledge of the Bible without a subsequent expression in action)

An early example of Pietist mission is found in the life of the wealthy Austrian baron, Justinian von Welz (1621–1668). Von Welz was converted to Protestantism at the age of forty, after living a life of luxury and excess. Deeply transformed by his conversion, he embraced a strict ascetic life and had a burden for the lost. He was disturbed by what he perceived as the clinical, unfeeling nature of the Lutheran Church of his day.

Herbert Kane writes that, in 1664, von Welz "issued a clarion call to the church to assume its missionary responsibilities. In three pamphlets, he set forth the missionary obligation of the church; called for the organization of a missionary society or association to get the job done; and advocated for the opening of a training school for missionary candidates."[9] In fact, von Welz was so committed to the establishment of a training college that he funded it himself. However, when it opened, it had not received any student applications. Kane says von Welz was called a dreamer, a fanatic, and a heretic. He continues the story: "Undeterred by opposition and ridicule, the disconcerted baron proceeded to Holland, where he abandoned his baronial title. Following ordination as an 'apostle to the Gentiles,' he sailed for Dutch Guiana (Suriname), where he died an early death before he could reap a harvest."[10]

A century later, the very missionary associations and training colleges von Welz advocated would be filled with students, but during his lifetime, he was a lone Spirit-seeker, trying to launch a missions movement in the midst of a spiritually dead state church. It took the spiritual renewal of Pietism to catalyze a rediscovery of mission. Indeed, I would suggest that no great missionary outreach has occurred without there first being a spiritual revival.

At the turn of the eighteenth century, more than thirty years after von Welz's death, his dreams were fulfilled at Halle University, established by two German Pietists—Philipp Spener (a Lutheran priest) and August Francke (a professor at Leipzig University before being dismissed for his Pietist beliefs).

Shortly after the school's founding, King Frederick IV of Denmark experienced his own Pietist conversion and pledged to fund the school. And because the king had a personal interest in sending missionaries to India, he also founded the Danish-Halle Mission in 1706. That year, two graduates of Halle University—Bartholomäus Ziegenbalg and Heinrich Plütschau—were ordained as the Danish-Halle Mission's first overseas missionaries.

Ziegenbalg and Plütschau made it to Tranquebar (now called Tharangambadi) in Tamil Nadu, South India, where the two men learned Tamil, set up a girls' school, and began a printing press for producing Tamil Bibles and other reading material. After five years in India, Plütschau passed away, leaving Ziegenbalg to carry on the work, which he did for another ten years before he too died in India. They left behind more than 350 believers, a Bible college, and most of the Bible translated into Tamil. And they had both traveled back to Europe on several occasions to recruit more missionaries for India.

During one visit to Halle University, Ziegenbalg was invited to speak to students about his missionary work. You've probably heard a "missionary speaker" make a presentation while home on furlough. These presentations often get a bad rap for being less-than interesting. I wonder whether returning missionaries sometimes question whether their presentations make any difference. Well, this one did. Ziegenbalg's speech set off a chain of events that would change history.

In God's providence, sitting in the audience that day was a young student of German aristocratic background named Nikolaus Ludwig, Imperial Count von Zinzendorf und Pottendorf. A Pietist himself, Zinzendorf (as he is known) was deeply influenced by Ziegenbalg's presentation and began to ask God whether he was called to abandon his civic duties as a count and submit to a life of missionary service.

THE COUNT AND THE MORAVIANS

Zinzendorf was born in 1700 to one of the most ancient of noble families in what is now lower Austria. His father died when he was an infant, and he was raised at Gros Hennersdorf, the castle of his Pietist grandmother.

Stories abound of his deep childhood faith. Influenced by his grandmother, the young Zinzendorf battled with his desire to study to be a Pietist minister and his family's expectations that he would fulfill his hereditary role as a count. It was during this internal battle that he began attending Halle University, where he heard Ziegenbalg's mission presentation, as well as being influenced by the enthusiastic faith of his lecturers and other students. The dilemma about which vocation to choose was incredibly painful for him.

After he graduated, Zinzendorf did what most aristocratic young men did at that time—he undertook a "grand tour." It was the custom in the seventeenth and eighteenth centuries that when wealthy upper-class young men and women came of age (about twenty-one years old), they were to undertake a tour of all the great galleries and museums and be presented in the great courts of Europe (young women were typically accompanied by a chaperone, such as a family member). It was an educational rite of passage for the nobility. This would have seemed like an awfully indulgent thing for a keen young Pietist like Zinzendorf to embark upon, but his grand tour ended up being very formative.

While on his travels, he visited Dusseldorf art museum, where he came across Domenico Feti's painting *Ecce Homo* ("Behold the Man"). As Zinzendorf stared at the image of the scarred and beaten Christ, the scene of humiliation touched him deeply. He later recounted that he heard the voice of Christ asking him, "This I have suffered for you, but what have you done for me?"[11] Note the strong Pietist spirituality in this incident. It illustrates the three values I mentioned earlier:

- the disciplined life (frugality, humility, restraint, sense of duty and order). It's understandable why an image of the humiliated Christ would affect him so deeply. Christ was more humble, more dutiful than Zinzendorf could ever be, and the young count heard Christ calling him to a similar form of self-sacrifice.
- the subjective experience of the individual (indwelling of the spirit, a sense of conviction). The experience at the Dusseldorf gallery was a highly subjective experience for Zinzendorf. By his own account, he broke down in tears at the sound of Christ's invocation.
- a preference for practice over theory (suspicious of a doctrinaire knowledge). Christ asks him, "What will you *do* for me?"

At the age of twenty-two, Zinzendorf was ready to do anything for Christ. This was not an untypical response to the movement of the Spirit among the Pietists, who believed the Holy Spirit was the Spirit of missions; the nearer they drew to Christ through the prompting of the Spirit, the more intensely missional they became. Young Zinzendorf's problem was his uncertainty as to where Christ wanted him to serve.

That's where the Moravians came in.

The Moravians were originally from Bohemia (now the Czech Republic) and had converted to Protestantism under the influence of the Czech reformer, Jan Huss. However, they were viciously persecuted by the Jesuits and fled in various directions, some ending up in Saxony where Zinzendorf lived.[12] One large group found refuge on Zinzendorf's huge estate, Herrnhut ("the Lord's Watch"), in 1722. Even though they were henceforth referred to as Moravians, only some of them were actually from Moravia. The rest included a rather disparate collection of Lutherans, Reformed, and Anabaptists from various parts of Europe. What united the group was their experience of persecution as Pietists and that they had been chased from their churches and their homes.

It was the custom of the day that aristocrats with tracts of land were obligated to allow refugees to "squat" (as we would say today) on their estates. And being a Pietist, Zinzendorf was especially welcoming of these Protestant refugees. Remember, at this time Zinzendorf was wrestling with a call to ministry himself, and because the count had been educated at a Pietist university, he was invited to teach the Bible to the refugee community.

Zinzendorf discovered that his pupils were a deeply committed community of Protestants, who were controlled by their emotions, both for good ("enthusiasm") and for ill (internal conflicts, limited Bible knowledge). In other words, the Moravians were a handful. He began teaching them in 1722, and by 1727 he had left public life to devote himself to pastoring the Moravians full time. As their pastor, Zinzendorf took it upon himself to bring some order to his unruly charges. He turned Herrnhut into a craftwork and farming estate, building a showcase village for his tenants and teaching them the disciplined life of a Pietist. However, he was not a hard taskmaster. Anglican priest and church historian David Edwards says that while Zinzendorf was "not afraid of being a dictatorial aristocrat," he was capable "of being lushly sentimental, of being innovative (every month there was a 'love feast' and a 'watch night'), of encouraging physical contact (his followers kissed each other and washed each other's feet)."[13]

Zinzendorf's decision to serve the Moravian community full time fulfilled his long-held desire to be a missionary-pastor, but it wasn't prompted merely by a personal longing. It arose from a spiritual revival that broke out among the Moravians.

On July 16, 1727, a group of the Moravians felt led to covenant to meet more often than weekly to pour out their hearts in prayer and song. Then, on August 5, following a large midnight prayer meeting, Zinzendorf himself spent the whole night in prayer with about twelve or fourteen others, during which many were overcome by the presence of the Holy Spirit. Five days later, one of the Moravians who was leading the Sunday service, became overwhelmed by the power of the Holy Spirit and collapsed to the floor. The whole congregation also fell down, and they continued in prayer and singing, weeping and praying until midnight. Something extraordinary was happening.

A few weeks later, on August 13, the so-called Moravian Pentecost was unleashed. During a communion service at Herrnhut, there was an outpouring of the Holy Spirit, and great signs and wonders took place in their midst for several days. The community increased in their hunger for the Word of God, and all their differences (remember, they were a fractious bunch) melted away. An overwhelming flood of grace swept over them all. Years later, Zinzendorf (who at the time of the outpouring was twenty-seven years old), described that day this way:

We needed to come to the Communion with a sense of the loving nearness of the Savior. This was the great comfort which has made this day a generation ago to be a festival, because on this day twenty-seven years ago the Congregation of Herrnhut, assembled for communion (at the Berthelsdorf church) were all dissatisfied with themselves. They had quit judging each other because they had become convinced, each one, of his lack of worth in the sight of God and each felt himself at this Communion to be unworthy of the noble countenance of the Savior. O head so full of bruises, So full of pain and scorn. In this view of the man of sorrows and acquainted with grief, their hearts told them that He would be their patron and their priest who was at once changing their tears into oil of gladness and their misery into happiness. This firm confidence changed them in a single moment into happy people which they are to this day, and into their happiness they have since led many thousands of others through the memory and help which the heavenly grace once given to themselves, so many thousand times confirmed to them since then.[14]

The effects of this revival were felt almost immediately. Just two weeks later, on August 26, twenty-four men and twenty-four women covenanted together to continue praying in intervals of one hour each, day and night, each hour allocated by lots to different people. This prayer meeting was maintained from 1727 until 1827—one hundred years of 24/7 prayer!

In 1747, a Moravian convert named Johann Haidt painted an imagined depiction of the Moravian Pentecost, which he titled *Zinzendorf as Teacher of the Peoples of the World*. In his interpretation, Zinzendorf is pierced by the light of God from the wounds of Jesus, surrounded by an amazed congregation of Moravian women, men, and children. But Haidt also included Indigenous North Americans and Africans in the gathering. Of course, they weren't actually present at Herrnhut in 1727, but because this very event resulted in more than one hundred missionaries being sent to the Caribbean and North America, they are symbolically depicted as beneficiaries of the Moravian revival.

THE LAUNCH OF THE PROTESTANT WORLD MISSION MOVEMENT

I think it is reasonable to say that the Moravian renewal launched the Protestant world mission movement. But how did a small, localized revival lead to a world mission movement?

As with everything in this story, the Moravians' overseas missionary activity began in an unusual manner. In 1731, Zinzendorf attended the coronation of the new Danish king, Christian VI. This in itself reveals the dual worlds Zinzendorf traversed: one day he was writhing in the dirt with the Moravians, the next he was at the court of the Danish king. No doubt about it, Zinzendorf was an extraordinary man, placed by God in an extraordinary situation for God's glory.

While at the coronation, Zinzendorf met a West Indian man named Anthony Ulrich, a converted African slave who had bought his own freedom and was living on the island of St Thomas (now the US Virgin Islands). Ulrich begged Zinzendorf to send Moravians as missionaries to his country. Shortly after, Moravian missionaries went to St Thomas, to live among the slaves and preach the gospel.

Soon, Moravians were heading to the North American colonies to proclaim Christ.

In 1736, an Anglican missionary, John Wesley, met some Moravians on a ship crossing the Atlantic. Wesley was what historian Diarmaid MacCulloch refers to as "a religious and intellectual omnivore."[15] By that, MacCulloch meant that Wesley was shaped by myriad influences. A high church Anglican priest, influenced by Lutheran pietism and Scottish-Irish Presbyterian revivalism, he was an avid reader of Catholic and Eastern Orthodox theology, as well as secular philosophy. He was soon to be deeply affected by the Moravians.

Wesley had set sail for America to preach the gospel to colonists and Indigenous North Americans, and the Moravians were headed there for the same purpose. On the treacherous sea journey, Wesley noticed the differences in the character of the Moravians (who he referred to as "Germans") and the English passengers. He wrote in his journal:

> At seven I went to the Germans. I had long before observed the great seriousness of their behavior. Of their humility they had given a continual proof, by performing those servile offices for the other passengers, which none of the English would undertake; for which they desired, and would receive no pay, saying, "it was good for their proud hearts," and "their loving Savior had done more for them." And every day had given them occasion of showing a meekness which no injury could move. If they were pushed,

struck, or thrown down, they rose again and went away; but no complaint was found in their mouth.[16]

Then, on January 25, 1736, while the passengers were all attending a Sunday service, a terrifying storm hit the ship, threatening the lives of all on board. Again, Wesley was astonished by the contrast between the Moravian response to impending disaster and that of the other passengers.

> There was now an opportunity of trying whether they were delivered from the Spirit of fear, as well as from that of pride, anger, and revenge. In the midst of the psalm wherewith their service began, the sea broke over, split the mainsail in pieces, covered the ship, and poured in between the decks, as if the great deep had already swallowed us up. A terrible screaming began among the English. The Germans calmly sung on.[17]

The Moravians' confidence in the hand of God, either to deliver them or to carry them to his bosom, was unshaken by any storm. John Wesley was so amazed by their tranquility and faith, he asked one of the Moravians whether they were afraid.

> He answered, "I thank God, no." I asked, "But were not your women and children afraid?" He replied, mildly, "No; our women and children are not afraid to die." From them I went to their crying, trembling neighbors, and pointed out to them the difference in the hour of trial, between him that feareth God, and him that feareth him not. At twelve the wind fell. This was the most glorious day which I have hitherto seen.[18]

The Moravians were filled with the Holy Spirit, following wherever the Spirit led. The impression this made on Wesley would eventually lead him to break from Anglicanism and found the Methodist Church. The Moravians went on to influence not only the Methodists but also the Salvation Army and eventually the Baptists. In 1792, when William Carey wrote his argument for why Baptists should become involved in foreign mission, he used information gleaned from the Moravians' Periodical Accounts—records of populations and church sizes in various countries. In his defense of that periodical at a subsequent Baptist Church Assembly, Carey exclaimed, "See what these Moravians have done.

Can we not follow their example, and in obedience to our Heavenly Master, go out into the world and preach the Gospel to the heathen?"[19]

From the 1740s, Moravian mission work spread rapidly to Africa, America, Russia, and other parts of the world. Zinzendorf himself traveled to the New World to convert Indigenous North Americans.

So synonymous had the term "Moravian" come to be with "missionary" that, in 1850, novelist Herman Melville, despairing the state of the world and church and yearning for renewal, wrote, "Are there no Moravians in the Moon, that not a missionary has yet visited this poor pagan planet of ours, to civilize civilization and Christianize Christendom?"[20]

All of this illustrates what we noted earlier—that God seems to use the most unlikely people to accomplish his purposes; in this case, to extend his kingdom.

First, God used a small movement of largely unlearned Jews from the far-flung eastern edge of the Roman Empire to bring the gospel to Rome.

Then, God used the wild, intemperate Celts from the far northern edges of the empire to re-Christianize Europe.

Next, he chose a group of despised outsiders—the Moravians—to be his messengers.

THE MORAVIAN WAY

The Moravians refused to establish a denominational missionary society and neither did they plant Moravian churches. Their motto became "In essentials, unity; in non-essentials, liberty; and in all things, love." What follows is an outline of their unusual approach to mission.

The centrality of the suffering and death of Christ. At the center of Moravian mission theology was the sacrifice of the Lamb. They spoke of Christ as "Brother Lambkin," and themselves as "little woundparsons," "worms in the wounds in his side," and "cross-wood little splinters." They fully expected that mission would bring suffering, and possibly persecution, and were willing to endure such for Christ.

Reliance on the power of the Holy Spirit. Naturally, a movement that was launched by a spiritual revival would emphasize a reliance on the Spirit's guidance. They would start by silently watching to see if any of the heathen (as they called them) were prepared, by the grace of God, to receive and believe the Word of life. Then, if even one was found, they would preach the gospel to her or him, trusting that God would open their ears and heart to receive the gospel. And finally, they focused on preaching chiefly to those who had never heard the gospel. They felt they were not to build on any foundation laid by other missionaries nor to disturb their work, but rather to seek the unreached and forsaken.

The concept of "first fruits." The Moravians sensed that the Indigenous people were already "bent" toward the gospel. Those who believed were called the "first fruit." They were to be baptized, trained, and given the task of leading the local churches. Not only did the Spirit prepare the hearts of those who would hear, but he would also care for those he called. If the Spirit cared for the new believers, then the missionary was not to remain with them permanently.

The unity of believers. Along with the church's belief that the Spirit's work was essential in the salvation and discipling of the first fruits, the initial Moravians emphasized the unity of all Christians in Christ. Therefore, as noted earlier, they chose not to set up "Moravian churches" in "competition" with other denominations, but instead preferred to send their converts to churches already established in the area.

Being guided by prayer and the casting of lots. When faced with a difficult decision about which tribe or community to reach out to, they cast lots, trusting God to direct them accordingly.

Work among the marginalized. In preaching Christ and his salvation, Moravians seemed to choose the most far-flung, neglected, and oppressed people and places of the world.

The practice of cultural humility. Visiting North America in 1742, Zinzendorf said, "Apart from this, they shall remain Indians,"[21] meaning that the Moravian mission did not intend to change the native culture. In this respect, the Moravians were a very early example of cultural contextualization (more on that in chapter eight). Their approach to local people was one of generosity and inclusion. Mark Noll refers to this in his book on the rise of evangelicalism, in which he reflects on the Moravians' work in the Caribbean colonies:

> Anglican Christianity remained resolutely hierarchical, made much of status and hereditary roles ... [and] maintained sharp racial divisions. By contrast the Moravians seemed to be offering a far more inclusive style of church life. They encouraged blacks to sing with whites, preached spiritual equality before God and welcomed the expression of religious emotion ...

So radical were the Moravians for their time that one of the early workers in
St Thomas actually took a bride [of mixed race], a step that brought down
the wrath of the island's white planters.[22]

The decision to preach the gospel in Indigenous languages. This might
seem obvious, but many Catholic missionaries up to that point had only
preached to those people who had learned Spanish or Portuguese, which left
Indigenous peoples with the distinct impression that Christianity was a foreign
religion.

Refusal to openly condemn polygamy and slavery. The Moravians didn't
condone polygamy or slavery, and instead saw their role as evangelists. They
were willing to overlook seemingly intractable social issues in preference for
calling people to salvation. It is commonly claimed that two pioneer Moravian
missionaries, Johann Leonhard Dober and David Nitschmann, who left
Germany for the Virgin Islands in 1732, voluntarily sold themselves into
slavery to evangelize the enslaved African community. The evidence that this
occurred is scant, although Dober did write that he was more than willing to
become a slave if that proved necessary.

We've noted the way St. Benedict and later Bernard of Clairvaux were
fresh springs from whom flowed a great river of Benedictine missionaries.
Similarly, we've seen the ways that Ignatius of Loyola and Francis Xavier
were taps from which the flood of Jesuit mission gushed. Now, Nikolaus
Ludwig (Count von Zinzendorf) joins their ranks. By the end of his life in
1760, there had sprung a deluge of Moravians who had established active
missions from Greenland to South Africa. And like water, the Moravians
seeped into every crack and crevice, disappearing from sight as a separate
entity in themselves. As Zinzendorf envisioned, his movement became not
a distinct denomination but a dynamic renewal society, which would serve
to revitalize existing denominations and help create new work in mission
areas.

There is much that early Moravian missions can teach us today, including
their desire to be led by the Spirt; their reliance on deep, long-term corporate
prayer; their allegiance to the example of Christ; their humility and gentleness;
their love for the least loved; and their willingness to be lost to history.

SPIRIT SEEKING TODAY

In 2005, a group of around a hundred British Christians converged at Holy Trinity, Clapham—the church of William Wilberforce and the Clapham Sect (a group that advocated for the abolition of slavery and supported missions at home and abroad). Their intent was to revive the prayer movement begun by the Moravians. There, they took vows and started a lay ecumenical religious order called the Order of the Mustard Seed (OMS).

In reality, this was the re-launching of a movement begun by Zinzendorf himself when he was studying at Halle. With five fellow students, he formed a society with the express purpose of inspiring all Christians "to labor for the salvation and fellowship of all regardless of denominations." They called themselves the Order of the Mustard Seed and adopted the motto, "No man liveth unto himself," eventually developing three central vows: to be true to Christ, to be kind to people, and to take the gospel to the nations. Because of the Moravian Pentecost we looked at earlier, and the subsequent hundred-year prayer meeting, the original OMS was also strongly associated with the idea of continual prayer.

The modern-day OMS used the same name for their order, as well as the Moravian focus on prayer and the Clapham Sect's vision for evangelical revival. In 2018, they were formally acknowledged by the Anglican House of Bishops as an ecumenical, lay-led international missional movement with a shared rule of life. They focus on prayer and seeking to make a measurable difference among the poor and the lost. Drawing their rule of life from the original OMS, they have developed six practices to express the three central vows:

Being true to Christ...

1. We live prayerfully.
2. We celebrate creativity to His glory.

Being kind to people...

3. We practice hospitality.
4. We express God's mercy and justice.

Taking the gospel to the nations...

5. We commit ourselves to lifelong learning that we might shape culture and
    make disciples by being discipled.
6. We engage in mission and evangelism.[23]

Pete Greig, one of the founders of OMS, says the rule of life "is a set of principles
and practices we build into the rhythm of our daily lives, helping us to deepen
our relationship with God and to serve him more faithfully. If creeds are what
we believe and Christ is why we believe, a rule is how we seek to live out that
faith, day to day as disciples in the power of the Holy Spirit."[24]

But it's not possible to talk about OMS without acknowledging not only
its historical roots but also its contemporary ones—in particular the 24-7
Prayer movement.

In September 1999, a small student-led prayer vigil went viral. Meeting in a
warehouse on a back street on the south coast of England, this group of young
people became inflamed with the Spirit and devoted to a life of prayer. They
committed themselves to a vision to revive the church and affect British culture
through non-stop, night-and-day prayer. They were Spirit-seekers, who had no
idea the Spirit would use them to launch an international prayer network with
over twenty thousand prayer rooms in more than seventy-five countries.

I began this chapter on Spirit seeking by quoting Ignatius IV and his
warning that the church should not over-rely on ecclesial strategy and technique
but instead draw on the power and guidance of the Holy Spirit. In the stories of
von Welz, Ziegenbalg and Plütschau, Zinzendorf, and Wesley, we can see what
it looks like when Christians do indeed draw on that very power. Their stories
remind us that good tactics can only take us so far; but when we seek the Spirit,
devoting ourselves to prayer—lots of prayer—God works through us in the
most surprising ways.

The contemporary 24-7 Prayer and OMS movements tell us the Spirit still
moves today, confounding our best management practice and striding over our
well-laid plans.

There seems to be a lot of self-indulgence when it comes to our views on the
work of the Holy Spirit today. Influenced as we are by our pervasive consumerist
culture, we tend to commodify everything, even turning people into objects of
trade or "human resources." In such a world it is tempting to also objectify the

Spirit into a useful tool for our own needs and purposes rather than seeing the Spirit as a Person—a Friend who fills us with the very life of Christ.

Now, more than ever, we need the Spirit to free us from the stultifying effects of consumerism and comfort. We need the Spirit's help to unify the church. We need the courage of the Holy Spirit to speak of God. We need the Spirit's wisdom to know when to speak up against culture's ills and when to be silent. We need the Holy Spirit to open eyes, hearts, and minds to shift us out of the immanent frame common to us all in the West.

And this applies to not only the more conservative evangelicals among us. Even the Spirit-filled charismatic renewal movements of today need to heed the example of the Moravians. At a time when charismatics and Pentecostals can be enamored by a kind of prosperity gospel, which tends to shun suffering, the Moravian readiness to endure persecution and extreme hardship for Christ is an important corrective.

Speaking of the journey of 24-7 Prayer, Pete Greig writes,

[The Spirit] really does do "immeasurably more than we can ask or imagine" (Eph. 3). He really is utterly and completely faithful. It's been a wild ride— much scarier, deeper, and more exciting than we could ever have possibly imagined in those first few hours trying to pray in that warehouse twenty years ago. We have made so many mistakes but the one thing we have got right is this: we have never stopped saying yes to the Holy Spirit. Whenever he has told us to do a thing, we have tried to do it and the results have been incredible! If he is asking you to do something today—do it.[25]

Never stop saying yes to the Holy Spirit. Be a Spirit-seeker.

The Fifth Shape

WORDSMITHING

To translate is to incarnate. To bring the Bible to a people in words they embrace, in a language their tongue can feel and articulate, is to say in no uncertain terms that Jesus also lives in their neighborhood.

BRIAN STILLER

In 1876, the adventurer/journalist Henry Morton Stanley wrote an article for Britain's *The Daily Telegraph* in which he described his meeting with Kabaka Mutesa, the feared ruler of remote Buganda (modern-day Uganda). Stanley reported that the king claimed he was willing to receive British missionaries, quoting him as saying, "White men will be welcome for the account of Christianity."[1]

The Daily Telegraph subsequently ran an appeal to fund missionary work in Uganda, and in just three days raised £5,000, which was offered to the Church Mission Society for this purpose.[2] (Try to imagine that happening today!) The news inspired Scottish missionary Alexander Murdoch Mackay to put himself forward to lead the expedition, and the following year he set out for Kampala with seven missionary companions.

Back then, the journey to Uganda involved sailing to Mombasa on the coast of Kenya and then trekking through to the shore of Lake Victoria before sailing the final leg to Kampala. Today, driving that 400 miles from the Kenyan coast

to the shore of Lake Victoria would take about fourteen hours. But Mackay
and his group had to make the journey on foot through thick jungle, which he
described this way:

> Imagine a forest of lofty, slender trees, with a cop between of thorny
> creepers, so dense below that a cat could scarcely creep along; and branched
> and intertwined above like green unraveled hemp. Through it winds a path,
> as if it had followed the trail of a reptile, and almost losing itself here and
> there, where the creeping wild vine and thorny acacia have encroached
> upon it. Now the densest jungle has yielded to the slashing strokes of a
> score of Snider sword bayonets and a road wide enough for two wagons to
> pass each other has been constructed, the nullahs [gullies, ravines] being
> bridged over, boulders removed, and rough places made smooth.[3]

The journey was brutal. They were not only traversing tough country, but they
were also building a road as they went! On the way, the group was beset by
illness and exhaustion. At one point Mackay himself had to be left behind
to recuperate while the others pressed on. In the end, only three of them—
Mackay, C. T. Wilson, and Lt. Shergold Smith—reached Uganda in June 1877.

So, why did they need to make this path to Lake Victoria so wide? Because
Alexander Mackay was transporting a very particular piece of missionary
equipment to Kampala, one that required him to get two large wagons to the
lake's edge.

He was hauling a printing press from London.

It is telling that a missionary expedition in the 1880s considered a printing
press such an essential piece of apparatus that they would lug it through the
most inhospitable, and sometimes almost impassible, countryside. Many
Protestant missionaries of the time viewed the translation, printing, and distribution of the Bible as their central task. They had come to bring words to their
audiences, both spoken and written. Mackay was just the latest in a long list of
nineteenth-century missionary-translators and printers.

In 1800, for example, William Carey established a printing works and paper
mill on the banks of the Hooghly River in Serampore, Bengal. One member of
his team was a professional printer. During his lifetime, Carey completed six
translations of the entire Bible and rendered portions of the New Testament
into nearly thirty additional languages.

In 1807, Robert Morrison became the first Protestant missionary to travel to China, where he lived for twenty-five years in Macau and Guangzhou, translating the whole Bible and baptizing ten persons. Morrison's team included two professional printers, Walter Henry Medhurst and William Milne.

Throughout the 1820s, missionaries Adoniram and Ann Judson endured years of suffering in Burma, including seventeen months of being tortured in prison. All the while, Judson continued his work on a Burmese translation of the Bible, which he completed in 1837.

In 1834, a Church Missionary Society (CMS) printer named William Colenso arrived in New Zealand's Bay of Islands with the nation's first printing press. Missionaries had been translating the Bible and the *Book of Common Prayer* into the Māori language *(te reo Māori)* for years prior to Colenso's arrival, and they were champing at the bit to start printing and distributing their work. It took just six weeks for Colenso to crank out copies of a sixteen-page pamphlet, containing two of Paul's epistles, in *te reo Māori*. Three years later, he produced five thousand copies of William Williams' 356-page *Māori New Testament*, followed by twenty-seven thousand copies of the *Book of Common Prayer*.

The CMS printing works at Kerikeri, on the western shore of the beautiful Bay of Islands, was in a hurry because it had come to their attention that, in 1838, French Catholic missionaries had established the Pompallier Mission at Kororareka (now Russell) directly across the bay. And the French meant business. They had built a grand two-story printery and tannery where church texts were translated from Latin to *te reo Māori*, then printed and bound in beautiful leather covers.

This meant war. A printing war.

As fast as the Catholics could churn out a translated version of the breviary, the Anglicans countered with a new pamphlet or tract. They were trying to out-print each other.

The European missionaries held such confidence in the power of the printed word that they believed whichever denomination could get their doctrine into the hearts and minds of the Māori first, would "win."

This isn't to say nineteenth-century missionaries weren't interested in other kinds of ministry. William Carey, for example, advocated strongly against child prostitution and the Indian practice of *sati* (widow burning). And Alexander Mackay was a tireless campaigner against slavery, cannibalism, and revenge

killings. But the key strategies of missionaries at that time were Bible translation, literature printing and distribution, evangelization, moral crusades, and
education—all of which the missionaries did with monumental effectiveness.

Where did this fervor for literature distribution come from? The Jesuit
missionaries to Japan in the sixteenth century made little attempt to translate
or distribute the Bible in the local language. In China during the Ming Dynasty
(1368–1644), the Franciscans and Dominicans prioritized other liturgical and
pastoral works over Bible translation. Indeed, Catholic canon law prohibited the
translation and publication of the Scriptures without the approval of the Apostolic
See or the conference of bishops. And yet, by the early 1800s, Protestant missionaries saw *wordsmithing* as their primary shape of mission. To help us understand
this dramatic change in strategy, we need to look back and see what forces were at
work, molding the missionaries of the 1800s into such wordsmiths.

THE ENLIGHTENMENT PARADIGM

The Enlightenment is defined as "a philosophical movement of the 18th
century, characterized by belief in the power of human reason and by innovations in political, religious, and educational doctrine."[4] It is said to have begun
with the death of Louis XIV of France in 1715, running until the outbreak of
the French Revolution in 1789, although some historians date its end as the
start of the nineteenth century. Regardless of when it began and ended, the
effects of the Enlightenment on Western society can't be overstated.

In 1700, a young man could grow up in a small village in Europe, be
apprenticed in the same trade as his father, marry a local girl, raise children,
attend the parish church, grow old, and be buried in the parish cemetery. He
would see himself as part of a fixed system of relationships rather than as an
individual with autonomy or agency. He wouldn't even contemplate the possibility of travel or education or choosing a different vocation. Women especially
wouldn't consider such choices as appropriate.

But a century later, young men and women would see themselves entirely
differently. They would dream of new horizons, of choosing their careers, of
pursuing education and travel opportunities. By the middle of the nineteenth
century, young people would consider the world their oyster and see themselves
as the masters of their own destinies.

The Age of Enlightenment brought this dramatic shift—and with it a new
kind of society and a new worldview. A worldview is an overall perspective that

includes, among other things, a view of God (or gods), of human power structures, of human beings, and of nature. As a whole, this way of seeing things tells people where they fit and what they are worth.

That hypothetical young person back in 1700 would have understood the unquestioned order of things to look like this:

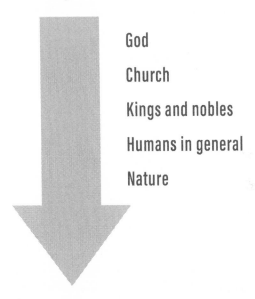

God

Church

Kings and nobles

Humans in general

Nature

God was perceived to be in heaven, ruling over everything. God conferred authority on the church (hierarchy), which in turn appointed kings to administer society. Our hypothetical young person wouldn't question a noblemen's jurisdiction over him. Neither would he dispute the pronouncements of his bishop. Beneath the young man was nature, which was ruled over by all humans. Whether he was a farmer or a stonemason or baker, he imposed his will on natural elements to produce the fruits of his labor.

The influence of the Enlightenment renegotiated that worldview, particularly in Protestant countries. The first shift was the reduction in the authority of the church. The Protestant revolution had shaken the church's foundations and caused ordinary people to question doctrines and practices they had previously accepted. But the subsequent corruption of the church, religious wars between Catholics and Protestants, and the increasing diversity of Protestant expressions significantly eroded confidence in Christianity. Church was therefore removed from the hierarchy of authority.

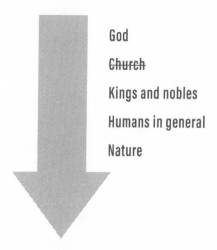

God

~~Church~~

Kings and nobles

Humans in general

Nature

The Enlightenment unfolded in waves, beginning in the academies and later affecting industry. The invention of the cotton gin, along with the emergence of city factories and mills and other technological innovations, set off what we now call the Industrial Revolution (1760–mid-1800s). People left the villages of their ancestors and moved to bigger towns for work. They felt dislocated from their own histories, from the land, and from tradition. The kings and nobles of Europe were not ready to navigate the complexities of this ever-changing era, and soon cries of revolution were ringing in the streets. The Age of Revolution (1764–1848), which included the American Revolution, the French Revolution, the Spanish-American Wars for Independence, the Italian Revolutions, the Greek War of Independence, and the Spring of Nations, destroyed the authority of monarchs.

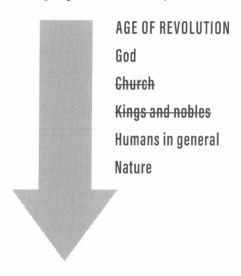

AGE OF REVOLUTION

God

~~Church~~

~~Kings and nobles~~

Humans in general

Nature

Europeans came to believe that, while God still held the ultimate authority, individuals had been given autonomy to choose their own destinies. Today, we take it for granted that the individual should be considered competent to determine what their life looks like; but the realization that no pope or bishop or king or duke could control a person's life was a whole new way of thinking in the early 1700s. Of course, this led to a deeply held belief in the right of human freedom and a confidence about the progress of human society. What followed was the overthrow of despots and the establishment of democratic rule. Another result was one of the grandest Enlightenment projects—the founding of what would become the United States of America. As it says in America's Declaration of Independence: "We hold these truths to be self-evident, that all men are created equal, that they are endowed by their creator with certain unalienable rights, that among these are life, liberty and the pursuit of happiness."

In the second wave of the Enlightenment, the Age of Reason, the worldview was adjusted even further, as trust in science and technology was elevated and belief in God was questioned. Since anything that couldn't be proven by the scientific method was doubted, God was removed from the hierarchy of authority.

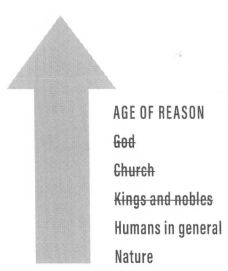

AGE OF REASON
~~God~~
~~Church~~
~~Kings and nobles~~
Humans in general
Nature

THE SHAPING OF A NEW KIND OF CHRISTIAN

Several threads of thought ran through the Age of Reason, which not only shaped society as a whole but also formed a new kind of Christian.

First, it was assumed that reason was based on the five human senses—that which could be physically observed and verified. No longer was it believed that humans had authority over nature. Rather, humans were under the authority of natural law—albeit detached from nature and capable of studying it. Scientific observation was based on the understanding that nature operates by reliable cause and effect, which is objective, factual, and value-free. Above all, people put their faith in humanity's ability to use rigorous scientific inquiry to unravel what had previously been unknowable or mysterious. It was assumed that the superstitious musings of the church and the so-called wisdom of God were no longer needed. An underlying assumption became prevalent: science dealt with facts, whereas the Bible was a book of opinions and values.

Some Christians in this era resisted this newfound devotion to reason and science by stubbornly claiming that the Bible was a collection of verifiable facts and that any scientific discovery that contradicted the Scriptures was illegitimate. But other Christians couldn't refute the scientific method. They acknowledged the discoveries of science and agreed that the Bible belonged to the world of opinions and values; but they still held the view that those opinions and values were superior to the results of scientific inquiry.

Second, Enlightenment-era Christians were deeply affected by the elevation of reason and science. More than just accommodating science and reason, some Christians in this era were deeply influenced by this new thinking. Often voracious readers and believing all truth to be God's truth, they hungrily devoured books on history, geography, science, and languages. For example, William Carey was fascinated by James Cook's account of his exploration of the South Seas. Adoniram Judson could read at the age of three, took navigation lessons at the age of ten, and studied theology as a child. And, as an infant, David Livingstone was an avid reader and loved looking for animal, plant, and geological specimens in local limestone quarries. For Enlightenment-era Christians, the world was a gigantic three-dimensional puzzle created by God for his glory and our pleasure.

Third, Enlightenment-era Christians developed great confidence in human ingenuity. It might seem like an ironic outcome, given how deeply aware Christians were of human sinfulness and the evils in society, but even though they held no faith in humanity itself, many came to believe that human ingenuity was capable of solving all manner of problems in the world. This mirrored what was happening in society, where Enlightenment thinkers were proposing that if people were just reason-able and put in the effort, anything was possible. While secular thinkers claimed humanity had been held back by tradition and religion, Enlightenment-era Christians came to believe that Christianity could rid the world of injustice and poverty. Indeed, mission came to be seen as a vehicle for progress and prosperity as well as for faith and eternal life.

In 1776, when Thomas Jefferson, Benjamin Franklin, John Adams, Roger Sherman, and Robert R. Livingston wrote that they held "these truths to be self-evident," they were referring to ideas that would certainly not have been considered self-evident to their own grandparents. Within a couple of generations, a whole new outlook had dawned on Western society.

Of course, as we know, the framers of the Declaration of Independence didn't fully embrace their lofty ideas. Women and people of color were not afforded the same equality, agency, or suffrage. But the American project was built on the foundation of the pillars of the Enlightenment—at least in theory.

The Enlightenment had a devastating effect on the church, leaching it of its institutional power, undermining its authority, casting doubt on its doctrines, and draining its congregations. But conversely, it also had a remarkably invigorating effect on the church, particularly on the pietistic and conservative sectors. It was impossible to grow up in the late eighteenth or early nineteenth centuries and not be shaped by Enlightenment thinking, and that was as true for devout Christians as anyone.

During this time, Christians embraced a belief in the primacy of individual agency and autonomy by emphasizing the idea of "personal salvation." A person wasn't a Christian just because they were raised in the church; they needed to experience—to feel in their soul—a sense of God's love for them (what was often called the "assurance of salvation"). Most Enlightenment-shaped missionaries had experienced a profound sense of conversion after reading an evangelistic tract or book or hearing a revivalist preacher.

Similarly, many Christians in this era took up the idea of human rights and championed causes such as abolition and universal suffrage. They found their way into the low-church tradition, eschewing the authority of bishops and boards, and preached that every person needed to follow whatever calling God placed in their heart.

What emerged in the late eighteenth century and into the nineteenth century was an incredible cohort of well-read, deeply motivated, hardy souls, willing to move any mountain to preach the good news to the lost. Herbert Kane says of them,

> Almost without exception the missionaries of the nineteenth century were men and women of deep conviction and compassion. They believed that the heathen were lost without a knowledge of Jesus Christ. They spared no pains to take the gospel to the lost and dying "before it was too late."[5]

With all that in mind, try to picture that intrepid Scot, Alexander Murdoch Mackay, hauling a huge printing press through the jungles of Kenya. Nothing could stop him. He and his colleagues built a highway from the coast to the lake. In Kampala, they built churches and houses, while Mackay translated the Bible and sent sections to the printing house they had established. The Ugandans nicknamed Mackay, *Muzunguwa Kazi*—"the white man of work." He was a true Enlightenment man; one who harnessed the best ideas from that era into humble service for Africans.

THE MOTIVATIONS OF ENLIGHTENMENT-ERA MISSIONARIES

Enlightenment-era thinking had a profound effect on missionary *practice*, but it is also worth looking at how this era affected the *motivations* of European and American missionaries, particularly in the nineteenth century. Those motivations can be grouped under three broad categories.

First, they were theologically motivated. An orientation toward individual agency led these missionaries to emphasize personal piety. Like the European Pietists we looked at earlier, they were compelled by a number of deeply held theological beliefs, such as:

- **Jesus' love:** Nineteenth-century missionaries were moved by a tremendous sense of personal gratitude for salvation and a genuine concern for those without Christ. This became a dominant theme. Missionaries would compile statistics on the populations of unreached nations to motivate others to join them in their work. The British missionary to China, Hudson Taylor, was famous for saying "A million a month in China are dying without God, and we who have received in trust the Word of Life—we are responsible."[6] While undoubtedly provoked by Jesus' love for the nations of the world, much of this approach was still laden with unhelpful assumptions about the "noble savage" waiting for the (superior, white) missionary to save them. But their love for Jesus and the world was undeniable.

- **Obedience to God's commission:** William Carey promoted the use of the Great Commission (Mt 28:18–20) to recruit missionaries. Enlightenment-era Christians took this passage seriously and came to see it as a personal call to obey the last command of Christ.

- **Beliefs about the Second Coming:** The complexity of these beliefs is beyond the scope of our discussion here, but it is enough to say that eschatology took on monumental significance. Amillennialists and postmillennialists were able to make room for the values of the Enlightenment and its belief in human flowering, and promoted Christianity as the means by which society would be renewed. Premillennialists, who came to dominate the world-mission scene, believed in a cataclysmic and imminent end to history and were motivated to save as many as possible before the return of Christ.

Second, they were imperialistically motivated. Loath as we might be to admit it, missionaries at this time were shaped by Western imperialism. Indeed, by the latter half of the nineteenth century, colonialism was an unstoppable force, and the context for all missionary activity.

Ultimately, the emphasis on individualism, freedom, science, and technology did fulfill the Enlightenment promise of progress. US and European societies experienced phenomenal economic growth and a solidified confidence in the idea of the democratic nation-state. But these beliefs also led to Western arrogance. Europeans and Americans came to believe that they had risen to a higher form of humanity and that there could be no end to their march to perfection.

Of course, this march to perfection was achieved on the backs of non-Western nations. Hungry for resources like rubber, spices, opium, gold, diamonds, and silver, the United States and European nations such as France, Britain, Spain, and the Netherlands, began colonizing other nations around the world. This Age of Imperialism (1800–1914) saw the systematic subjugation of Indigenous peoples in every continent of the world. Even Western countries that didn't technically establish foreign colonies, such as the US, acted toward other cultures with a sense of authority and superiority.

In *A History of Christianity*, Diarmaid MacCulloch notes that the goal of the church in this era was "to make the world Protestant" under the protective cloak of European colonialism; but he admits "there was a complex relationship between mission and this imperial expansion."[7]

Reflecting on this complexity, research professor Robert Woodberry writes, "One of the main stereotypes about missions is that they were closely connected to colonialism, but Protestant missionaries not funded by the state were regularly very critical of colonialism."[8]

Regardless, colonialism certainly helped Protestant mission to survive and thrive. Not long after Mackay got to Kampala, a ferocious wave of persecution broke out in Uganda, with hundreds of Christians barbarically executed. Mackay's work and that of his colleagues only survived when the British army arrived to overthrow the Ugandan king and annex the region to their East African colony in Kenya.

Even Hudson Taylor—regarded by many as the greatest nineteenth-century missionary—benefited from the power of Western imperialism. Taylor became a missionary to China in the 1850s, founding the China Inland Mission (CIM) in 1865. An extraordinary man by all accounts, Taylor was a dynamo of activity. He not only oversaw the establishment of 260 mission stations, but he also regularly traveled to the UK and US to recruit more missionaries and raise much-needed funds. By 1895, CIM numbered 641 missionaries, 462 Chinese helpers, and 5,211 communicants. The CIM was non-denominational, evangelical, and global.

But it must be noted that, ten years before Hudson Taylor arrived in China, the country had been dragged into a series of military conflicts known as the Opium Wars. The British East India Company had been successfully plying the opium trade in India and China for many years. Not only had opium flooded the streets of London, but it also swamped the Chinese villages that grew the poppies to sell to the British. The ensuing opium epidemic inflicted devastating social and economic damage on the Chinese. In 1841, a local governor, Lin Zexu, decided to end the opium trade altogether and ordered all poppy farms and cultivation factories to be burned to the ground. Opium dens were closed. Dealers of the drug were executed. It was a harsh program but, as Lin famously wrote to Queen Victoria, "I now give my assurance that we mean to cut this harmful drug forever."

And what was Britain's response? They sent in the Navy, of course.

British gunboats—including a new experimental gunboat named *Nemesis* that could fire 32-pounders—peppered the coastal cities with fire. The Royal Navy decimated the Chinese ships and crushed Canton before moving north to attack Nanjing (Nanking). The Chinese were easily defeated and were forced to sign the Treaty of Nanking, granting Western nations five ports for residence and trade. They also had to cede Hong Kong to British rule, compensate for the opium destroyed, and allow British monitoring of tariff rates.

David Lebedoff writes,

> Since history is written by the winners, this triumph of thuggery is known simply as the Opium War, which could leave the impression that England was trying to stop the Chinese from selling opium to *them*. It is as if, in the 1980s, the Colombians had destroyed all US border facilities and there-after, without restriction, hooked the American population on cocaine. This was, for wellborn Englishmen, the nineteenth-century version of the global economy.[9]

For our purposes, though, it is worth noting that one of the clauses of the Treaty of Nanking granted "the right of foreigners to travel in the internal regions of China for the purpose of travel, trade or missionary activities." Therefore, when Hudson Taylor arrived more than a decade later, the Chinese gave him and his compatriots unfettered access to any parts of their country they chose to travel. So, while it is true that the CIM didn't have a British military escort and were serving in places with no British garrison anywhere nearby, the reality is that their safety was assured by what British peer Lord Shaftesbury referred to as a "cruel and debasing war ... one of the most lawless, unnecessary and unfair struggles in the records of history."[10]

Taylor himself refused to align with British interests and campaigned vigor-ously against the opium trade. When the CIM suffered alongside other mission agencies during the Boxer uprising against foreigners in 1900, he refused the compensation extracted from the Chinese government by European forces. But his story does demonstrate how impossible it was for British and American missionaries to serve in foreign lands without the shadow of European colonialism.

Third, missionaries were motivated by various cultural movements. During this time, many movements enjoyed a widespread rise in volunteerism.

People offered their services to social movements such as abolitionism, temperance leagues, the trade union movement, and suffrage campaigns. In many respects, the formation of missionary societies and agencies was the same.

As implied earlier, this was also a time of incredible pragmatism. Every societal problem was seen as merely a challenge to be overcome. Optimism, enthusiasm, and activism led to great success in all fields, including the missionary endeavor. In fact, by the end of the nineteenth century, many in the missions world believed the evangelization of every nation was within reach.

One cultural movement of this time was patronizingly referred to as "the white man's burden." This phrase was drawn from the title of a Rudyard Kipling poem that is now considered misguided and racist. In it, Kipling called his European readers to "send forth the best ye breed" to "serve your captives' need."[11] In other words, Kipling was telling superior Europeans to assist the helpless people they had subjugated. As distasteful as this poem is today, it summed up the curious and contradictory attitude Europeans had toward colonized peoples in the nineteenth century. Christian missionaries weren't immune to this thinking. Some of them came to trust in the "manifest destiny" of Western nations, adopting the conviction that God, in his providence, had chosen the Western nations, because of their unique qualities, to be the standard bearers of his cause even to the uttermost parts of the earth.[12]

THESE LOVERS OF WORDS

How strange a sight these nineteenth-century missionaries with their printing presses and ink-stained fingers must have seemed. They were lovers of words— words they claimed to have received from God, and which contained the hope of eternal life. Up until that point, few missionaries emphasized hearing or reading the words of Scripture.

In India, for example, before 1800, missionaries denied Hindus certain employment opportunities and they were obliged to assemble periodically in churches to listen to preaching or to the refutation of their religion. The missionaries instigated mass baptisms, "making" Indians into Christians. These baptisms were "wordless" conversions. No gospel was preached. No faith was present. It was an almost magical ritual, completely unintelligible to its subjects.

But worse than that, Hindus were cruelly tricked into submitting to it. T. R. De Souza describes this insidious practice:

> A particularly grave abuse was practiced in Goa in the form of "mass baptism" and what went before it. The practice was begun by the Jesuits and was later initiated by the Franciscans also. The Jesuits staged an annual mass baptism on the Feast of the Conversion of St. Paul (25 January), and in order to secure as many neophytes as possible, a few days before the ceremony the Jesuits would go through the streets of the Hindu quarters in pairs, accompanied by their Negro slaves, whom they would urge to seize the Hindus. When the blacks caught up a fugitive, they would smear his lips with a piece of beef, making him an "untouchable" among his people. Conversion to Christianity was then his only option.[13]

Further east, in the area later occupied by William Carey, the conversion of the Bengalis involved a strange partnership between Catholic missionaries and Portuguese pirates. Whenever pirates captured local princes, missionaries forced them to convert. In one celebrated case, the Portuguese captured the young prince of Bhushna, an estate in Dhaka District. He was converted by Augustinians, and, in turn, demanded the conversion of twenty thousand Hindus in and around his estate.

In 1677, a report into the work in Bengali found nearly twenty-five thousand converts with hardly any knowledge of Christianity. It was also reported that many of them became Christians for personal gain—whether that be jobs, contracts, or access to business contacts.

These wordless, mass conversions came to an end as the Enlightenment-era missionaries, those lovers of words, arrived to print and preach the Word. The new wave of Protestant missionaries only offered baptism to those who had understood and assented to Christian belief.

William and Dorothy Carey arrived in India at the end of 1793. In 1800, a group of new missionaries came to assist them, including Joshua Marshman, a teacher, and William Ward, a printer. Carey relocated his base to Serampore and set about implementing a five-pronged approach to his work: (1) widespread preaching of the gospel by every possible method, (2) support of the preaching by the distribution of the Bible in the languages of the country,

(3) establishment, as soon as possible, of a church, (4) deep study of the background and thought of the non-Christian peoples, and (5) training, at earliest convenience, of indigenous leaders.

By 1818, approximately six hundred people had been baptized at Serampore, with several thousand regularly attending church and classes.

WITH WORDS COMES LIFE

These days it is common for people to make sweeping statements about the harm caused by colonial-era missionaries. We often assume they went blundering into foreign lands, trampling over long-held traditions, disrespecting the beliefs of Indigenous peoples, and destroying their cultures. As we've seen, there is no question that many saw the gospel as an intrinsic part of Western culture, and that evangelizing was often conflated with Westernizing.

But, in her *Christianity Today* article, "The Surprising Discovery About Those Colonialist, Proselytizing Missionaries," Andrea Palpant Dilley attempts to broaden that understanding, saying the overall effect of nineteenth-century mission was remarkably positive. She quotes scholar Robert Woodberry:

> We don't have to deny that there were and are racist missionaries. We don't have to deny there were and are missionaries who do self-centered things. But if that were the average effect, we would expect the places where missionaries had influence to be worse than places where missionaries weren't allowed or were restricted in action. We find exactly the opposite on all kinds of outcomes. Even in places where few people converted, [missionaries] had a profound economic and political impact.[14]

Dilley distinguishes between what she calls *conversionary* Protestant missionaries and those Protestant clergy financed by the state (as well as Catholic missionaries). In contrast with conversionary missionaries, she claims statechurch missionaries had little effect in the areas where they worked. So, how did these conversionary Protestants make such a difference to the societies they served? Dilley says the answer is twofold: social reform and mass education/literacy.

Social reform. We'll explore this aspect of mission more in the next chapter, but for now it is worth noting Dilley's examples of the ways missionaries contributed to the good of their host society. She lists the following:

- In Africa, missionaries campaigned to protect land from White settlers.
- In China, missionaries worked to end the opium trade.
- In India, they fought to curtail abuses by landlords.
- In the West Indies and other colonies, they played key roles in the abolition movement.
- In Australia and New Zealand, they protected tribes from being wiped out by settlers.

In the 1860s, when Boers (Dutch-speaking European settlers) started encroaching on lands owned by the Tswana, John Mackenzie, a Scottish-born London Missionary Society missionary to South Africa, started lobbying for the British government to adopt the Tswana territories as a protectorate. He even arranged for their chief, Kharma III, to travel with him to London, where Mackenzie translated for him at political rallies. There were petitions and meetings with members of parliament and even an audience with Queen Victoria. Ultimately, Mackenzie and Kharma obtained the British government's agreement to establish the protectorate of British Bechuanaland as a secure homeland for the Tswana. Now, it is known as Botswana, and without Mackenzie's efforts it might not exist as a nation today.

Mass education/literacy. Colonial-era Protestants were learning local languages and translating the Bible for the purpose of converting local people to Christianity. But for those very people to access the knowledge contained in Scripture, they needed to learn to read. Teaching communities how to read their own language inadvertently changed the future of their nations.

Dilley quotes historian Dana Roberts, saying, "They focused on teaching people to read. That sounds really basic, but if you look worldwide at poverty, literacy is the main thing that helps you rise out of poverty. Unless you have broad-based literacy, you can't have democratic movements."[15]

Furthermore, as true sons and daughters of the Enlightenment, these missionaries were also people with a deep love of knowledge, a hunger for learning, and a curiosity about the world. They instilled those qualities in the people among whom they ministered.

And so, while it is true that some missionaries saw the gospel as part of Western culture and assumed the "right" of Western nations to affect other cultures, and while it is true they labored within a colonialist context, there were also missionaries who saw personal sacrifice as primary. They loved those to whom God had sent them, and served them with fervor, optimism, and pragmatism. Their overarching motives were to bring God glory, to share the message of Jesus' love, and to prepare souls for eternity.

WORDSMITHING TODAY

The impact of nineteenth-century missions wasn't only felt in foreign mission fields. It also confirmed for generations of Christians in the West that words were the primary way of carrying the gospel to others. Evangelistic societies published thousands of tracts, booklets, and pamphlets for Christians to give out to unbelievers. The Gideons distributed Bibles to schools, hospitals, and hotel rooms around the world. Mission became an exercise in literacy.

But today, our culture is more accurately described as "post-literate." Scholars such as Marshall McLuhan and Walter Ong argue that the West is moving into what they term a "secondary orality"—a kind of merging of both oral and literate forms of expression—or something more commonly known as "post-literacy."

Ong explores these ideas in his book *Orality and Literacy: The Technologizing of the Word*. He insists that orality was much more common in human societies than literacy, and that writing is consistently regarded as a kind of alien technology when it is introduced into oral cultures. Indeed, he claims that the establishment of literacy irrevocably changes an oral culture. If this is the case, he posits, then similarly the introduction of new screen-based technologies such as television and video games will also irrevocably change literate cultures.

Walter Ong's book was published in 1982, but he rather prophetically saw the way writing (literacy) and talking (orality) were being merged by electronic media. As noted above, he referred to this as a period of secondary orality—a move away from literacy as our primary means of communication.

Ong writes, "Print encourages a sense of closure, a sense that what is found in a text has been finalized, has reached a state of completion."[16] This is unquestionably the way nineteenth-century evangelists saw the printed word. But today, it is open to interpretation. It is provisional. In an age of YouTube, fake news, and TikTok, truth claims are assessed based on who is presenting them and how sincerely they are posed.[17]

This doesn't make us illiterate people. Words still have meaning for us. But in our quest for meaning, we are looking beyond the printed page. In fact, far from making us illiterate, electronic media *increases* our use of writing and language. Researchers have shown that young people in particular write far more than any generation before them.[18] That's because so much socializing takes place online, and it almost always involves text.

Clive Thompson, writing on what he calls "the new literacy," says,

> Before the Internet came along, most Americans never wrote anything, ever, that wasn't a school assignment. Unless they got a job that required producing text (like in law, advertising, or media), they'd leave school and virtually never construct a paragraph again.[19]

Although the standard of grammar and syntax of online communications might be doubtful, it's inaccurate to say that people don't use words anymore. It's the *way* we use them that has changed. In the nineteenth-century, Westerners used words for the linear development of ideas. Written communicators were expected to shape a logical line of argumentation, presenting their main points as propositions and structuring ideas without needing context or relationship with the reader. The message was meant to be analytical and clear—an example of "left brain" communication.

But Ong and McLuhan point out that pre-literate (oral) people didn't engage analytically with ideas. As they became used to written communication, their brains were rewired to appreciate a more analytical approach. Previously, communication for them had been a more "right brain" activity. Ideas were always presented situationally and relationally. Nowadays, we might read a book written by someone from a completely different culture, in another part of the world. But in an oral culture, an individual would listen to someone else's insights because it was someone they knew and someone with whom they had shared life. Oral culture was more narrative based, with teachers stitching multiple stories together to present their wisdom. These stories were metaphors for participation. Listeners would enter the narrative and feel what the characters felt or see what they saw. In participating in the story, they learned something true and useful for their current lives.

Ong's secondary orality is a combination of both these ways of communication.

Post-literate people prefer information to be presented in smaller bites.

Contrary to what some might think, post-literate people don't have shorter attention spans. They can spend huge amounts of time reading text, but, given the nature of Internet communication, they have become wired to access it in smaller pieces.

Post-literate people are also more likely to engage with ideas when they are presented by someone they trust—with whom they have shared a common life experience. Truth claims that are presented conversationally, with emotion and conviction, are far more compelling than a clearly argued thesis by a stranger.

Post-literate people need to *hear*, not just see, what is being presented to them. For a post-literate generation, video is therefore much more effective than print alone. Walter Ong describes it this way:

> Sight isolates, sound incorporates. Whereas sight situates the observer outside what he views, at a distance, sound pours into the hearer ... Vision comes to a human being from one direction at a time: to look at a room or a landscape, I must move my eyes around from one part to another. When I hear, however, I gather sound simultaneously from all directions at once; I am at the center of my auditory world, which envelopes me, establishing me at a kind of core of sensation and existence ... You can immerse yourself in hearing, in sound. There is no way to immerse yourself similarly in sight.[20]

Just as the nineteenth-century missionaries embraced the new technologies of printing presses and literature distribution, so we must embrace the new technologies of our day. It will be necessary for us to share our faith using text, and to point to the Scriptures as the Word of God.

Even an old legacy mission like the Gideons, who have been distributing free Bibles since 1908, have embraced new technology and now promote their free Bible app in audio and over 1,500 languages.[21] Similarly, text-based mission agencies like the British and Foreign Bible Society[22] and the Scripture Gift Mission (now Lifewords) are utilizing online tools to share the Word of God with people.[23] Bible Society provides a fully online Bible along with reading support materials, and Lifewords hosts an interactive blog called VerseFirst to engage with younger readers.

Another use of text aimed at a post-literate culture is The Pour Over.[24] Offering a daily email digest of news stories, interspersed with Scripture, they aim to keep Christians informed on what's happening in the world while remaining focused on Christ. Every day they mail out a curation of the biggest news stories, regardless of their spiritual significance and seek to pair those stories with reminders of foundational Christian principles. They even host a podcast these days.

But most innovative is the work of people like Sydney-based online gaming chaplain, Pastor Ska.

It is estimated there are around 3 billion active gamers in the world today, using live streams on platforms such as Twitch (owned by Amazon), Mixer (owned by Microsoft), Facebook Gaming, and YouTube Gaming. When Baptist youth pastor Kiran Skariah discovered this, he knew he was just one click away from a massive unreached people group. Using Twitch, Kiran styled himself as Pastor Skar and began running a thrice-weekly, four-hour group on the live-streaming platform for gamers.

Skariah sits in front of a webcam in a purpose-built studio and plays online games as he broadcasts to the world. He narrates the games while playing and interacts with fellow gamers. Every session ends with a prayer. And on Thursdays, Pastor Skar opens the Bible in a sermon segment called Real Life. He now has twenty thousand followers with whom he interacts via Twitch's messaging facility.[25]

Kevin Schut, a game studies scholar at Canada's Trinity Western University and author of *Of Games and God: A Christian Exploration of Video Games*, says engaging gamers with the Bible makes perfect sense. He says, "Those of us who are gamers know that there is a unique form of friendship that results of playing games together. And once that friendship has started, it's possible to talk about faith with more integrity."[26]

There's much more that could be said about secondary orality, but hopefully we've delved into the subject enough to appreciate that the shape of mission embraced by the wordsmith missionaries of the nineteenth century is no longer appropriate for our day, and we must seek new alternatives by engaging with the multitude of media at our fingertips.

6

The Sixth Shape

FREEDOM FIGHTING

*"Doing justice" meant not only "not doing wrong," but also actively doing
right and restoring what is broken.*
JESSICA NICHOLAS

Alice Seeley Harris and her husband, John, left London for the Congo Free State in
1898, traveling inland to the remote mission station Ikau near Basankusu. They had
joined the Congo Balolo Mission (CBM), founded by the medical missionary Dr.
Harry Grattan Guinness, and were there to replace staff who had died from malaria
(only six of the first thirty-five CBM missionaries survived to 1900). What Alice
Harris would observe during her time in the Congo was far worse than the ravages
of tropical disease, though. She and her husband had unwittingly walked into the
middle of one of the worst human atrocities of the modern era.

During the 1880s, King Leopold II of Belgium managed to nefariously gain
private control of a large area in Central Africa by convincing the European
community that he was involved in humanitarian and philanthropic work.
Using several smokescreen organizations, he was able to lay claim to most of
the Congo Basin, which Leopold named the Congo Free State. However, it was
neither a state nor was it free.

For more than twenty years, Leopold extracted ivory, rubber, and minerals
from the upper Congo Basin for sale on the world market. He monopolized

trade by imposing huge export duties on other merchants and by constructing a rail line from the coast to the capital of Leopoldville (now Kinshasa). He then set the Congolese to work as serfs in their own country.

To ensure their subjugation, Leopold established a private army, named the Force Publique, made up of white Europeans (Belgian regular soldiers and mercenaries from other countries), as well as African fighters recruited from Zanzibar and West Africa. Their job was to enforce the crushing quotas on the collection of rubber placed on the Congolese workers, which the Force did with viciousness and cruelty. Failure to meet the collection quota was punishable by mutilation or death. It became the sordid practice to remove the hand of a worker who didn't yield the required amount of rubber. Sometimes the severed hands were collected by the soldiers as trophies.

One Congolese worker named Tswambe would later testify,

> A village which refused to provide rubber would be completely swept clean. As a young man, I saw the soldier Molili, then guarding the village of Boyeka, take a net, put ten arrested natives in it, attach big stones to the net, and make it tumble into the river ... Rubber causes these torments; that's why we no longer want to hear its name spoken. Soldiers made young men kill or rape their own mothers and sisters.[1]

It is estimated that, under Leopold's reign of terror, between five and ten million Congolese died collecting rubber for the tires of the bicycle craze that was sweeping Europe at the time.[2]

Meanwhile, Alice Seeley Harris was serving at the Ikau mission station where, in her spare time, she had taken up the relatively new hobby of photography. Initially, she was motivated by a desire to send photographs back to the UK to show her supporters what life was like in "darkest Africa." But over time she became quite an accomplished photographer.

Then one day, in 1904, two men arrived at Ikau from a far-flung village, claiming it had been attacked by the Force Publique for falling short of their rubber quota. One of the men, Nsala, was holding a small bundle of leaves in which were wrapped the severed hand and foot of a child. The Harrises were horrified. Nsala explained that the mercenaries had killed and mutilated his wife and daughter and that these two body parts were all he could salvage.

Appalled, Alice asked Nsala to place the tiny foot and hand on the wooden veranda of the mission building, and she photographed him seated beside them, staring forlornly at the remains of his family.

"Nsala of Wala in the Nsongo District (ABIR Concession)," by Alice Seely Harris, 1904.

Today, many regard this picture as one of the most iconic images in the history of the struggle for human rights. Both heart-rending and macabre, the photo shows Nsala staring dejectedly at the remains, while behind him, three young Congolese keep vigil, respectfully watching from a distance.

Outraged by the stories told by Nsala and his companion, Alice Seeley Harris took it upon herself to venture deeper and deeper into the Congo Basin to record the atrocities perpetrated by Leopold's regime. She went on to photograph hundreds of mutilated workers, many of whom were women and children, who had continued to satisfy the rubber quota, even after their hands had been severed.[3]

Back in London, the Congo Balolo Mission revealed the horror to a British audience by printing the pictures in a pamphlet. In 1904, the photos were published in a book, *King Leopold's Rule in Africa*. The Harrises returned to England to give lectures about the barbarism in the Congo, illustrating their story with images of Alice's pictures on an early-model projector. This was followed by a forty-nine-city tour of the United States. A daily newspaper, *The New York American*, devoted a week to publishing Harris's photographs to illustrate articles on atrocities in the Congo. Public outrage grew.

The Belgian government conducted a parliamentary enquiry in Brussels, and the CBM's Harry Guinness presented evidence saying, "We missionaries stand in the front row of those who demand that they shall be freed from their present oppression."[4]

Ultimately, Belgium would yield to international pressure. Their parliament wrested control of Congo Free State from Leopold, disbanded the Force Publique, and in 1908 took over the country's administration, changing its name to the Belgian Congo.

Alice Seeley Harris's photography was no mere hobby. Her pictures and her testimony had changed the course of history. Not unlike earlier missionaries who used translation and literature distribution to spread the good news, the Harrises did so using a very new form of technology. As we saw in the previous chapter, the printing press allowed missionaries to unleash the power of words. But in the twentieth century, the camera would facilitate a fresh kind of revelation through the power of the image. But more than that, the Harrises provide us with a dramatic story indicative of the shape Western mission had taken leading up to this era—*freedom fighting*.

In this chapter we will look at the varied ways missionaries took up the fight for human rights and liberation—including abolitionism, women's and children's rights, racial desegregation, and political liberty. Far from being agents of colonial subjugation, we will see that many Christians saw the mission of the church as directly concerned with freedom movements.

FIGHTING AGAINST THE SLAVE TRADE

The Harrises were part of a long line of activist-missionaries—Christians committed to righting the wrongs perpetrated by European colonists and businesses in other nations. From the late 1700s, much of the focus of these Christians was on fighting for the abolition of the slave trade.

Both the Enlightenment and Christianity led the world into a condemnation of slavery. The Enlightenment shaped a culture committed to the "rights of man," and many rationalist thinkers saw slavery as a direct violation of these rights. Humanist intellectuals showed the inadequacy of the arguments justifying slavery, particularly those that claimed that certain races were inferior and ripe for enslavement. At the same time, evangelical Christians drawn from Quaker, Anglican, and Baptist traditions condemned the practice of trading in humans as unchristian. As Diarmaid MacCulloch writes,

> The long struggle to abolish slavery remained throughout a curious collabo-
> ration of fervent evangelicals, who were most otherwise extremely politi-
> cally conservative, with radical children of the Enlightenment, many of
> whom had no great love of Christianity, though some were enthusiastic
> Unitarians.[5]

Christians such as William Lloyd Garrison, Julia Ward, and Frederick Douglass in America, and Granville Sharp, William Wilberforce, and Thomas Cookson in England, campaigned vigorously for slavery's end. By the late eighteenth century, moral disapproval of its practice was so widespread that it was considered a core Christian taboo.

The story of how John Newton penned the hymn *Amazing Grace* demon-strates how rapidly abolitionism became the Christian *cause du jour*. Newton had lived a wild and recalcitrant life as a young man before becoming a seafarer and eventually the captain of a slave ship. He would later write that the disci-pline of seafaring helped shape his adult life and instilled important skills he wouldn't have otherwise developed. In his autobiography, written in 1762 while in midlife, he offered no word of regret for shipping fellow humans from West Africa to America. Indeed, he claimed he was "upon the whole, satisfied with it."[6]

Bear in mind that Newton's Christian conversion occurred in 1748, but he continued to ply the slave trade for another seven years, retiring only after experiencing a stroke. In other words, it was possible in the 1750s to be a devout Calvinist, as Newton became, and still keep, or trade in, human beings.

But by 1788, the elderly John Newton recanted his position. He was no longer "satisfied" with his former life as a slaver, writing, "I am bound in conscience to take shame to myself by a public confession, which, however sincere, comes too late to present or repair the misery and mischief to which I have, formally been an accessory."[7] By that time, Granville Sharp, a devout Christian and civil servant, had published *A Representation of the Injustice and Dangerous Tendency of Tolerating Slavery*—the first tract in England attacking slavery. Sharp had secured the legal precedent that West Indian planters could not hold slaves in Britain because slavery was contrary to English law. The Quaker anti-slavery committee had also submitted its first petition to the British parliament to abolish the trade. British Christians were increasingly exercised by the issue, with committees and discussion groups forming across the country. The testimonies of former enslaved people were printed and distributed widely.

Newton's change of heart caused him not only to publish his regretful confession but also to befriend and mentor William Wilberforce, the leader of the parliamentary campaign to abolish the African slave trade. Newton was eighty-two, and in his last year of life, when the Slave Trade Act 1807 passed the parliament.

But the fight wasn't over. It continued to gather steam in the US, where both slavery and an anti-slavery movement had been entrenched in American colonial life for hundreds of years. In the period leading up to the American Civil War, abolitionism broke out of its Quaker beginnings and drew in northern Protestants. Two powerful influences were the 1852 publication of Harriet Beecher Stowe's *Uncle Tom's Cabin*, and William Lloyd Garrison's widely read anti-slavery newspaper *The Liberator*, which he launched in 1831.

For many nineteenth-century devout Protestants, bringing liberation to enslaved people was a key expression of their faith. In fact, possibly the most famous nineteenth-century missionary of all, David Livingstone, was an ardent abolitionist. Livingstone is revered today, as he was during his lifetime, as a celebrity explorer. His 1858 journey to navigate the African Zambezi River, and his unsuccessful expedition in 1865 to find the source of the Nile, made him a British national hero. On his death, he was honored with a state funeral and burial in Westminster Abbey. But Livingstone wasn't merely seeking fame and fortune as an adventurer. He had originally traveled to Africa as a pioneer medical missionary with the London Missionary Society.

Livingstone is often referred to as a particularly unsuccessful evangelist, having convinced just one African to convert to Christianity, only to see him later return to the religion of his tribe. But Livingstone had observed a peculiar challenge to the work of converting Africans.

He found that African people were so communal they would only convert to a new religion if their chief did so. For this reason, many missionaries focused their evangelistic efforts on tribal chieftains. But Livingstone also noticed that chieftains wouldn't embrace Christianity as long as abolitionism was required of them. They refused to repent of trading their own people because slavery was one of their tribe's primary sources of income. When they heard they had to abandon the practice in order to become a Christian, they reneged. Of course, Livingstone was uncompromising on this issue, writing, "The slave trade must be suppressed as the first step to any mission—that baffles every good effort."[8]

Ever the canny Scot, he came up with an interesting solution. He surmised that chieftains would only give up slavery if there was another way to fund the community, so he attempted to introduce farming as part of his three-phase approach to mission: Commercialize, Christianize, Civilize. Today, we consider this slogan a repugnant example of colonial missionary arrogance—and David Livingstone didn't help his cause by being an obnoxious, condescending character himself. But for all his flaws, he was genuinely motivated by a desire to end slavery. The problem with trying to introduce agriculture as an economic alternative was that the farmers had no way of transporting their crop to a major trading hub, all of which were on the African coast.

Livingstone then tried to figure out if the southern African river system could become a highway for remote farming villages to get their crops to market. Surely these surging rivers—the Zambezi, the Congo, the Limpopo, and the Okavango—could become transportation links for cargo ships to ferry crops to the coastal ports. In his quest, Livingstone abandoned his medical and evangelistic work to become an explorer, navigating the great rivers. Sadly, his explorations and those of other intrepid surveyors only proved that the river systems weren't reliable as commercial highways to the coast.

Livingstone's grandiose plans to end slavery by remaking the whole economic system of southern Africa might have come to naught, but his death inspired another missionary of note—who had greater success in her more modest campaign.

FIGHTING FOR THE RIGHTS OF WOMEN AND CHILDREN

Mary Slessor was a tall, robust woman from a working-class Scottish family. With her pale complexion, bright blue eyes, and shock of red hair, she was quite a curiosity in the villages of Calabar—a region in modern-day Nigeria—where in 1876 she went to work among the Efik and Okoyong people. Years later, she would be dubbed "the white queen of Okoyong."[9]

Like Livingstone—her fellow Scot and hero—Slessor was noted for her forthright manner and indefatigable personality, a facility she put to good use in what would become her successful campaign for women's rights in Calabar. When she arrived, Calabar was a small British protectorate ... and it was foundering. British colonial powers had little interest in the day-to-day management of the place or the welfare of its citizens. They maintained the port primarily for trading in the Gulf of Guinea. Slavery was newly illegal, but witchcraft, infanticide, and human sacrifice were still practiced; and women's rights were non-existent.

Unlike most missionaries, Slessor decided to live among the Efik people, becoming fluent in their language and familiar with local customs and culture. Also unusually, she went barefoot and undertook long canoe trips, deep into the interior, to preach the gospel to unreached tribes. She was shocked to discover that many of these tribal communities practiced cannibalism and twin sacrifice. The peoples of southeast Nigeria feared the birth of twins—viewing it as a bad omen—and believed the children would bring devastation upon society. In his acclaimed Nigerian novel, *Things Fall Apart*, Chinua Achebe details the belief that an earth goddess had decreed that twins "were an offence on the land and must be destroyed. And if the clan did not exact punishment for an offense against the great goddess, her wrath was loosed on all the land and not just on the offender."[10] In the novel, whenever twins are born, their terrified parents are forced to deposit the babies in earthenware pots and abandon them to die in a section of the jungle termed the "evil forest."[11]

In her missionary travels, Slessor regularly came upon these abandoned babies and felt compelled to rescue them. When their home villages refused to take them in, Slessor adopted them herself. She regularly traveled on her preaching tours through the jungle with up to five orphans by her side. It became a common sight for remote communities to see a tall, red-headed, bare-footed woman approaching their village with rescued babies in her arms or sleeping in her canoe.

But taking in these children couldn't go on. Mary Slessor didn't have the resources to feed the family she had already adopted, let alone the many others that needed rescuing. In 1888, she decided to leave Calabar and press further into the interior to establish a permanent settlement in Okoyong. This was an extraordinary feat. The Okoyong were a remote, primitive people who practiced head-hunting as a warning to their neighboring tribes. The village Slessor chose, Ekenge, was so feared by outsiders that when she arrived, her oarsmen refused to leave the boat. Slessor entered Ekenge with a troupe of tired children in tow and was welcomed by the Okoyong. Eventually, she supervised the erection of a mission compound that included mud-walled houses, a school, a church, and several outhouses for supplies. Soon the compound was full of rescued twins. Slessor also found that many of the twins' mothers had been driven into the jungle to fend for themselves. They too found refuge at Ekenge. Through evangelism, prayer, and her relentless commitment to fighting for the protection of human life, Slessor saw the conversion of the Okoyong people and with it an end to human sacrifice.

In 1890, the British decided to unite the Nigerian nations into a single colony, and the following year they appointed Slessor their vice-consul for Okoyong. After three years of combined missionary and civil service, she wrote,

> No tribe was formerly so feared because of their utter disregard of human life, but human life is now safe in Okoyong. No chief ever died without the sacrifice of many human lives, but this custom has now ceased. Some chiefs, in commenting on the wonderful change, said: "Ma, you white people are from God Almighty. No other power could have done this".[12]

As I mentioned earlier, the British press referred to Slessor as the white queen of Okoyong, but the Okoyong themselves called her the "Mother of All the Peoples."[13]

In many books on mission history, Mary Slessor is often grouped with her contemporaries Amy Carmichael, Lilias Trotter, and Lottie Moon, as representing a quaint new mission innovation—the single-female missionary. This diminishes their contribution. It is certainly true they were making different choices about their lifestyle and their future from other young women their age—choices based on their deep devotion to Christ and to the service of others. But in all four cases, these women lived in remote communities, far from conventional mission centers, at great personal cost. They learned local languages and embraced a similar lifestyle to the community they were serving. Their extraordinary achievement was not simply in being female but in courageously obeying Christ's call to spread the gospel.

Like Slessor, Amy Carmichael—who served in Dohnavur in Tamil Nadu, thirty miles from India's southern tip—was committed to human rights work as well as evangelism. She created a refuge for girls and young women rescued from forced temple prostitution. Families often felt they had no choice but to sell their children to the temples if they could not feed them or if they needed extra money. At its peak in the 1910s, Carmichael's refuge, the Dohnavur Fellowship, was housing 130 girls. Later, she added a home for young boys, many of them born to former temple prostitutes.

In both Slessor's and Carmichael's cases, the children were rescued after being utterly abandoned by their families and their villages. These women were engaging in critical emergency care. Sadly, many missionaries who followed them emulated their example and built orphanages without considering whether all children needed such a facility. The concept of the missionary orphanage took hold in people's imaginations. It was easy to "sell" the idea to donors in the West, who loved giving to such institutions.

But the rush to establish orphanages in poor countries was a mistake. Not all poor children needed them. This is still the case today. Evidence shows that children are raised more successfully in a family or family-like setting than in an institution like an orphanage, even one run with the best intentions.[14] In an orphanage, a child is isolated from their wider family and their kinship group. Language, culture, and history may be lost. Their sense of attachment and their mental health can be affected, which in turn affects their overall development. Even in well-managed orphanages, the staff struggle to provide healthy physical contact and care, especially for children with complex needs. In the worst cases, living in an orphanage can increase a child's exposure to abuse and put them at risk of future criminal activity.[15]

The present-day obsession with orphanages is a clear case of why we need to see mission like water. Mary Slessor and Amy Carmichael responded to the peculiar circumstances they encountered. But today our approach must differ. Merely mimicking their strategy—in contexts where children trapped in poverty could be better helped by remaining in their village or within their broader family system—shows how much we need to understand mission history.

FIGHTING AGAINST SEGREGATION

In 1875, the noted evangelist and abolitionist, Dwight Lyman Moody, violated his own principles by running segregated evangelistic meetings in Georgia. He had been convinced by local church leaders that the white people of the South would not only refuse to attend desegregated meetings, but they would also riot against them. Moody was noted for being conflict avoidant and decided it was more important to preach the gospel, even if that meant doing it to a whites-only gathering. It wasn't until the 1890s that his conscience troubled him enough to abandon segregated rallies in the South.

But by then the damage was done. Black leaders openly condemned Moody's hypocrisy. Frederick Douglass wrote,

> Of all the forms of negro hate in this world, save me from that one which clothes itself with the name of the loving Jesus ... The negro can go into the circus, the theatre, and can be admitted to the lectures of [the anti-Christian orator] Mr. Ingersoll, but he cannot go into an evangelical Christian meeting.[16]

Professor of theology Gregg Quiggle also highlights Moody's racial blind spot:

> From one angle, Dwight Moody towers as a man of great faith. Moody was a man with real limitations who gave himself fully to God. What God chose to do through Moody was astonishing. But, from another angle, this giant had clay feet. When faced with the besetting sin of his country, he backed down.[17]

Fortunately, there were many other Christians who did not back down.

In 1833, two Presbyterian ministers, John J. Shipherd and Philo P. Stewart, founded Oberlin College in Ohio, to educate ministers and schoolteachers. They were insistent that the college be desegregated and coeducational. But their commitment to abolitionism extended beyond their enrolment policy— the school was a station on the Underground Railroad, helping fugitive slaves escape to freedom in Canada.

Shipherd and Stewart recruited the noted New York evangelist Charles Grandison Finney to become the school's professor of theology. A red-hot revivalist, much maligned by conventional church ministers, Finney was an interesting choice. He had been a lawyer before experiencing a deep religious conversion, and then began preaching evangelistically in the villages of upstate New York, employing the same zeal on his congregations that he had previously used to convince juries. His unusual style and impassioned demeanor fomented a revival in the area. When he turned his attention to New York

City, he achieved spectacular success, launching an almost continuous revival at the Second Free Presbyterian Church, where he was appointed the minister. But Finney was never a committed Presbyterian, so in 1834, he and his supporters planted the Broadway Tabernacle where he continued his evangelistic campaign.

The following year, Shipherd and Stewart approached Finney to teach at Oberlin. Finney agreed. After spending a few years dividing his time between that post and the tabernacle, he eventually left New York in 1837 to become minister of Oberlin's First Congregational Church (closely related to Oberlin College), while teaching theology.

As a result, Oberlin developed an institutional culture that combined an unlikely set of Christian influences. Founded in Presbyterianism and committed to liberal social reform, the college was also shaped by revivalist theology. Finney became Oberlin's president in 1851, although he continued his itinerant preaching around the country. In this way he spread the Oberlin approach far and wide. He helped birth a generation of Christians who were committed to social justice, racial equality, and evangelism, and who believed they could right all wrongs in the world.

Finney's was a particularly Arminian theology. He berated the Calvinists at schools such as Princeton Theological Seminary for promoting a passive religion, one of waiting for God to initiate revival. In his view, "God helps those who help themselves" (to quote English politician Algernon Sidney). He taught that human depravity is a voluntary condition, one that the human will can overcome. As a preacher he believed his work was not simply to present Christ and invite audiences to believe; he had to help *make* them believe.

Those who fell under his influence were typically revivalist in their emphasis on common sense and humanity's innate ability to reform itself and save the world. Oberlin graduates fanned out across America and to mission fields in China and India. As historian Brent Morris writes,

> As the first college to admit men and women of all races, and with a faculty and community comprised of outspoken abolitionists, Oberlin supported a cadre of activist missionaries devoted to emancipation, even if that was through unconventional methods or via an abandonment of strict ideological consistency. Their philosophy was a colorblind composite of various schools of anti-slavery thought aimed at supporting the best hope of success.[18]

The work of opposing racial segregation wasn't just a North American issue. The South African system of apartheid that came to an end with the formation of a democratic government in 1994 is well known today, but its roots were established by the white Boer settlers in the nineteenth century. They had come to believe they were God's special elect, a peculiar people who could not mix with the "inferior" Africans around them. J. A. Templin explains,

> Afrikaner leaders saw themselves as a special people led as the pastoral children of Abraham in search of prosperity and religious peace or as followers of a new Moses or Joshua going to a promised land. They had made their covenant with God, and they believed implicitly that He was to be their God in a special way, and they were a special people in His sight. This interpretation soon ceased to be strictly theological and entered the realm more properly called legend, or even rationalization, as leaders attempted to justify their position in the last half of the nineteenth century.[19]

Missionaries from the UK were almost unanimous in their opposition to the kind of segregation proposed by the Boers. They advocated for equality and liberty for all Africans.

One of these desegregationist missionaries was the intrepid Johannes van der Kemp, a Dutchman who was sent to Cape Town, South Africa in 1799 by the London Missionary Society (LMS). Van der Kemp had spent time with Moravians in Holland before moving to London where he presented himself as a candidate to the LMS.

After a couple of years working among the Xhosa, van der Kemp heard that the Khoekhoe people were being exploited by Boer farmers, so he moved his outreach to their land. He soon discovered that, on white farms, the Khoekhoe were effectively enslaved workers. His initial calls for the South African government to act on behalf of the Khoekhoe fell on deaf ears. This might have been because van der Kemp made the unusual decision to assimilate into the Khoekhoe community—dressing as a Khoekhoe man and marrying an enslaved Malagasy woman. His detractors claimed he had "gone native."

Then, in 1803, van der Kemp founded Bethelsdorp, a mission station that became known as a refuge for runaway Khoekhoe slaves. The Dutch colonists were outraged by this. When slavery was abolished in the British parliament in 1807, van der Kemp held a day of public thanksgiving at Bethelsdorp to mark the occasion, only further enraging the settlers around him. His subsequent campaign demanding the Cape government pass laws against farmer cruelty to African workers was the last straw. White settlers brought accusations against van der Kemp, and he was recalled to Cape Town to answer the trumped-up charges. When it was found there was no real case against him, van der Kemp remained in the capital, lobbying politicians to crack down on worker exploitation until his death in 1811.

The funeral procession for Johannes van der Kemp was attended by huge numbers of Cape Town residents, Black and white, including leaders of church and state. It was a testimony to his courage and tenacity in serving his people and working tirelessly for a just and integrated society.

In 1828, British missionaries called for the passing of a law known as Ordinance 50, which ended the restrictions placed on Black South Africans, including removing the requirement for passes, and allowing them to choose their employers, to own land, and to move more freely. When it did pass, it caused an uproar. In 1834, the ratification of the 1833 Slavery Abolition Bill, emancipating all slaves in South Africa, also led to widespread protest. Because of the simmering tensions in the country, the authorities offered only modest protections to formerly enslaved people. It was left to a handful of mission stations to support them.

Ultimately, the Boer campaign for segregation would succeed, morphing in the twentieth century into a system of apartheid. We can only wonder what the history of South Africa might have been like had there been more brave missionaries like Johannes van der Kemp.

FIGHTING AS LIBERATION

In 1971, a Peruvian priest, Gustavo Gutiérrez published *A Theology of Liberation*, a seminal text that give rise to a new theological movement called liberation theology. Quickly adopted by Catholic missionaries in Latin America, it attempted to understand the Bible through the perspective of the poor, believing that God speaks particularly through them and for them. From that understanding, liberationists elevated the call for social justice from a minor thread—as it had been understood by many in the church—to be the central theme of Scripture. They demanded that the church support the marginalized and oppressed not only through works of charity but also by involvement in political and civic affairs.

Gutiérrez and other proponents, including Óscar Romero of El Salvador and Leonardo Boff and Helder Câmara from Brazil, saw oppressive socio-economic structures themselves as sinful and believed the work of Christian mission required active participation in extricating society from those structures. In order to achieve this, they established what they called "base communities"—small groups that not only studied the Bible but also attempted to actively change society by meeting their parishioners' practical needs.

Critics of liberation theology say it is a combination of Catholic mission practice and Marxist philosophy and that political revolution is its intended end point.[20] Nonetheless, the work of liberation theologians certainly woke up the church to the importance of biblical *social* ethics, not just individual ethics. There's no question that God has special concern for the poor, and the Bible is clear that those who oppress them will bear harsh judgment. (See Mt. 25:31–46, for example.) But a hundred years before *A Theology of Liberation* was published, Francophone missionaries in southern Africa were grappling with what role Christians should play in the protection and support of oppressed people groups.

Allow me to introduce you to the redoubtable Eugène Casalis. In 1833, Swiss-born Casalis was sent to South Africa by the Paris Evangelical Mission Society (PEMS), a French Reformed Church agency. He was commissioned to take up the now-dormant work of earlier French missionaries among the Basuto who were living in the high country of the northern Drakensberg mountains (some of the highest peaks in southern Africa). The Basuto were being threatened by the Boers and the British, who were pushing up from the southeast coastal lowlands of Africa, as well as by local African rivals. (The Zulu warlord, Shaka, ruled nearby and regularly threatened the Basuto.) As we saw with the vulnerable Xhosa and Khoekhoe peoples, these pressures had the potential to endanger their very existence.

But the Basuto's saving grace was that they were led by a warrior-king regarded as one of the most successful southern African leaders of the nineteenth century. King Moshoeshoe I was a formidable presence—a charismatic ruler who was not only a skilled military leader but also an adroit diplomat, capable of charming his colonial enemies. Moshoeshoe's diplomatic success with the British, however, would have been less fruitful if it weren't for his enduring friendship and key partnership with Eugène Casalis.

Casalis gained Moshoeshoe's permission to work in Basutoland, although the chief himself never became a Christian. In 1833, the chief granted land to the PEMS, at the base of the Makhoarane plateau, which had a plentiful water supply and an abundance of firewood. Casalis and his team—French missionaries Constant Gosselin and Thomas Arbousset—cleared the area, constructed mission buildings, and introduced European agricultural practices alongside indigenous ones. They established a school and a printing house, and set about translating the Bible into Sesotho, the language of the Basuto.

Over the following years, despite the great turmoil and warfare that was to ensue, Eugène Casalis and King Moshoeshoe developed such a trusting and genuine friendship that the Basuto began calling Casalis, *Mahloana-Matsoana*—"The man with the small black eyes," and "the friend of Moshesh." In fact, documents in the *Basuto Record* describe the PEMS missionaries this way:

> The French missionaries sent to our country for life pondered problems from the vantage point of the natives ... They did not seek to turn the Basotho into simple reproductions of the white man but rather encouraged them to progress in the furrow of their own conduct, adopting their way of thinking. This is the secret of their success as civilizers and of the great influence to which they attained in Lesotho.[21]

But Moshoeshoe was in trouble. In the mid-1830s, the Boers began their so-called "Great Trek," pushing deeper into Basuto territory where they fought for control of the fertile farming lands of the Caledon Valley. At Casalis's prompting, Moshoeshoe appealed to the British to step in, which they did, arbitrating in favor of the Basuto. But the peace didn't hold.

Over the next twenty years, Moshoeshoe was involved in a cycle of negotiations, military conflicts, and diplomatic appeals, during which time Casalis and Arbousset provided him with counsel on engaging with Western governors. They were effectively Moshoeshoe's ministers for foreign affairs. Casalis also helped to facilitate the purchase of modern weapons for the Basuto.

Missiologist Benjamin Beckner writes,

> The French mission to the Basotho is a clear counter-example of the largely imaginary and revisionist caricature of nineteenth century missions as the puppet and pawn of imperialist power. PEMS pioneer missionaries

Casalis and Arbousset, whose work issued in an authentic, autonomous and indigenous African church and, ultimately, in a nation, demonstrated exemplary anthropological methodology, linguistic skill, and cross-cultural aptitude.[22]

Aside from acting as state ministers, Casalis and Arbousset maintained their evangelical work, preaching the gospel to the Basuto and printing Sesotho language materials. Their first Sesotho translation of the Bible came out in 1878.

After losing the western lowlands to the Boers in 1868, Casalis advised Moshoeshoe that the best hope of survival for his nation was to appeal to Queen Victoria to proclaim Basutoland a British protectorate. Their appeal was successful. The Basuto enjoyed British protections until 1966 when they gained their independence as the new nation of Lesotho.

It is doubtful that Lesotho would exist today if it were not for the unlikely alliance of the fearsome warrior-king and his dark-eyed missionary-adviser.

FREEDOM FIGHTING TODAY

As mentioned earlier, while there were all kinds of mistakes made by nineteenth-century missionaries, the caricature of them always dutifully supporting their colonial masters doesn't hold. Referring to African missions, and using a clichéd expression from the 1970s, British missionary statesman Max Warren says,

> On one account the missionaries who went to Africa, whatever their other blunders, were uncompromising. They insisted that there was nothing in the world which the African could not achieve if he [sic] was given the opportunity. They believed this when nobody else believed it. And they acted on their belief. [They] demonstrated that "black is beautiful" long before anyone else dreamt of such an idea.[23]

Sadly, we need to acknowledge that none of the blights these eighteenth- and nineteenth-century missionaries addressed have been eradicated. There are still enslaved peoples today. There is still the need to fight for the rights of women and children. There are still segregating impulses in societies across the world. And there are still economic systems in place that perpetuate yawning gaps between the richest and poorest sectors of society. Despite the confidence of Enlightenment-era missionaries that they could reach every nation with the gospel and right every wrong, we have to acknowledge that we still have a long way to go on many of these issues.

Perhaps the first step for those of us who wish to fight injustice today is to recognize that the utopian vision of a completely repaired society is an unchristian dream. We can be helped in this respect by Lesslie Newbigin's threefold description of the mission of the church. He famously claimed the church is to be a sign, foretaste, and instrument of God's here-and-still-coming kingdom.[24] As a *sign*, we point to something that is real but not yet visible. As a *foretaste*, we are called to be the faithful "first fruit" of the kingdom. And as an *instrument*, we are agents in service of God's reign, to be used in the hands of God to steer history toward its true end. In other words, as a surgeon uses surgical tools, God uses the church to heal the world of injustice, bondage, and violence, as well as unbelief and idolatry.

However, Newbigin was quick to point out it is folly to imagine that our political or religious activity can establish the kingdom of God. Instead, we are to have a resolute belief that the coming reign of God is the framework for all missionary practice. We point to the reality of a kingdom that, while unfurling around us, won't ultimately be fulfilled until beyond history. We can't claim to be able to solve all the world's problems. Instead, as a sign, foretaste, and instrument of God's kingdom, we find our hope in a *coming* kingdom.

This in no way absolves us of the responsibility to pursue the justice, peace, and freedom of the kingdom in the here and now. It just frees us of the unbearable burden of being completely responsible for it.

Second, it is important to acknowledge that our well-intentioned efforts can sometimes contribute to disempowerment and even greater poverty. We need to check our motivations. This was powerfully highlighted by Steve Corbett and Brian Fikkert in their book, *When Helping Hurts*. They point out that, despite their best intentions, Westerners often fall into the temptation of a "god complex." They write,

> Why do you want to help the poor? Really think about it. What truly motivates you? Do you really love poor people and want to serve them? Or do you have other motives? I confess to you that part of what motivates me to help the poor is my felt need to accomplish something worthwhile with my life, to be a person of significance, to feel like I have pursued a noble cause … to be a bit like God. It makes me feel good to use my training in

economics to "save" poor people. And in the process, I sometimes uninten-
tionally reduce poor people to objects that I use to fulfill my own need to
accomplish something. It is a very ugly truth, and it pains me to admit it, but
"when I want to do good, evil is right there with me" (Rom. 7:21).[25]

The answer they propose is for us to recognize our mutual brokenness with the
poor. They continue:

> Until we embrace our mutual brokenness, our work with low-income
> people is likely to do more harm than good. I sometimes unintentionally
> reduce poor people to objects that I use to fulfill my own need to accom-
> plish something. I am not okay, and you are not okay. But Jesus can fix us
> both.[26]

Lastly, while we can be committed to freedom fighting by tweeting, posting,
and signing online petitions, the best of our work can't be done at a distance.
It involves the slow, monotonous, and sometimes dangerous work of those
whose stories we looked at in this chapter. They were people who entered
deeply into life with those they sought to liberate. We call this incarnational
mission. It involves sharing life with those to whom God has sent us. We are
not their saviors. We should become their friends and partners, adopting their
customs and life-rhythms insofar as our conscience will allow. Without this
proximity, it is easy for us to define poverty entirely in material terms, without
seeing the richness of community and the connection to earth, art, beauty, and
culture. When we just put a dollar amount on poverty, we fail to see the ways
we are so bereft in comparison with other societies. This in turn increases our
god complex when it comes to saving or "fixing" the poor. And that adds to the
sense of inferiority experienced by the recipients of our attempts at generosity.
This is also the case when we are engaging the issues of oppression, racism,
misogyny, and other ills from which people need liberation.

Being incarnational means being shaped by Jesus' priorities, lifestyle, and
practices. The Gospels contain not only the message we are called to preach but
also the means by which we are to do it. As missiologist Darrell Guder writes,

> By incarnational mission I mean the understanding and practice of Christian
> witness that is rooted in and shaped by the life, ministry, suffering, death and

resurrection of Jesus. The critical question is this: can and should the unique
event of the incarnation of Jesus that constitutes and defines the message
and mission of the church have concrete significance for the way in which
the church communicates that message and carries out that mission?[27]

To that question we can be certain Guder would answer yes—as should we.

Nonetheless, the accounts I've explored in this chapter are only half
the story. While white missionaries did toil for liberation and autonomy for
the peoples they served, there was also an indigenous Christian leadership
emerging around the world, struggling under the yoke of colonialism and often
viewed suspiciously by conservative Western missionaries. If in this chapter we
looked at freedom fighters, in the next we need to explore the mission work of
Indigenous peoples.

The Seventh Shape

UNSHACKLING

> *The whole country is opened to us, stations are occupied in different directions, churches are built, congregations are collected, and converts are numbered by hundreds.*
>
> SAMUEL AJAYI CROWTHER

By the mid-1800s, something unusual was happening in the small West African port city of Freetown. A boisterous, unshackled, distinctly African form of Christianity was being practiced with barely any involvement or oversight by British missionaries. Indeed, the head of the Church of England's Church Missionary Society (CMS) admitted that the missionaries sent out to minister in Freetown were not infrequently inferior to their African sisters and brothers in their knowledge of the Bible and Christian doctrine.

How did such a vibrant church spring so successfully from African soil in the early nineteenth century?

As mentioned in the previous chapter, the passage of Wilberforce's Slave Trade Act in 1807 outlawed the trade of humans throughout the British Empire. Slavery itself continued in British colonies until its final abolition in 1838, but the forced transportation, buying, and selling of humans was made illegal. Making a certain "commodity" illegal, however, doesn't automatically end its trade. Slavers continued to ply their evil trade across the Atlantic, but now they had to evade the Royal Navy who were commissioned to patrol the African coast and stamp them out.

When authorities today seize trafficked goods, such as drugs or weapons, they can impound and destroy those products. But at the turn of the nineteenth century, what were British naval officers to do with the cargo of a seized slave ship? The answer to that question lay in the West African nation of Sierra Leone.

In 1787, anticipating the passage of his anti-slavery bill, William Wilberforce helped found the Sierra Leone Company (SLC) with the express purpose of sending emancipated slaves and poor Africans from London and North America back to Africa. Together with British Navy Lieutenant John Clarkson and a group of freed American slaves from Nova Scotia, the SLC established the port of Granville Town (named after pioneer abolitionist Granville Sharp). Their initial plan was not only to provide safe haven for freed slaves but also to help stop the African slave trade by spreading Christianity through the continent.

Two years later, the British abolitionists sent a second, much larger, party of 1,100 former American slaves who had been resettled in Nova Scotia at the end of the American Revolution. They renamed their settlement Freetown. In 1800, the British landed five hundred Jamaican Maroons (descendants of Africans who had freed themselves from slavery in Jamaica). From 1808 to 1874, Freetown also became the headquarters for the Royal British Navy's West African Squadron, which captured slave ships headed for the Americas.

The Londoners, Nova Scotians, Jamaican Maroons, and newly freed West Africans intermarried to create a Creole population in Freetown. With no shared knowledge of native law or customs to unite them, the Creole community drew on their Christian background and Western culture to fashion a new society. In particular, the Jamaicans brought their very dynamic way of expressing their Christian faith—which soon came to dominate the religious life of Freetown. The British referred to the churches of Sierra Leone as practicing a "boisterous Christianity." They were *unshackled*.

UNSHACKLED MISSION IN WEST AFRICA

Henry Venn, the superintendent of the CMS in London, took an active interest in the churches in Sierra Leone. His father, John Venn, had been William Wilberforce's minister in Clapham, London, and the Venn family were noted evangelicals and abolitionists. As the head of CMS, Venn developed a new theory—namely that the establishment of a genuinely indigenous church was a key goal of Christian mission. Instead of planting Western churches in African or Indian or Chinese soil, CMS missionaries were told their goal was to foster localized forms of Christianity.

In Venn's thinking, a church was determined to be truly indigenous when it fulfilled what became known as the "three selfs." That is, when it was self-propagating, self-supporting, and self-governing. In other words, for as long as a national church relied on missionaries, theologians, and funding from Britain to survive, the CMS had not yet fulfilled its mission in that field.

The irony here, of course, is that what was fomenting in Freetown at that very time was exactly the kind of church Henry Venn was proposing. And it was emerging without any help from British missionaries. The unshackled churches of Freetown were not only growing in number and knowledge, but they were also itching to start sending out their own missionaries. A significant number of the Christians in Freetown were Yoruba speakers from the Niger Delta area, and many of them yearned to make their way back to their home villages to be reunited with their families and to share Christ with them. The best-known of these was a man named Ajayi, who was born in Nigeria around 1806. He was captured by slave traders, but his ship was intercepted by the British Navy. Taken to Sierra Leone, he joined a church, heard the gospel, and was converted to Christianity. He was baptized and, as was the unfortunate custom of the time, took a British-sounding name: Samuel Crowther. He joined CMS, studied at an Anglican missionary college, and became a Bible teacher at a Yoruba service in Freetown. In 1841, Crowther began his first missionary work in Nigeria.

Crowther was a shining example of Henry Venn's missionary strategy, so CMS decided to make an example of him. They sent him to England for further theological study, which culminated in his ordination by the Anglican Church in 1843.

Crowther believed that the evangelization of Africans must be carried out by Africans, so he requested an appointment to head up a new Anglican mission in the Niger territories. The story of his missionary journeys to his homeland—including being reunited with his family and friends—make for heartwarming reading, especially the account of how his long-lost mother and sister were among his first converts. In 1864, he was appointed as the first African bishop and set about forming an all-African staff to evangelize the Yoruba people.

Samuel Ajayi Crowther became a great linguist, translator, scholar, and mission teacher. He is also credited with producing the Yoruba Bible and played a key role in improving the British government's perception of Africa in the 1800s. Crowther was lionized as a success story of Anglican mission. His biography, *Samuel Crowther, the Slave Boy who became Bishop of the Niger*, became a bestseller in England.

Nonetheless, Samuel Ajayi Crowther became a target of the racist aspersions that British settlers, including some missionaries, cast on his all-African staff. There were vague charges of poor recordkeeping and possible misappropriation of finances, none of which were ever proved. A shadow descended on Crowther's mission, and it was subsequently dismantled.

He retired in shame.

In 2015, on the 150th anniversary of Crowther's ordination, Archbishop Justin Welby offered this apology:

> We in the Church of England need to say sorry that someone was properly and rightly consecrated Bishop and then betrayed and let down and undermined. It was wrong. In spite of immense hardship and despite the racism of many whites, Samuel Ajayi Crowther evangelized so effectively that he was eventually ordained Bishop, over much protest. He led his missionary diocese brilliantly, but was in the end falsely accused and had to resign, not long before his death. Crowther did not make himself grand. He lived out the commands of the words he took at his consecration. And from his time forward, God has demonstrated his grace through that ministry. Today well over 70 million Christians in Nigeria are his spiritual heirs. Today we honor him and in so doing The Lord Jesus Christ whom he served. We are sorry for his suffering at the hands of Anglicans in this country. Learning from their foolishness and from his heroism, we seek to be a church that does not again exclude those whom God is calling. We seek new apostles, and the grace to recognize them when they come.[1]

Crowther's mistreatment notwithstanding, Henry Venn's vision of a self-propagating, self-supporting, and self-governing church was a noble one. Many years later, South African missiologist David Bosch would add a fourth "self"—self-theologizing—insisting that non-Western ways of understanding the Scriptures and tradition were essential for indigenous churches. Up until this point, European and American missionaries had, in some cases inadvertently, transplanted Western ways of being a Christian and doing church into foreign soil.

A tropical fruit that is indigenous to Asia or South America can technically be grown in a cold climate like Scotland or Canada. It just needs to be planted in a heated greenhouse and attended to year-round. However, because this process is so labor-intensive, it's cheaper and simpler to import tropical fruit from Thailand or Brazil. Similarly, a British church can be planted in India or Africa; it just requires continual attention. It can survive, but is unlikely to become self-propagating, self-supporting, self-governing, and self-theologizing. It needs the metaphoric greenhouse of foreign missionaries to maintain it. An indigenous church, on the other hand, is one that is "generated from within," according to missionary pioneer David Garrison.[2]

William Smalley, an anthropologist and former missionary to the Hmong people, defines an indigenous church as, "A group of believers who live out their life, including their socialized Christian activity, in the patterns of the local society, and for whom a transformation of that society comes out of their felt needs under the guidance of the Holy Spirit and the Scriptures."[3]

We've already looked at the ways that people like Hudson Taylor and Mary Slessor lived among the people to whom they were sent, adopting their diets and dress, and embracing their rhythm of life. But Henry Venn was calling for more than this. His three-self approach was so radical that many missionaries found it impossible to implement ... though some tried.

In 1895, Roland Allen, a missionary to China, advised his coworkers to base their work on the three selfs. In his 1927 book, *The Spontaneous Expansion of the Church*, he insisted that churches thrived when put into the hands of "indigenous, biblical, apostolic witnesses."[4] He dreamed that "in every market town in China, in every center of population all over the world [there would be] the church which could grow and expand without any direction from foreigners."[5]

This is what makes the story of Samuel Ajayi Crowther so galling. Here was one of the first examples of an indigenous church combusting into missionary endeavor, only to be snuffed out by racist attacks. Crowther's mission to the Niger Delta was a truly unshackled moment in mission history, not only because many of its proponents, like Crowther himself, were literally unshackled, formerly enslaved people, but also because it was a spiritually and culturally unshackled movement of God. And the churches of Freetown weren't the only example of this spontaneous, unshackled birth of an indigenous church.

UNSHACKLED LEADERSHIP IN SOUTHERN AFRICA

Four-thousand miles south of Freetown, the Xhosa people were coming into conflict with Afrikaner trekboers (Dutch-descended nomadic pastoralists) who were migrating eastward from Cape Town. In a series of wars in the early 1800s, the trekboers pushed the Xhosa progressively east and claimed their lands. Furthermore, the Zulu nation was pushing south, squeezing the Xhosa, the Khoekhoe, and other ethnic tribes into an ever-smaller region of modern-day Eastern Cape. Caught in the vice between these two aggressors, the Xhosa were further weakened by famine and resorted to stealing cattle from European pastoralists to survive. They were routed in yet another frontier war in 1856.

One of their only refuges at that time were the South African mission stations. These were farming villages made up of a series of houses, a chapel, and agricultural buildings. The missionaries offered a measure of safety and security to the Xhosa in exchange for farm labor. The missionaries also expected their visitors to wear cotton clothing, learn to read and write, and attend church services. By the 1850s, sixteen thousand Xhosa lived in mission stations.

The missionaries in South Africa at that time intended to Christianize the Xhosa, teach them agricultural skills, and subsequently assist them in establishing their own farms. And it appears their aims were successful. In her book *A History of Christianity in Africa*, Nigerian author Elizabeth Isichei says the Xhosa "enthusiastically adopted modernity in all its guises—including Christianity, education, and commercial agriculture."[6]

However, this put them in direct conflict with the British pastoralists and the Boers—who didn't want the Xhosa as farming competitors, and who refused to accept them as their Christian brothers and sisters. Considered too Christian and Westernized by other Africans, and too African by their colonial neighbors, the Xhosa found themselves in a kind of cultural limbo.

It was at this time that God raised up an extraordinary prophetic figure.

Ntsikana was born around 1760 and grew up in a traditional Xhosa family. He became a noted orator, singer, and rain dancer. During his ceremonial dancing, he covered his body in red ochre, the recognized symbol of a holy man or diviner.

For the missionaries, rain dancing had become one of the central taboos for African converts. The dancer was moved into an ecstatic frenzy by his association with the spirits that governed the weather, and the missionaries regarded this as an unacceptable pagan practice. One day, while performing a traditional rain dance for his village, Ntsikana began to feel unwell and excused himself, retiring to a nearby stream to wash the ochre from his body. While in the water, he claims to have had a mystical experience. He suddenly prophesied, *"Lento indingenileyo ithi makuthandazwe!"* ("This thing that has entered me, it says 'Let there be prayer! Let everything bow the knee!'").[7] So profound was this "thing" that had come over him that he renounced traditional Xhosa ways, including rain dances and polygamy. He called his two wives to him and said to them, "It does not agree with this thing which has entered me that I have two wives."[8] He then sent one wife away with a share of his property to support her family.

With no Bible, no contact with missionaries, and no knowledge of Jesus, Ntsikana simply followed the "thing" that was directing him to adopt a new way of thinking that consisted of belief in a sovereign God, acknowledgement of human sin, river baptism, rejection of the red ochre, pacifism, monogamy, and prayer.

When he later encountered Christian missionaries, Ntsikana was astonished to find them like-minded brothers and sisters. He attended their church services and believed in Christ, but he refused their baptism, saying he had already had his own. He also refused to take on an additional Christian (Western) name. South African writer Mphuthumi Ntabeni says of him, "In Ntsikana, Xhosa tradition and Christian religion fused into a world and religious view that didn't betray what was most important in both."[9]

In 1812, Ntsikana was compelled to act when a false prophet-diviner named Nxele began proclaiming that the Xhosa should revolt against British rule, promising that an army of Xhosa ancestors was going to rise from the dead, bringing with them new cattle stock and wealth for the nation. Nxele attracted a huge crowd of followers to the riverside at a place called Gompo, where they readied themselves for war. Ntsikana rushed to the river to calm the mob. Mphuthumi Ntabeni writes,

> Ntsikana went around exclaiming that Nxele has turned upside down! Why does he mislead the people? He said Nxele was wrong in saying God is on earth: God is in the heavens! He told those who were coming from Gompo

under Nxele's influence; You only go to wash yourselves with seawater at
Gompo! But the real witchcraft is the badness of the heart, which you need
to repent against.[10]

Ntsikana's impassioned appeal to repentance and peace quelled a pointless
rebellion and saved thousands of lives.

Ntsikana died in 1821, leaving a legacy of sacred songs—the first hymns
composed in the Xhosa language. His best-known hymns were "Life Creator"
and "*Ulo Thixo omkhulu ngosezulwini*" ("He, the Great God in Heaven").

Today, Ntsikana is revered in South Africa not as a great Christian leader
of the past but as a symbol of Xhosa nationalism and Christian separatism.
This inaccurate perception arises largely from Western missionaries who did
not know what to do with him, and even questioned whether Ntsikana was a
Christian. His form of Christianity was unshackled. He wasn't converted or
baptized by missionaries. He refused membership in any denomination. He
expressed his beliefs in distinctly Xhosa ways, with references to hunting and
pastoralism. His talk about ecstatic experiences, voices, and healings concerned
Westerners. As Brian Stiller writes of the missionaries at that time, "Many of
them were tutored in the assumptions of the Enlightenment and rationalistic
nineteenth-century theologians: anything outside of a rational explanation was
seen as superstition."[11]

In many ways Samuel Ajayi Crowther and Ntsikana could not have been
more different. One was an enslaved man, the other was free. One embraced
Western (Anglican) Christianity and was baptized and ordained, the other
refused baptism and church membership. One took on an English name,
the other would not. But in other ways, they were remarkably similar. They
were both influential African men who attracted followers willing to embrace
the radical teaching of the gospel. What might have happened if colonial-era
missionaries had supported and assisted the work of such men? Could their
distinctly African leadership have led to greater growth and blessing for the
churches in their respective nations?

UNSHACKLED LEADERSHIP IN NEW ZEALAND

A third example of unshackled Christian leadership can be found in
New Zealand in the story of the extraordinary Māori leader, Te Whiti o
Rongomai III.

The son of a great Māori warrior, Te Whiti was born into the Waikato tribe in 1832 on the night before the battle of Ōtaka—an intertribal war in which his father lost his life. Following that defeat, and fearing reprisals by their enemies, the surviving Waikato fled south. Te Whiti's family took refuge among the Patukai people under the leadership of Te Whiti's uncle.

Even as a young boy, Te Whiti was recognized as possessing a special spiritual authority in teaching and prophecy. As a result, the Patukai people saw it as their responsibility to keep him safe and teach him traditional Māori knowledge as his spiritual abilities developed.

During his childhood, more conflict broke out in New Zealand, but this time it wasn't intertribal; it was between the New Zealand colonial government and allied Māori tribes. Previously known as the Māori Wars (now the New Zealand Wars), these were a series of battles and skirmishes that took place between 1845 and 1872 and involved up to four thousand allied Māori warriors fighting eighteen thousand British Army troops, supported by artillery, cavalry, and local militia. Grossly outnumbered, the Māori fought valiantly for nearly twenty years; but, in the end, they lost thousands of lives and had tracts of land confiscated as punishment for their "rebellion." After so much bloodshed and decades of upheaval, all New Zealanders, both Indigenous and white, were traumatized. People were looking for hope.

Meanwhile, Te Whiti was growing in his knowledge of local lore, as well as another source of spiritual knowledge he'd encountered: the Bible. It is supposed that Te Whiti was introduced to Christian teaching by a Māori Wesleyan evangelist named Minarapa Rangihatuake around 1842. Several years later, Te Whiti became an ardent pupil of the German Lutheran missionary Johann Riemenschneider. However, as he grew to manhood, Te Whiti strove to develop a distinctly Māori form of the Christian faith—one that acknowledged traditional beliefs and practices without watering down biblical doctrines.

Around this time, after the peak of the New Zealand Wars, Te Whiti emerged as a national figure. He started prophesying about a day of restoration and peace for the disillusioned Māori peoples, but not until after a great tribulation. Telling them he had "heard a thunder and sensed an approaching flood"—a reference to encroaching European settlement—he believed he was to pursue a special mission to deal with the white colonists.[12] In the *Dictionary of New Zealand Biography*, Danny Keenan writes,

Te Whiti developed an oratory which addressed Māori misgivings over the loss of their land. He skillfully utilized a spiritual Māori idiom and the rhetoric of Christianity, imbued with a knowledge of the [European] world. Robert Stout, writing of Te Whiti in 1883, observed that he preached temperance and peace. His only literature was the Bible. His favorite book was said to be Revelation ... He developed an especial belief in the affinity of Māori and Jew, once telling James Cowan, "We come from the land of Canaan."[13]

In 1867, Te Whiti established a village at Parihaka, on the very southern tip of New Zealand's north island. He wanted his people to regain their land, pride, and self-respect after the confiscations in other parts of the country. His aim seems to have been to establish a new way for Māori to resist European attempts to take what was left of Māori culture.

But European settlers continued to encroach on Māori land, even sections of the country that had been legally allocated for Māori use. Te Whiti made multiple appeals to the New Zealand government, demanding they stop the continued intrusion onto their property, but to no avail. Some Māori leaders readied for another war, but Te Whiti preached peace and developed a strategy that was unheard of at that time—civil disobedience, or nonviolent resistance.

Today, when people hear a phrase like nonviolent direct action (NVDA), they might think of things like sit-ins, tree sitting, strikes, occupying workplaces, and street blockades. They might think of Martin Luther King Jr.'s boycotts and marches in 1950s Alabama, or Mahatma Gandhi's tactics of withdrawal in early twentieth-century India. But Te Whiti pioneered peaceful resistance as early as the 1870s. He had seen that war with British forces achieved nothing, and his Christian faith counseled him toward peace at all costs.

The tipping point occurred when the government began surveying sixteen thousand acres of land intended as a Māori reserve with the intention of selling it to colonists. Te Whiti and his followers disrupted the surveyors by plowing the land to make it less saleable. They did the same on other tracts of land around the country, enraging the settlers, and the New Zealand police began arresting Te Whiti's followers. His sit-ins and field-plowing were so disruptive that the government had to negotiate with Te Whiti—promising various concessions without pledging to cease their encroachment on unoccupied land. Te Whiti refused to accept their terms. He guaranteed the government that his followers would not resort to the use of arms, but the campaign of "plow and protest" intensified. He pronounced:

> Though some, in darkness of heart, seeing their land ravished, might wish to take arms and kill the aggressors, I say it must not be. Let not the [whites] think to succeed by reason of their guns ... I want not war, but they do. The flashes of their guns have singed our eyelashes, and yet they say they do not want war ... The government come not hither to reason, but go to out-of-the-way places. They work secretly, but I speak in public so that all may hear.[14]

Despite this, after a series of proclamations forbidding peaceful protest, on November 5,1881 the government sent a huge force of more than 1,500 armed police to Parihaka where they were met by about two thousand peaceful Māori. No one had ever seen such a protest before. It bewildered the New Zealand police, who weren't sure what to do with thousands of passive protesters. One attending officer, Col. W. B. Messenger, described it this way:

> Their attitude of passive resistance and patient obedience to Te Whiti's orders was extraordinary. There was a line of children across the entrance to the big village, a kind of singing class directed by an old man with a stick. The children sat there unmoving, droning away, and even when a mounted officer galloped up and pulled his horse up so short that the dirt from its forefeet spattered the children they still went on chanting, perfectly oblivious, apparently, to the [white settlers] ... There were skipping-parties of girls on the road ... There were six hundred women and children there, and our reception was perfectly peaceful.[15]

Inside the village, the police encountered the great Te Whiti, dressed in a *korowai*—the traditional feathered chieftain's cloak. He too remained seated, refusing to move even when directed to do so. Although later a New Zealand court would cast doubt on the legality of the police's actions at Parihaka, Te Whiti was arrested and charged with "wickedly, maliciously, and seditiously contriving and intending to disturb the peace."[16] Due to a lack of evidence, the judiciary continued to delay his trial, despite his demand to have his day in court. He was held in custody for nearly three years without trial, during which time the village at Parihaka fell into disrepair.

Te Whiti was a Christian brother to the churchgoing colonists who had imprisoned and humiliated him. He was a man of peace, a godly leader full of compassion and with a deep desire for justice. His pioneering work in nonviolent direct action would later inspire the British Suffragette movement, the Indian independence campaign, the Dutch anti-Nazi general strike of 1941, the American Civil Rights movement, Greenpeace, and the Global Climate Strike. His political campaign of resistance against the colonization of his nation was clearly shaped by his Christian convictions. And yet, despite some support from Western missionaries, he was reviled and despised by the white-settler churches. He died among the ruins of Parihaka in 1907.

Yet again, Western missionaries could not cope with an unshackled indigenous church emerging beyond their control.

UNSHACKLED MISSION IN NORTH AMERICA

In North America, Native American missionaries have been at the forefront of calling for justice for Indigenous people. Foremost among them is the Pequot Indian evangelist, William Apess. Known by some today as the leader of the Bloodless Mashpee Revolt of 1833, Apess is another example of indigenous Christian leadership fusing the work of evangelism and preaching with peaceful political activism. Born into poverty in Massachusetts in 1798, William Apess began life as an indentured servant, but served in Quebec during the War of 1812. A hard-drinking soldier, Apess appears to have reformed his ways, and in 1829 he was ordained as an itinerant Methodist minister. That same year, he wrote the first published Native American autobiography, *A Son of the Forest.*

His memoir not only describes his journey from soldiering and alcohol abuse to the piety of Methodist ministry, but also rails against the injustices he had seen perpetrated against his people. Apess writes about how the elders in the church hierarchy placed barriers in his way, and how the army didn't pay promised bonuses to soldiers like himself. Although critical of some aspects of Native American cultures, he was uncompromising in his evaluation of white settlers, writing, "They introduced among my countrymen ardent spirits; seduced them into a love for it, and when under its baleful influence, wronged them out of their lawful possession—that land where reposed the ashes of their sires."[17] Furthermore "they committed violence of the most revolting and basest kind upon the persons of the female portion of the tribe, who until the arts, and vices, and debauchery of the whites were introduced among them, were happy, and peaceable, and cheerful, as they roamed over their goodly possessions."[18]

Apess saw no reason why his preaching of the gospel shouldn't include a call to personal devotion to Christ as well as a rallying cry for social and racial justice. This combination of motivations is often at the heart of unshackled mission.

In 1833, as part of his preaching circuit, Apess visited the Mashpee-Wampanoag people on Cape Cod—a community of several hundred people living in sub-standard conditions on an Indian reservation. What Apess encountered was the age-old story of land confiscation, withheld wages, government corruption, and limited education for the Mashpee children. But to top it off, Apess found a crooked missionary holding sway over the township. Rev. Phineas Fish, a Congregational minister assigned to the town, and funded and overseen by Harvard College, was found to be taking hundreds of dollars of aid intended for the Mashpee. His only form of service was to preach to a small group of white people who attended his church. Apess was infuriated.

Although a Pequot, Apess asked the Mashpee to accept him as one of their own and grant him standing in their tribe. He then helped his new tribe to write what amounted to a Mashpee declaration of independence. In it, they resolved to have complete sovereignty over their own lands and to no longer permit any white people to enter or carry off wood or hay. They also discharged the odious Rev. Fish, claimed the right to have their own Christian meeting house "and place in the pulpit whom we please to preach to us."[19]

You can imagine how these declarations went down at the Massachusetts state house and Harvard College. The latter refused to stand Fish down, allowing him to continue serving his white church. As for the Massachusetts governor, he sent a contingent of negotiators to meet with the Mashpee to try to find a solution to their grievances. But while there, the government forces arrested Apess and six others, charging them with inciting a violent uprising. Apess was indignant, protesting that the Mashpee were engaged in a nonviolent revolt against white rule.

To the white citizens of Cape Cod, a revolt was a revolt, nonviolent or not. William Apess was locked up, and his anger at the treatment of Indigenous people continued to simmer. Disheartened by his short incarceration, Apess turned to alcohol again. Frequently drunk, his family split up. He lost his Massachusetts property and died in New York City in 1839, a broken man.

William Apess's story is not an unfamiliar one for indigenous leaders. Ground down by an entrenched system of prejudice and exclusion, they fade away, crushed by the enormity of the struggle they have enjoined. But Apess's writings are still available, and his voice is as eloquent and as passionate as that of better-known orators of the time, such as Thomas Paine or Frederick Douglass. In 1833, the year of the Mashpee uprising, Apess published an essay titled "An Indian's Looking-Glass for the White Man," in which he outlined his vision for social and political equality between the races. He offered a mirror in which white readers could examine their own actions. The essay begins,

> Having a desire to place a few things before my fellow creatures who are traveling with me to the grave, and to that God who is the maker and preserver both of the white man and the Indian, whose abilities are the same and who are to be judged by one God, who will show no favor to outward appearances but will judge righteousness. Now I ask if degradation has not been heaped long enough upon the Indians? And if so, can there not be a compromise? Is it right to hold and promote prejudices? If not, why not put them all away?[20]

Ultimately, he writes, his deepest desire is that white American settlers look at themselves and their treatment of his people and take steps to end their discrimination, concluding with, "Pray you stop not till this tree of distinction shall be leveled to the earth, and the mantle of prejudice turn from every American heart."[21]

UNSHACKLED MISSION IN THE PACIFIC

Evangelism and advocacy went hand in hand for people like Te Whiti and William Apess. This was also the case in Australia. Because of the 1850s gold rush, Australia attracted prospectors from around the world, including a large number of Chinese immigrants. Three Christian evangelists—Lo Sam-yuen, Ho A Low, and Chu A Luk—ministered among them. Hundreds were baptized, many of whom returned to China with their newfound faith. So successful was evangelism among Chinese miners, cooks, and laundry workers that the Australian Anglican Church formed a permanent Chinese mission. Its superintendent, Cheok Hong Cheong, was not only a highly effective evangelist but was also active in protesting racist and discriminatory laws against Chinese workers. He also made it clear he would resist the "Europeanization" of Christianity among the Chinese. His outspokenness created tensions within the church, and he complained that Australian Anglicans seemed uninterested in supporting his vital ministry. When in 1885 Hudson Taylor conducted a speaking tour of Australia, attempting to recruit people to join him in the China Inland Mission, Cheong noted that white Australians were interested in evangelizing the Chinese, as long as it wasn't the Chinese across the street.

This was a time of widespread discrimination against the Chinese in Australia. Rumors circulated that China was preparing to invade and that Chinese migrant workers were agents and spies sent to get the country addicted to opium so the attacking army would meet no resistance. (Racism and hysteria are always a combustible combination.) In response, Cheong published a booklet, *Chinese Remonstrance to the Parliament and People of Victoria*, challenging the government's disregard of Chinese rights, refuting myths of any Chinese invasion, and calling for better treatment of Chinese citizens. Cheong even implored Australia's first prime minister, Sir Edmund Barton, to address racism and discrimination and relax the immigration laws for the Chinese.

Another example of unshackled mission in the Pacific by a person of color is that of Betsey Stockton. Born in New Jersey in 1798, Stockton found herself indentured as a domestic slave at a young age. She grew to be a woman of deep faith with an abiding sense that she had been called to missionary work. When granted her freedom in 1815, she immediately presented herself to the American Board of Commissions for Foreign Missions to serve as a missionary in Africa. In their wisdom, the ABCFM suggested she consider Hawaii instead. After some training, in 1823 Betsey Stockton set out for a mission station on Maui. There she convinced her team leader to allow her to start a school for the Maka'ainana—those considered the "common people" by the islanders. It took a woman familiar with discrimination and marginalization to feel an affinity with the Maka'ainana. Eventually, Stockton also trained the Maka'ainana as teachers, so they could break free of their reliance on missionaries. In so doing, it is likely that Betsey Stockton gave generations of native Hawaiians the opportunity to receive an education and hear the gospel in their own language.

But perhaps the most impressive story of the unshackled spread of the gospel is that of the evangelization of South Pacific nations—such as Tahiti, Fiji,

Tonga, Samoa, and the Cook Islands—where a truly indigenous missionary movement moved across Polynesia into Melanesia.

In 1797, thirty British missionaries arrived in Tahiti—one of the most eastern of the Pacific nations—under the leadership of British missionary Henry Nott. The Tahitians received them warmly and responded favorably to their ministry, but the widespread conversion of the Tahitians didn't begin until King Pomare II announced he had become a Christian and was baptized.

During a civil war in Tahiti in 1808, Pomare II was overthrown and forced to flee to a nearby island. The British missionaries, uncertain of their own fate, fled there with him. In his book *The Great Century,* historian Kenneth Scott Latourette takes up the story:

> While on that island, in close company with the missionaries, Pomare II, perhaps in part because of loss of faith in the religion which had failed to save him from his fate, professed Christianity and asked for baptism. While that was not at once given him, he henceforth sided with Christianity. When in 1815 Pomare II succeeded in restoring his authority over Tahiti, his victory meant the triumph of the new faith.[22]

By 1821, the Tahitian church was so large, it was preparing to send missionaries to the nearby Cook Islands. Two years later, they commissioned missionaries to go to Tonga. Then, in 1830, British missionaries arrived in Samoa, accompanied by missionary teachers from Tahiti and the Cook Islands and a Samoan couple from Tonga. This set off a chain reaction, with each island nation sending missionaries westward toward Australia and Melanesia.

To be sure, these efforts were assisted by British missionaries, such as David Cargill from Scotland and George Brown from England, who was the most dominant pioneering figure in Methodist missions history after 1860. But as remarkable as Brown was, the success of his work in Samoa was due to the devotion of his Samoan, Fijian, and Tahitian coworkers. And Brown knew it. Rather than shackling the Samoan church—which underwent a revival in the 1860s, growing by more than 100 percent—Brown saw his role as that of a support person or theological consultant. He also impressed upon the Samoans their duty to evangelize nearby island nations. In 1875, he took a team of Fijians and Samoans to the last unreached nation in the region—the remote and inhospitable Papua New Guinea (PNG).

Because the rugged mountains of the interior were nearly impassible, European missionaries had only reached the coastal regions of PNG by the nineteenth century. Many tribes were isolated until well into the twentieth century. Reputed to be fierce warriors and plagued by constant intertribal warfare, PNG tribespeople still practiced cannibalism, especially toward their vanquished foes. PNG women had no right to have or to desire spiritual knowledge. Religion was only for men, so when the first missionaries arrived in teams that included women, the tribesmen were taken aback.

One of these teams was headed up by a Cook Islander missionary named Ruatoka. His parents were Christian converts, and he embraced the calling to missionary service as a young man, eventually being sent to Takamoa Theological College in New Zealand to prepare for service in PNG.

In 1872, Ruatoka, his wife, Tungane, and his team arrived at Manumanu village near Port Moresby. Within a year, four members of the team were dead; the rest were starving and abandoned the mission. Ruatoka and Tungane retreated to the British colonial port of Somerset to regroup and plan their next move.

Five months later, along with three British missionaries, they sailed back to Manumanu where they encountered some Motu traders who recognized Ruatoka and Tungane from their earlier trip. The Moto people invited the group to stay at their villages, and Ruatoka advised the British missionaries this could be an opportune opening for the gospel. Though he was never appointed the official leader of the party, Ruatoka clearly took command. The English missionaries depended on him to interpret, advise, and supervise when they were away.

Early in his time among the Moto, Ruatoka saw a breakthrough when he intervened to save a young girl who was about to be offered as a human sacrifice to a neighboring tribe. The tribal chief marveled that the missionary should take so much trouble over a girl from his tribe. Despite not being a relative of hers, Ruatoka still saved her life, which led her chief to conclude that Ruatoka's *lotu* (religion) must be good.

In 1878, gold was discovered at the nearby Laloki River, attracting a rush of miners from around the region and even nearby Australia. Ruatoka, already noted as an evangelist and pastor, now found himself acting as a mediator in land disputes between immigrant miners, local tribes, and the colonial government. As a result, the Moto and other neighboring tribes accepted

Ruatoka as a leader. He was even called on to help administer justice within the community. Unfortunately, Ruatoka was often unwell, having never fully recovered from an illness he suffered before becoming a missionary. In 1885 Tungane died, and Ruatoka eventually succumbed in 1903. His was not an easy life, but he had made such an impression that he is now a part of PNG history, with a permanent memorial to him, streets and schools named after him, and a postage stamp with his image on it.

NEVER QUITE FULLY UNSHACKLED

Each of the stories we've encountered in this chapter shows us that mission not only involves people of color, but also that mission must never be about transplanting British or American forms of Christianity into foreign fields. The people we've looked at were unshackled men and women, but they also unshackle our understanding of mission. They pry open the gilded cage in which mission had been trapped, showing us that the work of God's people includes social reform, political activism, peacemaking, and mediation as well as the more traditional evangelism, translation work, and literature distribution.

Samuel Ajayi Crowther's example in the Niger teaches us that indigenous cultural forms need to be respected and that new churches need to be equipped and unleashed to self-theologize in their own contexts.

Similarly, Ntsikana's work in Southern Africa as a prophet-diviner and peacemaker invites us not to fear indigenous forms of ministry that look different from what we are used to in the West.

Te Whiti's pioneering work in nonviolent direct action in New Zealand, William Apess' peaceful uprising on Cape Cod, and Cheok Hong Cheong's fervent advocacy for Chinese immigrants in Australia reveal the essentially Christian work of standing with the poor and speaking truth to power.

And finally, the selfless, hard work of Betsey Stockton in Hawaii and Ruatoka in PNG show us how it is often those who are familiar with marginalization who are best placed to seek and humbly serve the marginalized.

But perhaps you also noted as you read this chapter that none of these people of color were able to operate in a completely unshackled manner. Each of them struggled against racist societies with entrenched discrimination. Some of them suffered at the hands of colonial rulers, including church authorities. Some were broken by their experience. Most of them saw very little fruit for their costly labors.

And yet today, African and South Pacific Christianity are among the most vital, dynamic, and growing expressions of the faith in the world, along with those in South Korea, Southeast Asia, and Latin America. Christianity, contrary to popular opinion, is not dying, even though it is in decline in the West. In fact, the nineteenth-century assumption that Christianity is strictly a European religion no longer holds.

But for now, it is worth asking ourselves whether we are willing to do what William Apess asked his readers to do back in 1833 and peer through the looking glass held up to us by people of color. Are we humble enough to learn from our Black neighbors and from Christians in the Global South? Are we willing to undertake the necessary work of educating ourselves to the effects of systemic racism around the world? More than that, could we learn from Cheok Hong Cheong's rebuke to colonial Australians who were excited by Hudson Taylor's attempts to recruit missionaries for China but weren't even willing to befriend their Chinese neighbors? Many of us today live in culturally diverse cities, thanks to the effects of migration and globalization. We have more opportunity than ever to understand indigenous forms of Christianity and to learn from the Global South within our own neighborhoods. We need to unshackle ourselves from our cultural blind spots to see where God is at work in the world, even if its forms and expressions are different from what we might imagine.

In his book *Holy Anarchy*, English missiologist Graham Adams calls on his readers to do exactly this—to unshackle ourselves from the imperialistic assumptions behind so much of our understanding of mission. This involves not only learning from Christians in the Majority World but also repenting of the ways the structures and patterns of Empire have shaped us and working intentionally to transform those patterns. Adams notes these five marks of anti-imperial mission:

1. Hear the groans of creation to discern the damage done to it by the structures and practices of Empire. Expose, subvert and transform those patterns.
2. Hear the cries of the oppressed, exploited and excluded to discern the harm caused by the structures and practices of Empire. Expose, subvert and transform those patterns.

3. Attend to the needs of those bruised by such systems of domination, in all
    their forms … and to all who are grieving, wearied and unwell.

4. Build community in which we learn together how to decolonize our (un)
    consciousness and commit to an alternative solidarity that has room for
    all.

5. Witness to this alternative solidarity in the stories we tell, believing in
    the good news of the Empire's subversion at the hands of God's awesome
    weakness.[23]

The Eighth Shape

CONTEXTUALIZING

Contextualizing the gospel involves presenting it in such a way that if it causes offense in its hearers, it is for the right, biblical reasons, not for the wrong cultural ones.

ANON.

In his book *The Lamb Enters the Dreaming,* historian Robert Kenny tells the story of the Ebenezer mission, established by Moravians in the 1850s to evangelize the Wotjobaluk people in southern Australia.[1] Like many Indigenous peoples across the continent, the Wotjobaluk practiced totemism, a belief system in which humans develop a mystical kinship with a spirit-being, usually an animal. Different spirit animals, or totems, were adopted by different kinship groups as their emblem or symbol. In Australia, spirit animals include the fleet-footed kangaroo, the ferocious saltwater crocodile, and the majestic eagle.

Kenny points out that the Moravians' preaching focused on references to Jesus as the "Lamb of God" and the "Good Shepherd." As we saw back in chapter four, the Moravians even spoke of Christ as "Brother Lambkin." This, writes Kenny, gave the Wotjobaluk the impression that the lamb was the Moravian's spirit animal. The Wotjobaluk assumed the missionaries saw sheep as sacred and symbolic. Their assumption was only confirmed when white pastoralists invaded their land, establishing huge sheep stations across the Wimmera. So, you can imagine their confusion when they saw these same missionaries and settlers slaughtering and eating the lambs they had previously been tending. Also, having been told that Jesus was a shepherd, it must have disturbed them to imagine him eating his own totem.

Not only that, the running of huge flocks of sheep on the Wotjobaluk's land degraded the previously fertile soil, and the Wotjobaluk therefore saw the white man's spirit animal as a destructive presence in their country. The Wotjobaluk believed that the brutality of white pastoralists toward them must have been derived from their harmful spirit animal. What ensued was a spate of attacks on flocks across the Wimmera, followed by aggression against the Wotjobaluk—who came to despise the wretched sheep.

The missionaries' message about the loving sacrifice of the Lamb of God was largely lost on the Wotjobaluk (although Kenny's book does note the 1860 conversion of the first tribal man from their nation). Not understanding how their totemic belief system worked, the Moravian missionaries had no idea how all their talk of shepherds and lambs was affecting their Indigenous audience.

Something similar happened in southern Africa when British missionaries first preached the message of the gospel to the Xhosa nation. In the early nineteenth century, it was not uncommon for evangelists in Britain to use Revelation 3:20 as the key text for their sermons: "Here I am! I stand at the door and knock. If anyone hears my voice and opens the door, I will come in and eat with that person, and they with me." British evangelists, taking the verse somewhat out of context, directed it at unbelievers, asking them to "open the doors of their hearts" to the Christ who was knocking patiently outside. When British missionaries arrived in southern Africa, preaching Revelation 3:20 to the Xhosa in the same way, they evoked a very different reaction. For a start, Xhosa houses didn't have doors. The entrances to their huts were always open. When a relative or neighbor approached another person's home, they would call out as they drew near. Knowing their voice, the house owner would bid them to enter. The only people who "knocked" were thieves who would rap on the side of the house and listen for movement inside. If not, they would sneak in and steal property. By preaching that Jesus is the one who knocks, the missionaries were presenting Christ as a malevolent, untrustworthy presence in their village.

Getting the host language right—as well as understanding customs, culture, and the vernacular—is essential work for missionaries. Even one of history's greatest missionaries, the Jesuit Francis Xavier, made some missteps in this regard. In 1551, while in Japan, Francis asked a local convert for a Japanese word that would be the equivalent of *Deus* (Latin for "God"). The convert offered the word *dainichi*, meaning "the Cosmic Lord," in the tradition of the Japanese theism. But Francis rejected the term because of its connections with esoteric Buddhist belief. He chose instead to use a simple phonetic equivalent: *daiusu*. This turned out to be disastrous, because Francis's new word was phonetically very similar to the Japanese term *dai uso*, meaning "Great Lie."

Even contemporary fiction is peopled with ignorant missionaries who get key words wrong or don't understand the local culture. In her 1998 bestseller, *The Poisonwood Bible*, Barbara Kingsolver tells the story of a hapless American missionary named Nathan Price who tries to baptize new Congolese Christians in a river which, unbeknownst to him, is filled with crocodiles. He tells his wife he is disappointed that so few people responded to his appeal to join him in the river, believing their reticence is due to hard-heartedness. Later, Price proclaims "Tata Jesus is *bängala*!" thinking he is saying, "Jesus is beloved," when in fact his mispronunciation means he is actually saying "Jesus is poisonwood."[2] Despite being corrected many times, Price repeats the phrase continually, hence the book's title. Nathan Price is Kingsolver's none-too-subtle metaphor for the cultural insensitivity of missionaries.

A NEW MISSIONAL STRATEGY

As we saw in the previous chapter, the nineteenth century saw the emergence of a number of indigenous missionaries in various parts of America, Africa, and the South Pacific. However, they were a tiny minority of the missionaries serving around the world at that time. In the latter half of the century, inspired by people such as Hudson Taylor and Dwight Moody, thousands of young women and men were sent out from Western countries to almost every corner of the globe. But as the 1800s drew to a close and a new century dawned, many of them faced the growing challenge of trying to "fit" the gospel into non-Western cultures. By the early twentieth century, colonized countries were bucking against the yoke of oppression they had been subjected to, and the dreadful conflagration of World War I only undermined the idea that the "West is best." Missionaries were rethinking their whole strategy. At this time, a group of innovative young missionaries began to engage in this new shape of mission: *contextualizing*.

This process assumes there is no such thing as a universal Christianity—a single version of the faith that can be transplanted into different cultures.

Instead, all forms of Christianity are local. Wherever in the world we encounter Christianity, we will find it in what British historian of mission Andrew Walls calls a "historically, culturally conditioned form."[3] The early missionaries believed they were taking a universal Christianity with them from, say, London to India. However, these newer missionaries realized that they were in fact taking a localized British form of the faith and transplanting it in India. They believed there was nothing to fear in acknowledging this fact because, in the incarnation of Christ, we see God becoming human in a particular time, culture, and place. Whereas the first wave of Western missionaries was concerned with translating Christianity into the *language* of their host country, this new wave was concerned with translating it into the *culture* of that country. They were contextualizing it.

Missiologist René Padilla defines the work this way:

> To contextualize the gospel is so to translate it that the Lordship of Jesus Christ is not an abstract principle or a mere doctrine, but the determining factor of life in all its dimensions and the basic criterion in relation to which all the cultural values that form the very substance of human life are evaluated. Without contextualization the gospel will become tangential or even entirely irrelevant.[4]

Timothy Keller puts it more simply: to contextualize the gospel means "to resonate with yet defy the culture around you."[5]

A NEW KIND OF MISSIONARY

In the summer of 1886, the famous evangelist Dwight Moody was scheduled to speak at a Christian student convention in Mount Hermon, Massachusetts. More than 250 students from eighty-seven colleges across the country were enjoying camp life and listening to presentations by preachers and seminary professors. But Moody was the star attraction.

Moody appealed to the students to give their all to the service of God, whatever career path they chose. But as a strong supporter of Hudson Taylor's China Inland Mission, he also insisted they seriously consider whether God might be calling them to an overseas mission field.

Some of the students wanted to explore foreign mission service, so early in the four-week convention, one of the students, Robert Wilder, called a meeting of anyone interested in learning more. He invited a well-known mission enthusiast, Arthur Pierson, to speak to the group. Pierson's address was titled "Christ means that all shall go, and shall go to all." Twenty-one students showed up and were greatly inspired by what Pierson shared. They wanted everyone at the convention to hear about the need for foreign missionaries, so they approached the convention organizers to ask for a spot on the main stage to share their new-found convictions. Ultimately, ten students spoke at one of the sessions, each one talking about the needs of a different foreign nation. They concluded their series of brief talks with a call to serve God overseas.

The result was electrifying. Later, Robert Wilder wrote, "Seldom have I seen an audience under the sway of God's spirit as it was that night. The delegates withdrew to their rooms or went out under the great trees to wait on God for guidance."[6]

By the end of the Mount Hermon convention, one hundred students had signed a pledge committing themselves to become foreign missionaries.

Flushed with the success of his efforts and deeply convicted about the priority of foreign missions, Wilder suspended his studies and spent the following academic year touring 167 college campuses, telling the story of the "Mount Hermon 100" and urging students to pledge themselves to become missionaries. That year Wilder recruited 2,106 student volunteers. Two years later—in 1888—2,894 students signed the pledge: "It is my purpose, if God permit, to become a foreign missionary."

That same year, Wilder and others formed the Student Volunteer Movement (SVM) with the purpose of establishing student groups on campuses across the nation in order to study missions, develop strategies, and promote the Mount Hermon pledge. They took as their motto "Evangelization of the world in this generation." (Never mind that over 130 years later we still haven't evangelized the whole world.)

The energy and enthusiasm of the SVM was infectious. Within five years there were 6,200 new missionaries on the field. Prior to the formation of the SVM, American Protestants supported less than one thousand missionaries throughout the world. By 1945, when the movement was in decline, 20,500 students had volunteered for the mission field.

But more than just being great recruiters, the SVM was developing a new kind of missionary. These volunteers weren't cobblers, as William Carey was, or the sons of bricklayers, like Moody. They weren't from poor, working-class backgrounds. They were America's brightest and best. They were talented and driven, as well as culturally adaptable and somewhat liberal socially. They had enough education to be more aware of global issues and more respectful of foreign cultures and indigenous faiths than their parents' generation. And they possessed all the brashness and energy of America's Gilded Age.

As Michael Parker writes, "Their goal was to create a missionary force large enough to evangelize every nation. They thought in military terms. Missionaries were soldiers in God's army. The SVM sought to recruit, to support, and to place these soldiers strategically around the world. If done shrewdly, they thought they would surely conquer the world."[7]

The SVM even produced their own "celebrity" missionaries. People like C. T. Studd, Eric Liddell, and Jim Elliot were all student volunteers. But here, we will consider the story of just one: Eli Stanley Jones.

BROTHER STANLEY AND THE
CHRISTIAN ASHRAM MOVEMENT

Stan Jones, as he was known, was born in 1884. His father was an alcoholic and largely absent from his son's life, which might explain why Jones became a rebellious teenager and got involved in gang activity on the streets of Baltimore. However, his father's premature death had a powerful effect on the young man. He enrolled at City College and began selling insurance to support his mother. Initially intending to become a lawyer, Jones experienced a dramatic conversion in 1901 and wanted to transfer to a Christian college. He chose Asbury College—a small Methodist school in Wilmore, Kentucky.

Jones joined the SVM group on campus and was encouraged to consider foreign mission service. When he told his mother he was contemplating becoming a missionary, she gasped, "What! A poor Methodist preacher?"

Then in February 1905, Jones was attending a prayer meeting on campus with a few other members of the SVM group when, as he described it, the Holy Spirit seemed to enter the room. From this meeting, a small revival swept across the Asbury campus and the nearby town of Wilmore. As the Asbury University website explains it,

> There were confessions of sin, powerful prayers, and new deeper commit-
> ments to the Lord. In his spiritual autobiography, Jones said that this revival

liberated him from a sense of superiority, which prepared him for future
work as a missionary, opened his ears to the Holy Spirit, and led directly to
his calling to the mission field.[8]

In 1907, the twenty-three-year-old Stan Jones arrived in India, ready to
contribute to the SVM vision of evangelizing the whole world within a
generation. On his journey to Lucknow, northern India, he found himself
sharing a train compartment with a well-educated English-speaking
Muslim. Ready to begin evangelizing, Jones read the Sermon on the Mount
to his traveling companion, expecting him to be impressed by the unique
wisdom of Christ. The young missionary was taken aback when his new
friend told him that Islam has the same teaching in their sacred book. It
suddenly dawned on him that he had arrived in a foreign land and had very
little knowledge of Islam or Hinduism. On his first day as a missionary,
he realized he needed to know more about other religions in order to find
bridges between them.

Jones resolved to disentangle the gospel of Jesus Christ from Western
systems, culture, and their sometimes-non-Christian expressions. After all, as
he said, "Western civilization is only partly Christianized."[9] A natural contextualizer, he began dialogue meetings with judges, lawyers, and politicians, honing
his ability to speak about Jesus in everyday ways, as the universal Christ, for all
races and cultures and as the answer to all human need.

During his sixty years in India, Jones took a keen interest in the burgeoning
independence movement, befriending its leaders, Jawaharlal Nehru and
Mahatma Gandhi, who called him "Brother Stanley." In 1948, Jones wrote one
of the first biographies of Gandhi for an American audience. Much later, Martin
Luther King Jr. told Jones's daughter, Eunice, that it was reading her father's
book about Gandhi that convinced him to adopt the strict non-violent method
in the civil rights struggle. In his earlier book, *The Christ of the Indian Road*,
Jones attributed much of the thinking of the Indian independence movement
to the influence of Christianity:

> Call the roll of the reforms that are sweeping across India and whether they
> be economic, social, moral, or religious, they are all tending straight toward
> Jesus Christ and his thought. Not one of them is going away from him, that
> is, if it be reform and not reaction.[10]

One of his most notable feats of contextualization was his creation of the Christian Ashram movement.[11] Traditionally, an ashram is a hermitage or monastery for Hindus—often located in remote areas away from busy towns and cities, usually in forests or mountains, so that the faithful can find the peace and quiet necessary for spiritual instruction and meditation. Each ashram consists of basic living quarters, a dining hall, a yoga hall, library, and gardens, and is headed by a resident spiritual master or teacher. Visitors to the ashram are expected to become part of the teacher's family, following his daily routine, which includes teaching, meditation, yoga, and chores.

Jones studied ashrams in India and was moved by their serenity and the seriousness with which visitors undertook the spiritual exercises required by their teacher. He contrasted this with the often-ornate Christian churches and the way their leaders only required the observant to attend a single meeting each Sunday morning, largely to witness a ritual performed by the clergy. He decided to experiment with developing a Christian ashram, a live-in experience like the Hindu versions in style and schedule but promoting the Christian faith instead. His first ashram was founded in 1930 on the shores of the beautiful Sattal freshwater lake at the foot of the Lower Himalayan Range. Set among dense forests of oak and pine trees, the Sattal Christian Ashram still exists today and is a year-round center for spiritual development based on the ashram model. Sattal inspired a wave of various other Christian ashrams across India.

It's hard to imagine what missionaries such as Hudson Taylor, David Livingstone, or William Carey would have made of the idea of a Christian ashram in India. Indeed, for many of Stan Jones's contemporaries—especially fundamentalist and evangelical church leaders—a form of Christian community inspired and shaped by Hindu spiritual practice would have been unacceptable. Perceiving of a form of Christianity that didn't *look* Western, especially one that resembled the practice of another religion like Hinduism, was beyond many Christians. So how radical was Stan Jones's ashram movement? To help us understand, let's back up and briefly explore the stages of the development of contextualized Christian mission.

THE JOURNEY TO CONTEXTUALIZATION

Although questions of contextualization gathered pace in the early twentieth century, they didn't appear from nowhere. A slow process of missionaries taking culture more seriously had unfolded throughout the previous century. That process included several stages:

Cultural adaptation. Our caricatures of colonial-era missionaries often depict them as white men, wearing pith helmets and woolen suits and wilting in the African sun. But some of the more progressive thinkers were willing to embrace forms of cultural adaptation. Missionaries usually focused on outward appearances and behaviors, as an attempt to assimilate into their host culture. You might have heard of Hudson Taylor growing a Chinese "pigtail" and dying his hair black, wearing traditional Chinese dress, and eating local foods. In Algeria, the British missionary Lilias Trotter rejected the European strategy of evangelistic meetings and fervent preaching. Instead, she held discussions with Muslims in cafés, with readings of the Bible in a rhythmical recitative accompanied by a drum—much like the Qur'an readings in a mosque. Local people no doubt appreciated these attempts at adaptation, but they were still keenly aware that they were bring introduced to a Western religion by outsiders.

Indigenization. This strategy involved Western missionaries starting churches, schools, colleges, and hospitals and slowly but deliberately handing them over to local Christians to manage. It was sometimes referred to as "making something more native." Local people would take on various roles and thereby contribute to the transformation of some service to better suit the culture. This was Henry Venn's dream with his "three selfs" strategy that we looked at in the previous chapter. The great challenge of this approach was that the services developed by Westerners often created a form of cultural codependence among local societies, and the process of completely handing them over to local leadership and withdrawing was rarely achieved.

Inculturation. This term was used by Catholic missionaries to describe the way Christian teachings and Western ways of thinking gradually shaped the surrounding culture, particularly through institutions such as the education system and civil service, as well as the political sphere. Key (Christianized) institutions in turn would mold society toward Christianity in implicit ways. In parts of the world colonized by Catholic powers, such as Spain and Portugal, this appeared to be successful until independence movements caused the withdrawal of the colonizers, and it was revealed that very little "heart" transformation of the culture had occurred.

Contextualization. Going further than other techniques, this approach sought to use the gospel to address the key social, political, and economic questions posed by local people, and asked how those questions could shape our understanding of the gospel. Those, like Jones, who took up the task of contextualization hoped to not only explore how Christian teachings were to be presented to non-Christian cultures but to also gauge the influence of those cultures on the teachings. In doing this, foreign missionaries did not create churches but simply helped local converts develop their own spiritual gifts and leadership abilities and gradually develop their own assemblies. Missionaries provided teaching and pastoral care. The churches that resulted were thus indigenous from the start, shaped by their surrounding culture. In his chapter in *Appropriate Christianity*, Charles Van Engen quotes Indian priest Regunta Yesurathnam saying,

> Contextualization both extends and corrects the older terminology [indigenization and inculturation]. While indigenization tends to focus on the purely cultural dimension of human experience, contextualization broadens the understanding of culture to include social, political, and economic questions. In this way, culture is understood in more dynamic and flexible ways, and is seen not as closed and self-contained, but as open and able to be enriched by an encounter with other cultures and movements.[12]

Syncretism. If the great danger of adaptation, indigenization, and inculturation is that local people will still consider the gospel to be a foreign religion, the big danger for contextualization is that of syncretism. The term just means the combining of separate concepts into one new idea. When we talk about cultural syncretism, we're referring to the way two or more distinct cultures blend together to create a new custom, idea, practice, or philosophy. Cultural syncretism happens all the time. Immigration, intermarriage, or even military conquest result in blended customs such as Americans celebrating St. Patrick's Day or reading fortune cookies.

More concerning for Christian missionaries is religious syncretism, or the blending of Christian belief with non-Christian belief in ways that compromise Christianity. A missionary to Thailand was once translating Bible study materials from English to Thai when she came across the word "syncretism." There is no Thai word that conveys its meaning, so the missionary used a term that translates as "a bird with two heads." In their attempts to adopt cultural forms, language, and practices from their host culture, contextualizing

missionaries can go too far, creating something unrecognizable or deformed—
a two-headed religion. That said, the line between deep contextualization and
syncretism is a fine one. British missionary to India Lesslie Newbigin referred
to it as a perilous path between opposing dangers:

> There are always two opposite dangers … between which one must steer.
> On the one side there is the danger that one finds no point of contact for the
> message as the missionary preaches it, [so that] to the people of the local
> culture the message appears irrelevant and meaningless [while at the other
> extreme] is the danger that the point of contact determines entirely the way
> the message is received, and the result is syncretism. Every missionary path
> has to find the way between these two dangers: irrelevance and syncretism.
> And if one is more afraid of one danger than the other, one will certainly fall
> into the opposite.[13]

Did Stanley Jones's ashram movement fall into syncretism? One of the ways to
answer that is to compare it with another Christian ashram strategy. Around
the turn of the twentieth century, Brahmabandhab Upadhyay, a young man
from a religious Hindu Brahmin family in Bengal, converted to Catholicism.
He soon declared himself a Christian *sannyasi* (monk) and went about barefoot
and wearing saffron robes, with a large ebony cross around his neck. Calling
himself a Hindu Catholic, he established an ashram to teach his followers his
new blended Hindu-Catholic belief system. When asked if he was no longer
a Hindu, Upadhyay replied, "By birth we are Hindu and shall remain Hindu
till death. We are Hindus so far as our physical and mental constitution is
concerned, but in regard to our immortal souls we are Catholic."[14]

Upadhyay's vision for an indigenous Indian church embracing the *sannyasi*
lifestyle of Hinduism was later taken up by various Catholic missionaries, most
notably the British Benedictine monk, Bede Griffiths. Although sent to India
as a Christian missionary, Griffiths confessed to a friend at the time, "I am
going to discover the other half of my soul," something he felt could be found
in Hinduism. Eventually, Griffiths would migrate from his Christian faith to
a kind of Hindu-Catholic belief system. He established an ashram and styled
himself as a "Christian yogi," taking on the name Swami Dayananda. Later in
life, his thinking took him even beyond his Catholic-Hindu views to a belief in
a coming world religion in which all the great religions would merge toward

a kind of unity-in-truth. In his vision, Christianity would contribute as much to this new "universal wisdom" as Islam, Hinduism, and Buddhism. He saw himself as an interfaith and interspiritual pioneer, writing, "This is the destiny of all humanity, to realize its essential unity in the Godhead, by whatever name it is known, to be one with the absolute Reality, the absolute Truth, the infinite, the eternal Life and Light."[15]

In 2005, the *National Catholic Reporter* declared Griffiths to be a "dangerous man ... who found nature first, and through nature God, and through God Catholicism, and through Catholicism Benedictinism, and through the monastic life, Eastern mysticism."[16] We might conclude that his idea of a Hindu-Catholic ashram is an example of a bird with two heads.

If we compare Stan Jones's ashrams with that founded by Bede Griffiths, we see a world of difference. Jones did not see his ashrams as anything but Christian communities. In his autobiography, Jones wrote,

> Some might surmise [that] because we have a Hindu term that therefore the Christian Ashram is an amalgamation of Christianity and Hinduism. Nothing could be further from the reality. The Christian faith, being life, assimilates. The Christian faith reaches into the culture of every nation and takes out things, which can be assimilated into its purpose, but in doing so makes something entirely new and different.[17]

What Jones wanted to see emerge was what he termed "an Indianized Christianity for Indians." He wrote, "I am frank to say that I would not turn over my hand to westernize the East, but I trust I would give my life to Christianize it. It cannot be too clearly said that they are not synonymous."[18] In saying this he revealed his deep desire to see Indian Christians disassociate Christ from the West and take him as their own.

As anthropologist Nadya Pohran explains, "It was [Jones's] conviction that the categories of 'Christianization' and 'westernization' were not congruent which enabled him to consider establishing a Christian ashram which would be imbued with an Indian ethos. And yet, at the same time, Jones held on to certain (Protestant) Christian convictions regarding the theological uniqueness of Christ, and he never veered away from this Christocentric standpoint."[19]

As you can see from these examples, there are a range of ways of thinking about contextualization—from the very Western-style churches that were planted in many places to E. Stanley Jones's distinctly Christian ashram to the Hindu-Catholic ashram of Bede Griffiths.

THE SPECTRUM OF CONTEXTUALIZATION

In 1998, an American missionary to India named Phil Parshall, writing under the pseudonym John Travis, devised a framework for assessing how contextualized or syncretistic a ministry was. It has become known as the C-Spectrum.[20]

The C-Spectrum is a series of six postures a church might take to its surrounding culture—C-1 being the least contextualized to C-6 being Christ-centered communities of secret/underground believers. Here is a summary of the model. (These descriptions refer to Muslim contexts because that was who Parshall was working among in India.)

The C-1 church. A C-1 church is one that, despite being in the Muslim world, uses distinctly non-Muslim, or "Christian" forms of music, liturgy, architecture, prayer posture, and so forth, and holds its public worship services in languages other than the language of the host culture. According to Parshall, there were thousands of such churches in the Middle East, Asia, and Africa.

The C-2 church. This isn't very different from a C-1 church, except that the worship is conducted in the language of the surrounding population. It still uses Western forms of liturgy and architecture, but at least local people can understand what is being said.

The C-3 church. These churches have dropped their Western or "Christian" ways of doing church and attempt to adopt local cultural forms—such as music, dress, and imagery—rather than distinctively Western or Christian ones. They aim to reduce the foreign-ness of the gospel by contextualizing to biblically permissible cultural forms. C-3 churches sometimes meet in a religiously neutral location. They aim to develop indigenous expressions of congregational life while avoiding anything that appears distinctly "Islamic."

The C-4 church. Instead of avoiding anything that appears distinctly "Islamic," C-4 churches retain them where they are neutral or can be filled with new biblical meaning. This includes things such as religious terminology, holidays, personal names, avoiding pork and alcohol, keeping the fasts, praying with raised hands, not keeping dogs as pets, and using Islamic terms and dress. In general, C-4 Christians tend to avoid the label "Christian" due to the unfortunate cultural baggage it carries, preferring to refer to themselves as "followers of Isa [Jesus]."

The C-5 church. C-5 churches are made up of people who follow Jesus as Lord and Savior and view the Bible as God's Word without taking the step of leaving the religious community of their birth. Some C-5 Christians will engage with Christian-background believers (for example, missionaries) for friendship and spiritual interaction but form and lead their own groups for prayer, fellowship, and Bible study. They will also still attend the mosque with their broader community. By remaining part of the Muslim community, they are attempting to be a source of salt and light for their family and friends. Some cross-cultural missions-literature refers to C-5 churches as an "insider movement."

The C-6 church. Parshall's sixth posture refers to the many tiny and isolated groups of Jesus-followers who are forced to meet underground because of state persecution of Christians. These C-6 believers are severely restricted in their ability to meet or witness and will appear to their friends and neighbors as Muslims. Nonetheless, many of them find creative ways to connect with other Jesus-followers and share the good news discreetly as God's Spirit leads.

The C-Spectrum has received criticism in recent years, but it nevertheless provides a useful continuum of the varying degrees of contextualization. Using Parshall's tool, Stan Jones's Christian ashram is represented somewhere between a C-4 and C-5 approach. Jones had modified Hindu or Eastern practices to give them explicitly Christian meanings while also introducing new, fresh expressions of the Christian experience, drawn from indigenous forms, symbols, practices, and customs.

Stan Jones's bestselling books and his association with Mahatma Gandhi led to his worldwide fame. In later life he was called upon as a peace negotiator in Burma, Korea, and the Belgian Congo, as well as between China and Japan, and between Japan and the United States. In fact, in the months prior to the Japanese attack on Pearl Harbor, he was a constant confidant of Franklin D. Roosevelt and Japanese leaders trying to avert war in the Pacific. He received the Gandhi Peace Prize in 1961 and was nominated twice for the Nobel Peace Prize.[21]

Meanwhile, without any help from Western missionaries or any understanding of the theory of contextualization, an indigenous African movement was emerging that took seriously the need to develop a historically and culturally conditioned form of African Christianity.

CONTEXTUALIZED AFRICAN CHURCHES

When missionaries first began their work in Africa, they encountered a variety of highly complex religions across the continent. Many Africans believed in a supreme god who ruled over a multitude of deities. These lesser gods had no power of their own, except what they derived from the supreme god. Nonetheless, in African cosmology, each was very important to the orderly function of the universe. Under these gods existed an even greater number of ancestor spirits who had the power to bless, protect, or punish the families from which they came. They acted as intermediaries between the supreme god and their families. The missionaries quickly discovered that, for Africans, keeping the spirits of their ancestors happy was paramount—which they did by invoking the spirits' presence at family gatherings, ceremonies, and rituals, and asking the spirits to shower them with peace, unity, and prosperity.

There were also countless other spirits to contend with. These were apparitional entities who emerged from the unseen world. In fact, many African nations still believe everything has spirits. These spirits even have categories— ghost-spirits, born-to-die spirits, spirits of witches, guardian spirits, diviner spirits, and so on. Belief in these spirits permeates the lives of many Africans and should be taken seriously.

In such a worldview, things like drought, famine, misfortune, illness, and tragedy are all put down to unhappy gods or spirits. Unless satisfied by propitiatory sacrifices and rituals, the spirits will bring great evil upon the village.

The earliest European missionaries responded to African indigenous religions in a variety of ways, none of them particularly good. These methods included:

Hostility. Missionaries adopted the position of cultural superiority and condescension toward indigenous religions, calling them, "primitive religions of animism and polytheism." Some referred to African cosmology as the "empire of Satan." They labeled Africans themselves as pagans, heathen, idolators, polytheists, and barbarians, complaining about their superstitions and fetishism. To most missionaries, African religions were synonymous with misery and delusion.

Ignorance. Many European missionaries were uninterested in learning African belief systems. In their ignorance, they saw African cosmology as undeserving of study and therefore unworthy of dialogue.

Aggression. Whatever we are willfully ignorant about, we are usually deeply threatened by. Both Christianity and Islam are aggressively proselytizing religions, but Africans in general were not evangelistic about their beliefs. Thinking they would be easily converted, Christian missionaries saw Africans as targets rather than dialogue partners.

Fear. For all their bravado, many European Christians harbored an underlying fear about African beliefs. There were racist anxieties about "black magic" and cultic practices, some arising from sexual repression at the sight of writhing bodies moving ecstatically in ritual dances. Many Christian missionaries also feared religious dialogue would lead to syncretism. In fact, Africanizing Christianity was seen as a corruption of biblical truth. So, if they became Christians, Africans were expected to give up all their traditional beliefs and practices.

Many colonial-era missionaries reduced African religious belief to superstition, pointless rain dances, curses, and immoral polygamy. Christian missionaries tried to ban all these practices. Whether consciously or not, many missionaries communicated to Africans that to be Christian meant acting like a European Christian, which meant taking a European name, adopting monogamy, wearing Western clothing, and speaking European languages. But when the early African church leaders read the Scriptures for themselves, they found it was full of examples of miracles, curses, demons, manipulation of the weather, and even polygamy. Not only that, but God had been raising up prophets from among their number for generations (remember Ntsikana from the previous chapter?). These leaders had ecstatic prophetic experiences and performed exorcisms and miracles, including raising people from the dead. And they were devoted to the task of Africanizing Christianity for their followers.

One such leader was Simon Kimbangu, who was born in the late 1880s in Congo Free State during Leopold II's reign of terror (which we looked at in chapter six). Kimbangu was raised in a British Baptist Missionary Society mission but was only semi-literate in both English and French. In 1921, he became famous among the Bakongo people of Lower Congo. The 1918 influenza epidemic in Europe had spread to southern Africa, and Kimbangu said he had received a vision from God, calling him to become a healer and a prophet to his people. He began touching the sick and seeing them miraculously healed. Reports spread that he could even raise people from the dead. As he toured the region, followers would bring hundreds of stretchers bearing the sick to the roadside as he passed by. Thousands attended his rallies to hear his preaching. He was proclaimed *ngunza*, the Kikongo word for "prophet," and soon his followers numbered over ten thousand.

More than a miracle-worker, Kimbangu was a radical contextualizer. His hymns and sermons affirmed his listeners' blackness, and he insisted that they Africanize their faith. In doing so, Kimbangu was overturning the perception of light as good, and dark as evil; and demanding that Black people see themselves as every bit as Christian as fairer-skinned ministers. One hymn attributed to Simon Kimbangu reads:

> God's messenger has come.
> To show men God's love for the race which broke the Law.
> Keep the Law, do exactly as you are told, Black person, wake up!
> Cultivate love, do exactly as you are told, Black person, wake up!
> Keep working, do exactly as you are told, Black person, wake up![22]

As remarkable as Simon Kimbangu's ministry was, it was its brevity that proved most astounding. After barely six months of preaching and healing, Kimbangu was arrested by Belgian authorities and charged with subversion, even though his preaching had no political content. His large following alone made him a threat as far as the colonizers were concerned.

After initially being condemned to death, Kimbangu's sentence was commuted to life in prison. But "Ngunzism"—or, as it came to be called, Kimbanguism—wouldn't die. The prophet's followers maintained his vision, and, led by the youngest of Kimbangu's three sons, Kimbanguism continued to flourish in the Belgian Congo and the neighboring French Congo and Angola. As Diarmaid MacCulloch writes, "His thirty years of silence did not stop other imprisoned disciples from cherishing his memory as good news for multitudes silenced by 'the prophets of Satan, missionaries, the Belgian government.'"[23]

Eventually, Kimbangu's son, Joseph Diangienda, would lead the movement from an underground network into official recognition in 1959 as the Kimbanguist Church. French ethnologist Jean-Claude Froelich says, "Of all the African churches ... born from a reaction to colonial domination, the Kimbanguist Church is, no doubt, the most remarkable."[24] This is because, according to Asonzeh Ukah, professor of Christianity and African Religion at the University of Cape Town, "Kimbanguism takes African culture seriously by providing a structure upon which Christianity can exist in Africa and transmitting Christian messages into the idioms of the place."[25]

THE RISE OF AFRICAN INDEPENDENT CHURCHES

In 1958, the All-Africa Church Conference was held in Ibadan, Nigeria. In *Twentieth Century Christianity*, Stephen Neill describes the groundbreaking event this way:

> The guidance of that conference was wholly in African hands and it was impressive. Its members made it clear that they felt sufficiently mature to dispense with the guiding rein from Europe. They also set up an organization to ensure the work of that conference would continue. It all becomes the more significant when it is remembered that just a century before, Livingstone was calling for pioneers to venture into dark gaps on the map.[26]

The event was also significant considering how African leaders such as Samuel Ajayi Crowther, Ntsikana, and Simon Kimbangu were treated by Western missionaries and their colonial governments.

But, as mentioned in the previous chapter, the seeds these African leaders sowed in their home soil have yielded a remarkable harvest. Churches founded by African initiative rather than by foreign missionaries claim over twenty million adherents and are growing faster than any other churches in Africa. Often grouped together under the name African Independent Churches (AICs), there are an estimated ten thousand networks or denominations across the continent, mainly in the south and the west. Though they vary, all AICs emphasize the need to include African cultural norms in their modes of worship, theology, and practice. Some African scholars claim that several AICs are syncretistic in that they combine indigenous African religion with Christian beliefs, but the degree to which this occurs varies. Despite criticisms of some AICs, it is indisputable that they constitute one of the most remarkable examples of church growth in the twentieth century.

How have they been so successful? Whereas Western missionaries were largely negative about African culture, AICs have developed an Africanized Christianity for Africans, representing a truly indigenizing movement. Their approach incorporates several distinctive elements.

First, the AIC is a place for Africans to feel at home. Rejecting the highly verbal and cerebral modes of Western Christianity, which put the faith beyond the reach of many people's comprehension, the AICs offer a joyous religion, expressed in music, dancing, and with African symbols. Thus, they more faithfully represent their own culture, as opposed to the cultural imperialism of the historic churches.

Second, the AICs emphasize the role of the Holy Spirit much more than the Western missionaries did. Of course, some of those missionaries—particularly the Methodists for example—affirmed the Holy Spirit's role in aiding personal holiness, but the AICs also see the Spirit working powerfully in healings, exorcisms, and glossolalia. They take seriously the promise of Christ to send his Spirit.

Third, AICs represent a radically biblicist movement. This is a feature that disturbs Western observers. Biblicism refers to an overly rigid adherence to certain Bible texts while ignoring their context and the rest of Scripture—as revealed by the tendency to appeal to an individual verse or passage to the exclusion of the wider (and far more complex) truths of the Bible. We sometimes call this "prooftexting." You can find examples of this in AICs (as you can in churches in the US or UK, admittedly), but often it is expressed as a deep affiliation with the plight of God's people. For example, in southern Africa, the biblical stories regarding the bondage of Israel are viewed as a meaningful parallel of their own circumstances. The Old Testament accounts of dreams, visions, and trances as means of God's revelation (cf. Gn 40; Mt 1:18–24) are also emphasized.

And fourth, AICs are deeply communitarian. The churches of the West are highly individualistic, but that goes against the ethos of African societies, which view life more communally. The AICs reflect this communal nature, and in some ways, come to fulfill the role that tribal groupings had in African society. This sense of community manifests in pilgrimages to their holy cities, mutual aid in resources, and the sharing of a common vocabulary.

Western theologians often dismiss the AICs as "a mile wide and an inch deep," meaning that while they might be large numerically, they are shallow theologically. But is it really appropriate for theologians from the West, those shaped by Enlightenment thinking and serving a rapidly shrinking church, to judge the largely non-literate and poor members of AICs so harshly? The AICs don't fit into the West's neatly defined theological positions. And besides, the Western churches demonstrate more than enough theological shallowness.

The churches of Africa, India, and the South American continent aren't perfect, but their vibrancy and growth call for a new approach to the metrics of being church—an approach that would have been unheard of just half a century earlier.

CONTEXTUALIZING TODAY

Earlier, I shared a story from Barbara Kingsolver's novel *The Poisonwood Bible* about the fictional missionary Nathan Price. You'll recall he uses a word he thinks means Jesus is "beloved," but the way he pronounces it leads his Congolese congregation to think he's saying Jesus is "poisonwood." Like poison ivy, contact with a poisonwood tree causes skin rashes, so Price's daughter Adah, the narrator of the novel, facetiously refers to his congregation scratching themselves in bewilderment. She imagines the Congolese Christians hearing something like, "Jesus will make you itch like nobody's business."[27]

This is exactly what uncontextualized ministry does. It causes others "to scratch themselves in wonder." But the work of contextualization concerns more than postcolonial contexts. Here in the post-Christian West, we too must do the work of reading our culture and being church in ways that connect with secular people.

We need to embrace the challenge mentioned by Lesslie Newbigin earlier in this chapter, to walk the line between irrelevance and syncretism. We must engage in the difficult work of cultural exegesis. The word "exegesis" means "to draw out." It is the act of studying something (a text, art, language) and extracting meaning from within. The opposite is "eisegesis" (literally "to draw in"), where the observer interprets through his or her own presuppositions. To exegete culture involves putting aside our presuppositions (easier said than done) and reading the context so we can understand how to share Christ faithfully in that setting. In Acts 17:22–33, Paul perceived that the Athenians were religious. He exegeted the Athenians' culture and told their own story back to them in light of the gospel.

Similarly, today we are called to the work of cultural exegesis. And we can take some courage in doing this from Andrew Walls's reminder that every culture needs to do this work. He writes,

> We need not fear this; when God became man he became historically, cultural conditioned man in a particular time and place. What he became, we need not fear to be. There is nothing wrong in having local forms of Christianity—provided that we remember that they are *local*.[28]

This is the first step in the process of critical contextualization. It involves an analysis of the beliefs, ideologies, stories, art, customs, institutions, lifestyles, and norms of the host culture. It's the kind of work that cross-cultural workers do every day. They are continually learning language and customs and trying to read the new setting in which they find themselves. But when attempting to contextualize in our own cultures, it's easy to become complacent. We must not be lazy with this work. It's important to get a reading on our own society's hopes, desires, and fears.

When trying to make sense of people in your own culture, consider asking the following questions:

- **Values/customs:** What is important to them? How do they spend time, money, energy? What is the importance of family, work, group, money, power, respect, land, independence?
- **Conflicts/needs:** What challenges their values? What tensions do they feel? War/peace, social issues, oppression, natural disasters, enemies, economy?
- **Outlook:** Is their outlook generally positive/negative, victor/victim, hopeful/hopeless?
- **Stories:** What movies, books, TV shows, mythology, folk tales/songs are popular? What are favorite themes? Redemption, overcoming oppression, rebellion, hope, good vs evil?
- **Idols:** What do they worship? What are their (dis)functional saviors? Religion, tradition, systems/structures, technology, money, materialism, education?
- **Fears:** What are their cultural extremes? What do they run from/defend against/avoid? War, oppression, loss of culture, loss of status, disease, exploitation, loss of face?
- **Narrative:** How do they make sense of the world around them? What is their national story? What do social commentators and historians say about their narrative?
- **Tribes:** How do they organize socially? Where do they find their social identity? Sub-cultures, affinities, clubs, neighborhoods, stereotypes, friends, cliques?[29]

Having collated these reflections, we have three options. First, we can disregard the local culture and present a version of the gospel that sounds foreign to those we've been sent to reach. Second, we can uncritically accept the culture and try to reshape the gospel to fit its preferences and priorities. These options lead either to rejection or syncretism, as presented at the top and bottom of the following diagram.

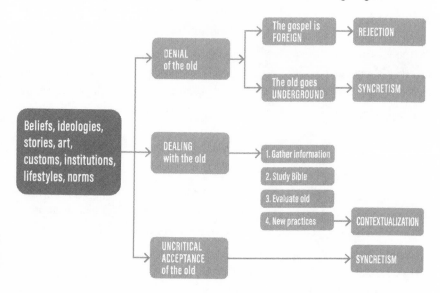

The third option is in the middle of the diagram. It requires us to deal with the culture, taking seriously the customs, idols, narratives, and ways of organizing we've discovered. This middle way—what missiologist Paul Hiebert called "critical contextualization"—is the most challenging approach, but it is the only way for the gospel to become embedded within a host culture in a way that neither clashes with that culture nor compromises its truth.[30] As you can see in the diagram, this work involves not only exegeting culture but also exploring what the Bible says about the information you're gathering. The central task is to evaluate the culture in light of Scripture, keeping that which is not unbiblical, rejecting that which is unbecoming, modifying some practices to give them explicitly Christian meaning, and creating new symbols and rituals to replace the old. Hiebert called this, "building a hermeneutical bridge" between the old and the new.[31]

For Timothy Keller, contextualization means "to antagonize a society's idols while showing respect for its peoples and many of its hopes and aspirations. It means expressing the gospel in a way that is not only comprehensible but also convincing."[32] And, as we'll see in the next chapter, this very work was at the center of a new school of missiologists and practitioners—people committed to the task of remissioning the post-Christian West.

The Ninth Shape

REMISSIONING

Postmodernism is the Enlightenment gone mad.

STANLEY ROSEN

In 1901, after reading Charles Darwin's *On the Origin of Species*, the millionaire industrialist and Enlightenment proponent Andrew Carnegie recorded this reaction in his diary:

> I remember that light came as in a flood and all was clear. Not only had I got rid of theology and the supernatural, but I had found the truth. "All is well since all grows better," became my motto, my true source of comfort. Man has risen to the higher forms [and there can be no] conceivable end to his march to perfection.[1]

The Enlightenment initiated world-changing ideas such as abolitionism, workers' rights, universal education, democracy, and women's suffrage, as well as an invigorated interest in science and technology. It also gave rise to what has been termed "the Great Century" of Christian mission. However, as Europe lay in ruins, torn to shreds by a brutal, pointless war between so-called civilized nations, it became clear to many that the Enlightenment was not all it had been cracked up to be. In 1915, upon re-reading his 1901 entry with some embarrassment, Carnegie wrote in his diary, "As I read this today, what a change! The world convulsed by war as never before! Men slaying each other like wild beasts! I dare not relinquish all hope."[2]

But relinquishing all hope is what many people were doing that year. By the time World War I ended in 1918, there was utter devastation across Europe, with eighteen million dead and twenty-three million wounded in one of the bloodiest conflicts in human history. "Christian Europe" had been shown to be not very Christian at all. As the English writer Thomas Hardy quipped, "After two thousand years of mass, we've got as far as poison-gas."[3]

Europeans were asking what good Christianity was if it didn't make us better people. Indeed, what good were the lofty ideas of the Enlightenment if all we built on them was a continent littered with bodies and tanks and criss-crossed with blood-soaked trenches.

Those who survived the war came to be known as the Lost Generation, mired in cynicism and rage. And their outlook became only more calloused by the outbreak of the Great Depression in 1929 and World War II ten years later. That Nazism and Fascism could take root in the soil of Christian nations such as Germany and Italy raised questions about the superiority of Western civilization and the efficacy of Christianity in shaping good societies. Immanuel Kant, one of the architects of the Enlightenment, had this unfulfilled expectation:

> Gradually violence on the part of the powers will diminish and obedience to the laws will increase. There will arise in the body politic perhaps more charity and less strife in lawsuits, more reliability in keeping one's word, etc., partly out of love of honor, partly out of well-understood self interest. And eventually this will also extend to nations in their external relations toward one another up to the realization of the cosmopolitan society.[4]

POST-ENLIGHTENMENT, POST-CHRISTENDOM, POST-COLONIALISM

All the hopes and dreams of the Enlightenment era had come to a crashing halt. The West was shaken. Although its political, military, and economic dominance would continue throughout the twentieth century, the West was increasingly unable to see itself as a paragon of Christian virtue or a model society. The world was entering a new era—that of post-Enlightenment, post-Christendom, and post-colonialism. These are more complex realities than we have space to explore here, but let's look at each of them briefly as part of unpacking *remissioning*—a key shape of mission during this period.

POST-ENLIGHTENMENT

During the Enlightenment, people put their hope in reason, and they championed the importance of science, technology, and education. As we've seen, these ideas were embraced by many Christian missionaries. However it was a double-edged sword for the church, which was forced to either embrace all scientific objections to faith or try to "prove" faith claims such as the existence of God or a six-day creation. But Enlightenment reason began to wane in the twentieth century, and although post-Enlightenment thinkers today still embrace rationality, they tend to do so in ways that leave room for experience, metaphor, myth, and analogy.

Furthermore, the Enlightenment viewed nature as a "machine" to study. This was supposed to liberate humans by giving them control over nature. Instead, by the mid-1900s, people began to see how Enlightenment thinking was being used to destroy life, enslave humans, and ruin nature. A post-Enlightenment way of thinking affirms that humans are not objects, technology is not God, and nature is not property.

The Enlightenment also put absolute trust in humanity as the savior of the world, but people began to realize this was gravely misplaced. In the post-Enlightenment era, the belief in unending progress was abandoned. Twentieth-century people remained pessimistic about all human solutions to "save" the world, especially those solutions espoused by those holding wealth and power.

And finally, the Enlightenment belief in value-free objective knowledge, together with the points above, opened the door to some of the worst curses of the twentieth century—the ideologies of Marxism, Capitalism, Fascism, and Nazism. Post-Enlightenment people became resistant to utopian ideologies and insisted others also be freed from self-deception and false hope.

As the Enlightenment project unraveled, the seismic shifts that occurred (and continue to occur) shaped (and continue to shape) people as powerfully as the Enlightenment itself.

POST-CHRISTENDOM

Alongside the broader changes in thinking listed above lie some specific changes in how Europeans perceived the church. As we saw back in chapter three, the role of the church in European societies was set in stone with the establishment of the Holy Roman Empire in 800—an alliance between the Frankish King Charlemagne and Pope Leo III. The era of Christendom was characterized by a theocratic understanding of society and a close partnership between church and state as its two main pillars.

Throughout European history, this alliance resulted in Christian baptism becoming a de facto form of imperial birth registration, tithing as a state-imposed tax, the banning or "Christianizing" of pagan practices, and, at times, compulsory attendance at mass and forced baptisms of immigrants. It also provided the means for the church's influence to grow in the West, and the opportunity for missionaries to gain access to colonial outposts.

But by the twentieth century, the alliance between church and state was being challenged. Even though church buildings remained prominent, and clergy were involved in various aspects of civil life, the church itself was becoming marginalized. Europeans began to question why the church, in which they had so little personal interest, remained so powerful in the culture as a whole. In his book *Post-Christendom*, Stuart Murray lists a number of reasons for this disillusionment:

- Disappointment with religion resulting from incessant warfare between supposedly Christian nations
- Reliance of philosophers and scientists on reason and experimentation rather than revelation
- The impact of industrialization and urbanization on traditional beliefs and structures
- Postmodernism, pluralism, and fragmentation
- The persistence of dissent and emergence of the Free Church tradition
- The globalization of the church and its mission[5]

These reasons and more brought on the era we call "post-Christendom"—a socio-political situation where the Christian story no longer provides the prevailing cultural narrative in the way it once did. As historian Callum Brown concludes, "What emerges is a story not merely of church decline, but of the end of Christianity as a means by which men and women, as individuals, construct their identities and their sense of 'self.'"[6]

This can't be overstated. The term post-Christendom is often used to refer to Western societies where church attendance has dropped, but it actually indicates something more complex and concerning. In post-Christendom, the church and its faith are seen as bearing no relevance or influence on how society chooses to conduct itself or form its values.

POST-COLONIALISM

By the mid-twentieth century, across the globe, an emerging post-colonial world rejected the involvement of Christian missions. Weakened by the cost of war and economic collapse, European colonizers were less able to maintain control of their empires far afield, and throughout the 1950s and '60s, independence movements developed in India, Africa, Southeast Asia, and South America.

Indonesia proclaimed independence from Dutch rule in 1945, and Indian independence from Great Britain came two years later. A cascading series of revolutions and upheavals quickly followed. Algeria ejected France in 1954, Malaysia broke free from Britain in 1957, as did Cameroon in 1960, Tanganyika in 1961, Kenya in 1963, Rhodesia in 1964, and on and on.

These new post-colonial nations now found themselves struggling with the challenge of developing a national identity after generations of outside rule. They needed to learn how to articulate and celebrate that identity, which meant examining the ways colonizers had previously dehumanized and exploited them. This was not a simple process. At times it led to the rejection of all things Western, including an imported Christian faith.

In newly formed Indonesia, the Christianity of their Dutch colonists was soundly rejected in favor of Islam as the new state religion. In other parts of the world, indigenous forms of religion were rediscovered. Soon people began to wonder—if the West was no longer best and indigenous religions were preferable in post-colonial nations—why Christian missionaries were needed.

This was met by a familiar cry within independence movements in those parts of the world: "Missionary, go home!"

The three shifts we have just explored were characterized as dark days by many mission agencies. At the same time, the church's outlook in the West continued to worsen—with attendance rapidly declining.

You might think this reality would have awoken the church to a need for radical change. But, as Stuart Murray points out, there were more signs that the church in the West was, and still is, avoiding the problem rather than confronting it. Those signs included:

- an orientation towards maintaining (but perhaps tweaking) the status quo rather than advocating radical and disturbing change;
- over-emphasizing church and internal ecclesial issues at the expense of God's mission and kingdom;
- disgruntlement that Christian festivals (particularly Christmas and Easter) are no longer accorded the spiritual significance they once enjoyed;
- a predilection for large congregations that support a "professional" standard of ministry and exercise influence on local power structures;
- approaches to evangelism that rely excessively on "come'" rather than "go" initiatives;
- assuming churchgoing is normal social activity and that most people feel comfortable in church buildings and services; and
- attitudes towards church buildings that imply these are the focal points of God's presence.[7]

Echoing Murray's concern about the church's avoidance of the challenges it faces, Darrell Guder writes:

The obvious fact that what we once regarded as Christendom is now a post-Constantinian, post-Christendom, and even post-Christian mission field stands in bold contrast today with the apparent lethargy of established church traditions in addressing their situation both creatively and faithfully. Yet this helpfully highlights the need for and providential appearance of a theological revolution in missional thinking that centers the body of Christ on God's mission rather than post-Christendom's concern for the church's institutional maintenance.[8]

Interestingly, responses to this crisis initially came not from Western Christian leaders but from Christians working in post-colonial settings. In the latter part of the twentieth century, there was an explosion of Christian missionaries being sent into the West from countries such as South Korea, Nigeria, Kenya, and Brazil, changing the shape of the church in Europe and America.

All three of these movements—post-Enlightenment, post-Christendom, and post-colonialism—not only completely changed the world, but they also completely changed the shape of mission. The West was no longer seen as the Christian portion of the globe, sending missionaries to dark, unevangelized peoples. It was now seen as needing missionaries. It needed to be *remissioned*. And one of the first voices to announce this was a retired British Church of South India bishop named Lesslie Newbigin.

NEWBIGIN PROCLAIMS BRITAIN A MISSION FIELD

Though known by many for his work as a global Christian statesman, Newbigin was primarily a cross-cultural missionary. Indeed, even when he moved to Geneva in 1963 to work with the World Council of Churches, he planted a house church in his spare time, believing he couldn't claim to be a leader in world mission if he wasn't a practicing missionary in the place where he lived.

Born in Newcastle, England in 1909, Newbigin's father enrolled him in a Quaker boarding school because he wanted him to be a pacifist. In 1929, Newbigin started at Cambridge University where he became involved with the Student Christian Movement (SCM). After graduation, he remained with the SCM as a staff member.

Sensing a calling to missionary service, Newbigin commenced theological study at Westminster College in 1933. Three years later, he was ordained by the Presbytery of Edinburgh to work as a Church of Scotland missionary at their Madras Mission on the Bay of Bengal in eastern India. His first impression of the mission, however, was not positive. He was horrified by the missionaries' reticence to get along with their new neighbors, observing British missionaries constantly finding fault with Indians and rarely offering a word of encouragement.

Newbigin resolved to see himself primarily as a servant to Indian church leaders, eventually encouraging them to fulfill their desire for an indigenous Indian church. For nearly two decades, the Indian church had tried to sever itself from its ecclesial umbilical cord to British denominations. Newbigin lobbied on their behalf for another ten years before they achieved their goal.

In 1947, Indian leaders from the Anglican, Methodist, and the South India United Church (itself a 1908 merger of Presbyterian, Dutch Reformed, and Congregationalist groups) formed the Church of South India (CSI). Newbigin was overwhelmed with joy. Writing about the first worship service of the newly formed church, he said,

> There came a greatest moment in the service when the whole of the great congregation rose and burst into *Te Deum*. It was as though all the agonizing fears and delays of these twenty-eight years had dammed up a flood that was now bursting through. I have never heard such singing; I think there were many like myself who found it hard to keep back tears of joy as one remembered all that had gone before and all that might lie ahead.[9]

However, the harsh reality of smoothing over a combination of so many differing ecclesiologies caused some initial problems for the group. They turned to Newbigin and his wise, gentle leadership for help in uniting the movement. After initially resisting, he was elected bishop of the CSI on August 21, 1947.

Sadly, but perhaps inevitably, considering what we've seen before, English church leaders looked at the CSI askance, focusing on inconsistencies and questioning their theology. Newbigin was recalled to the UK to attend a Presbyterian assembly where he was grilled by the delegates about whether this new Indian church was heretical.

One of his interrogators seized upon the fact that while baptismal candidates were required to affirm the Apostles Creed, candidates for ordination in the CSI were asked to accept the Nicene Creed. He asked Newbigin to account for this apparent inconsistency. In that moment, Newbigin thought about the Christian women of Tamil Nadu who attended the new CSI churches. Reflecting on his time at the Presbyterian assembly, he later wrote,

> These women were real amazons, tough, shrewd but—of course—illiterate. I tried to imagine the bishop in front of me sitting on the ground in that village and explaining to these women all the differences between the Nicene and Apostles Creeds. I realized that this was not a discussion about

the Church of South India at all. It was about the English ecclesiastical and social and cultural differences.[10]

In other words, it was about prejudice and condescension.

In the 1950s, Newbigin's star began to rise beyond India. He was chosen as the chair of the working group of the World Council of Church's assembly on the theme "Christ the Hope for the World," and oversaw a committee that included Karl Barth, Emil Brunner, and Edmund Schlink. He chaired the International Missionary Council and became the editor of the *International Review of Mission*. In 1960, he shared the platform of an ecumenical student conference on world missions with Martin Luther King Jr. and D. T. Niles. He left India in 1963 to take up the earlier-mentioned role in Geneva. During this time, he struck up friendships with Hans Kung and Mother Teresa. In 1972, he retired to the UK and began teaching missiology at Selly Oaks College in Birmingham.

Had that been all Lesslie Newbigin achieved, it would have been a fruitful ministry. But it was in his "retirement" that Newbigin had his most lasting impact.

In Britain, Newbigin was surprised to find a rapidly declining church—a church in desperate need of remissioning. In the thirty years he had been away, he detected a significant drop in English Christians' confidence in the gospel. He couldn't understand the timidity Christians had about sharing their faith, something he had never encountered in Madras. There, despite opposition from Hindu neighbors and the authorities, Indian Christians were bold in sharing their beliefs and pleased to admit they attended a church.

In 1978, Newbigin became the moderator of the United Reformed Church, the denomination he had joined upon returning home. In his first address as their leader, he announced, "I am not ashamed of the gospel"—a message he went on to share all over the country. It was during this period that Newbigin said he found Britain to be as challenging a mission field as India.

Today, we don't find it unusual for people to say the church needs to entirely rethink its stance and become a missionary church within the West. But in 1978 that thought was repugnant to many British Christians. In their minds, Britain was still a "Christian nation"—the country that *sent* missionaries, not received them. Indeed, to call Britain a mission field was considered tantamount to calling the English "savages" or "pagans." Newbigin was vilified by many conservative Christians. But that didn't stop him.

That same year, he published *The Open Secret: An Introduction to the Theology of Mission*, in which he outlined his vision for a commitment to a new era of mission to the West. His argument was irrefutable. Mission, he wrote, was a distinctly Trinitarian activity that involved "proclaiming the kingdom of the Father, sharing the life of the Son, and bearing the witness of the Spirit."[11] How could this not apply to the West as much as to anywhere in the world?

Then in 1983, he followed that up with what he called a "brief, hastily written paper" for the British Council of Churches (BCC), spelling out what a mission-to-the-West stance would look like. The BCC launched a year-long study group committed to exploring the issues Newbigin raised—namely the shape of Christian mission within Western culture. They called the initiative the British Council of Churches 1984 Project. (George Orwell's book, *1984*, had become a kind of code word for "the future" in the same way the year 2000 later became.) Newbigin's paper was published as a book, titled *The Other Side of 1984*.

After the year 1984, the initiative changed its name to the Gospel and Culture Network (GCN).

THE GOSPEL IN WESTERN CULTURE

The work of the GCN promoted what would later be called the "Newbiginian project"—an attempt to awaken churches to the realities of remissioning the West. Nowhere is that vision more simply expressed than in Newbigin's 1988 book, *Foolishness to the Greeks*, which begins with this question: "What would be involved in a missionary encounter between the gospel and this whole way of perceiving, thinking, and living that we call 'modern Western culture'?"[12]

Newbigin was asking his readers to try to distance themselves from Western culture, to see it as no longer Christian, to critically identify its key features, and to develop missionary responses to that culture. He wrote,

> A missionary encounter with our culture must bring us face to face with the central citadel of our culture, which is the belief that is based on the immense achievements of the scientific method and, to a limited but increasing extent, embodied in our political, economic, and social practice—the belief that the real world, the reality with which we have to do, is a world to be understood

in terms of efficient causes and not of final causes, a world that is not governed by an intelligible purpose, and thus a world in which the answer to the question of what is good has to be left to the private opinion of each individual and cannot be included in the body of accepted facts that control public life ... The twin dogmas of Incarnation and Trinity thus form the starting point for a way of understanding reality as a whole ... at the center of this disclosure, providing the clue to the whole, there stands the cross [and the] resurrection, in which that very death became the source of life.[13]

His prescription for remissioning secular Western culture was thorough. It included:

- A recovery of an eschatology that recognizes that our political or religious activity cannot establish the kingdom of God. Rather, the coming reign of God is the framework for all missionary practice.
- A rediscovery of the freedom of the Christian life, based on the grace of Jesus.
- A "declericalizing" of the church and an equal rediscovery of the importance of so-called lay leaders who help congregations "to share with one another the actual experience of their weekday work and to seek illumination from the gospel for their daily secular duty."[14]
- A radical theological critique of the theory and practice of denominationalism. [Newbigin became famous for claiming this was the religious aspect of secularization.]
- An objective and distanced examination of Western culture with the help of views of those from other cultures.
- A resolute preparedness to hold fast to the core beliefs of the Christian gospel, bearing in mind that "[t]he gospel is not a set of beliefs that arise, or could arise, from empirical observation of the whole human experience. It is the announcement of a name and a fact that offer the starting point for a new and life-long enterprise of understanding and coping with experience. It is a new starting point. To accept it means a new beginning, a radical conversion."[15]
- A commitment to the belief that mission must proceed from a dynamic, worshiping community of faith and not merely from innovation or new methods and techniques.[16]

176

6 6

In the 1990s, the Newbiginian project to remission the West was embraced by practitioners and missiologists in the US and called the Gospel and Our Culture Network (GOCN). Its proponents included Lois Barrett, Darrell Guder, Alan Roxburgh, George Hunsberger, Inagrace Dietterich, and Craig Van Gelder. They invented a different adjective to describe their approach ("Newbiginian" is quite a mouthful after all), preferring instead to urge the American church to become a "missional church."

In 1998, the leaders of the GOCN published *Missional Church: A Vision for the Sending of the Church in North America*. Acknowledging that the US was founded on the principle of the separation of church and state, and therefore not on Christendom, they nonetheless pointed out that American churches assumed a "system of church-state partnership and cultural hegemony in which the Christian religion was the protected and privileged religion of society and the church its legally established institutional form. Even when the legal structures of Christendom have been removed (as in North America), the legacy continues as a pattern of powerful traditions, attitudes, and social structures that we describe as 'functional Christendom.'"[17]

Now is the time, they declared, for the American church to do what Newbigin called the British church to do: to see themselves as strangers and aliens in a post-Christian society, and to adopt the posture of missionaries to their own land. Central to this task, they argued, was the need for the church to not simply see itself as *doing* mission, but to reconceptualize the church *as* missional. They wrote, "Mission is not merely an activity of the church. Rather, mission is the result of God's initiative, rooted in God's purposes to restore and heal creation."[18]

The GOCN authors claimed that the missional identity of the church shouldn't be *situational*—that is, occurring just because the American church is in decline. Instead, they argued, mission should be the *permanent* theology of the church. God is always a missional God, so God's people should always be a sent people. They called this a "missional ecclesiology" and listed several of its characteristics:

- A missional ecclesiology is *biblical*—It must be based explicitly on what the Bible teaches.
- A missional ecclesiology is *historical*—Shaping an ecclesiology for a particular culture, in this case North America, must demonstrate respect for the historical development of other ecclesiologies.

- A missional ecclesiology is *contextual*—The only way to be a church is incarnationally, within a specific culture.

- A missional ecclesiology is *eschatological*—The church represents the dynamic and creative work of the Spirit in moving us toward God's promised consummation of all things.

- A missional ecclesiology can be *translated into practice*—"The basic function of all theology is to equip the church for its calling ... A missional ecclesiology serves the church's witness as it 'makes disciples of all nations ... teaching them to obey everything that [Jesus has] commanded you' (Matthew 28:19–20)."[19]

Newbigin's vision not only resulted in the GCN/GOCN, but also extends into the twenty-first century, as practitioners and missiologists still struggle to understand what remissioning the West looks like. In some measure, movements such as the emerging church, the missional church, the current church-planting movement, Fresh Expressions, Missio Alliance, and Forge can trace their theoretical framework back to Lesslie Newbigin.

TO THE POST-CHRISTENDOM WEST FROM THE POST-COLONIAL REST

It wasn't only Western voices calling the West to see itself as a mission field. Soon, a trickle and then a steady flow of missionaries from the Majority World would start moving to Britain, Europe, the US, and other Western countries.

At the turn of the twenty-first century, the US was still the leading mission-sending nation in the world; but the vast majority of total missionaries in the world now come from the Global South. In 2020, the *International Bulletin of Mission Research* stated, "the United States (135,000) continues to send the bulk of long-term cross-cultural missionaries today (with over half coming from North America and Europe), but Brazil (40,000), South Korea (35,000), the Philippines (25,000), and China (15,000) each send large numbers as well."[20]

Westerners who imagine that missionaries look like David Livingstone in a pith helmet will be surprised to discover that, by the end of the twentieth century, a missionary was far more likely to be from Korea or Nigeria than from Great Britain. Indeed, not only do the Korean and Nigerian churches send missionaries to Majority World countries, but they are also now sending them to the US, Britain, and Europe.

One scholar who has been tracking these changes in recent years is Graham Hill of the Global Church Project. Paraphrasing the thoughts of Lamin Senneh from Yale Divinity School from an interview in 2020, Hill says,

> We in the West are confident and articulate people. Theology has served us well as a vehicle of our aspirations, desires, and goals. There is no shortage of theological books on all sorts of imaginable subjects. There are how-to-do manuals instructing us about effective ministry. These manuals tell us how to fix our emotions. They affirm our individual identity and promote our choices and preferences. They tell us how to change society by political action. They show us how to raise funds and build bigger churches. They teach us to invest in strategic coalitions. All this language leaves us little time or space to listen to God. What if God has something else to say to us? What if that something else challenges what we want to hear? Yet, without reciprocity in the moral and spiritual life, of hearing and responding to the intimations of the Spirit, it is hard to see how God can be salient in the lives of modern men and women.[21]

It is Hill's hope that the "de-Westernized" form of Christianity coming from Africa, Asia, the Caribbean, Eastern Europe, Oceania, the Middle East, Latin America, as well as First Nations and Indigenous thinkers, could help release the Western church from the cultural captivity mentioned by Senneh above.

So, what do these missionaries from the Global South look like? Here are a few examples.

KOREA

In the early years of the twentieth century, a series of revivals swept through Protestant communities on the Korean peninsula, culminating in 1907 with what is called the "Pyongyang Revival." It was a dramatic awakening akin to the old camp meetings of the US Second Great Awakening in the late eighteenth and early nineteenth centuries. Thousands of Koreans experienced a deep sense of contrition over sin, and many found themselves prostrate on the ground, beating their fists on the floor and screaming out as if in agony. Revival meetings were noisy affairs, with people praying out loud and wailing, in behaviors that would later be characterized as Pentecostal in nature. Thousands were converted and joined the church. Missionaries began referring to Pyongyang as the "Jerusalem of the East."

Three years later, Japan invaded and annexed the peninsula, ruling until 1945. But despite this, the Korean church sent out over eighty missionaries to neighboring China between 1907 and 1955.

But it wasn't until the 1980s that the great wave of Korean missions began to crest. This was in no small measure due to the launch in 1988 of the Mission Korea student conference—a biannual event that attracted up to five thousand attendees. Edward Smither writes, "This conference encouraged intercessory prayer movements for global mission and mobilized many young Korean people to commit their lives to serving in mission."[22]

In 1980, there were just under one hundred Koreans serving as full-time missionaries, but by 2013 that number had exploded to over twenty thousand. There is a current vision among the Korean churches to send out one hundred thousand missionaries by 2030.[23]

CHINA

In 1942, Chinese evangelists coined the phrase "Back to Jerusalem" to denote their vision of sending Chinese missionaries westward along the famed Silk Road toward Jerusalem.[24] Such a route would take them through some of the least-reached nations of eastern and central Asia and the Middle East. Between China and Jerusalem lie nations such as Pakistan, Afghanistan, northern India, Iran, Iraq, and Syria, as well as most of the other "Stans" that were formerly part of the USSR. These countries are dominated by Islam, Hinduism, and Buddhism.

While stymied by the establishment of the communist regime in China, the vision was treasured privately by the Chinese church for decades until the 1990s when it was revived publicly. The Back to Jerusalem movement (BTJ) believes the evangelizing of these least-reached nations is the responsibility of Chinese Christians. The region between Jerusalem and China covers not only the least evangelized countries but also the most dangerous for Westerners—especially Western missionaries, because persecution of Christians is rife.

The BTJ movement believes the Chinese church is not tarnished in the same way the Western church is. They also believe their decades of communist persecution have especially prepared them for this task, so they have committed to sending westward twenty thousand bi-vocational evangelists and church planters.[25]

NIGERIA

It is estimated that there are more than eighty-five million Christians in Nigeria.[26] The two largest groups are Catholic and Anglican, but the biggest growth in recent decades has been among those who identify as Evangelical or Pentecostal.

In 1982, the Nigerian Evangelical Mission (NEM) was established and within five years had sent out five hundred missionaries to foreign nations. This was at a time when Nigeria had five thousand foreign missionaries working in their country. By 2005, there were five thousand Nigerian missionaries serving in sixty-five different countries around the world. NEM adopted a vision to release fifty thousand missionaries by 2021.

THE MOTIVATIONS FOR REVERSE MISSION

These numbers reported from South Korea, China, and Nigeria are big. But are missionaries from the Global South or Majority World effective in re-Christianizing the West? In his analysis of what he calls "reverse mission," church planter Sandro de Oliveira explores the general impulses, limitations, and the opportunities for missionaries from the Global South. He points out three motivating factors.

First, these missionaries feel a burden of gratitude to the West for the way they have benefited from historical European missionary activity. In many senses, "reverse mission" is about the formerly colonized going to their former colonizing nation to take the gospel back to them. Aside from convenient visa arrangements, this is why Nigerians often serve in Britain, Brazilians in Portugal, and Filipinos in Spain or the US.

Second, says Oliveira, "these Christians are aware of the much-spoken-about decline of Christianity in the West and consider secular Europe a 'dark continent' … and a 'spiritual desert' in need of re-evangelization."[27]

Third, Oliveira points out that these Global South Christians feel a deep sense of calling. They believe that God has commissioned them to evangelize in Western contexts, and their work is a response to such divine leading.

Interestingly, Oliveira is also frank about what some scholars perceive to be less noble motivators. These include seeing mission in the West as a way to "boost the self-image of postcolonial nations and their diasporas,"[28] and using their missionary status as a way to fund themselves as they get established in the West.[29] However, Oliveira concludes, "While there may be some truth in such criticisms, they appear to be based more on the judgment of the scholar than in research findings."[30]

THE LIMITATIONS OF REVERSE MISSION

Oliveira is also frank about the challenges facing those undertaking reverse mission. He identifies a huge cultural gap between Europeans and missionaries from the Global South—a gulf so great it is as if they come from very different worlds. This gap is felt by both sides and is the same gulf that existed when European missionaries went to the Global South. Native Europeans say the missionaries aren't adept at acculturating themselves to their new contexts. On the other side of the gulf, reverse missionaries often attribute their lack of relational connection with Europeans to socio-economic and racial factors.

Oliveira believes that many scholars see the validity of the European argument. He quotes several of them who complain that missionaries from the Global South have no clear, premeditated cross-cultural missionary plan[31] and that they are hampered by "a widespread inability to overcome cross-cultural communication barriers."[32] He refers to a scholar who says that many Dutch people say that reverse missionaries' lack of cultural sensitivity mirrors the same mistakes Europeans made when going to Africa in the nineteenth century.[33]

I have heard similar complaints from Cambodian pastors who feel that the Korean missionaries to their nation are using a shape of mission borrowed from a previous era. Furthermore, aside from cultural insensitivities, they told me that the Korean missionaries were presenting a theologically and politically conservative form of Christianity—one that was not only anti-charismatic and anti-egalitarian but was also critical of anti-government protests regarding issues of injustice.

Oliveira says Europeans were similarly perplexed by the gospel preached by African evangelists and by their preference for techniques such as street preaching, door-to-door evangelism, and evangelizing people on public transportation. He points out that some European scholars are concerned about the African missionaries' lack of theological training, and writes, "References to witches, demons, end times, hell, divine punishment, and ancestral curses are ... unpalatable to Europeans' sensibilities."[34]

But before we blame everything on the missionaries from the Global South, we should take some time to see it from their perspective. Many of them say that Europeans are highly resistant to the gospel, even when it is presented in appropriately contextual ways. They say Europeans see a return to Christianity as a regressive attack on modernity. But worse than that, they identify a theme of racial prejudice in the complaints made against them. Nigerian-born lecturer and church leader Joseph Ola says bluntly, "Racism is still deeply entrenched into the cultural fabric of the global north, perhaps only modernized and cloaked in newer lingo."[35] He condemns the European use of labels such as "white and black Christianity," or "local and immigrant churches" as forms of "othering" non-European Christians.

Oliveira says these issues are expressions of a European superiority complex, with Europeans believing themselves to be smarter and better than those from the Global South. He notes that even when Europeans are open to the Christian message, they resist receiving it from non-European missionaries. Oliveira quotes one missionary who says that the English claim they are "the grandfathers of mission" and don't need Africans preaching to them.

THE OPPORTUNITIES FOR REVERSE MISSION

Despite all this, missionaries from the Global South haven't stopped coming to the West. One Kenyan megachurch, Nairobi Chapel, is sending hundreds of missionaries to foreign lands. Their goal is to plant three hundred churches worldwide, with twenty of those in capital cities across Africa and ten in international cities of influence. Their pastor of global partnerships, Faith Mugera, says,

> For a long time, we felt like the Great Commission was a mandate given to the Western world. But do we believe that we are part of the global body of Christ? If so, then we absolutely cannot dismiss ourselves from that. If we as the African church are not functioning right, then the global body is missing out.[36]

Oliveira himself is positive about the impact of reverse mission, writing, "Despite the strong voices questioning the tangible impact of reverse missionary efforts in the revitalization of faith in Europe, there is significant evidence for affirming that Global South Christian migrants and the formation of diaspora churches are having a positive impact on the religious milieu in the continent."[37]

He also sees hope in the successive waves of migration and the formation of ethnic diasporas in the West, as does the Lausanne movement. They write,

> Global diasporas and migration have been and will continue to be a significant and indispensable means by which God accomplishes his redemptive purposes in this world through Jesus Christ. The developmental process of the Church's expansion—inclusive of past, present, and future—cannot be explained without taking into consideration 'God's sovereignty, ruling over the nations, and the moving of His people' from everyone to everywhere.[38]

REMISSIONING TODAY

It remains to be seen whether the West is humble enough to embrace the transition from being the sending center of the world to becoming a receiving center. But it is also doubtful as to whether the church in the West can do as British scholar Martin Robinson recommends and "rethink its stance entirely and become a missionary church within the West."[39] Even though Lesslie Newbigin's critiques of the Western church are over thirty years old, we are still struggling to fully understand and embrace his prescription for the future—a remissionalizing of the church's agenda, a re-gospeling of the church itself, and ultimately a re-Christianizing of Western society, all with the help of voices from the Majority World.

And here we need to distinguish between Newbigin's vision of a re-Christianized West and the old paradigm of Christian domination and control. Many voices today call us to the latter, whether they be proponents of Kingdom Now or the Seven Mountain Mandate or the New Apostolic Reformation. Collectively referred to as "dominionists," these people seek a return to the Christendom paradigm by trying to institute a nation governed by Christians and based on their understandings of biblical law. As the name implies, they seek Christian dominion over the culture. They are not satisfied with a voice or influence in society; they are after total authority.[40]

Newbigin envisioned a renewed Christian influence in society but not a return to political and legal domination. Earlier, I shared the seven points of his vision, which included the need for the church to abandon the notion that our political activity can establish the kingdom of God. Instead, he promoted an understanding of the church freed from its partnership with the state, distanced from Western culture, unraveled from its denominational straightjackets, and released from its addiction to clericalism.

His vision was for a church remissioned; a church that lived out the freedom of the Christian life, drenched in the grace of Jesus, motivated by the coming reign of God, and holding fast to the central beliefs of the gospel. He seemed to believe that society is infected positively by the gospel when it is lived out by dynamic, worshiping communities of faith. Re-Christianization of the West today—rather than by a grasping attempt to wield political power and lord it over those who don't share our faith—can occur gently, lovingly, by the burgeoning growth of multiethnic communities of God's humble, peace-loving people.

10

The Tenth Shape

UNEARTHING

One un-vents something; one unearths it; one digs it up; one runs it down
in whatever recesses of the eternal consciousness it has gone to ground.
ELIZABETH ZIMMERMANN

In her 1927 novel, *Death Comes for the Archbishop*, Willa Cather tells the story of two missionaries who travel from Rome to the southwestern deserts of New Mexico to re-evangelize the formerly Catholic frontier communities. Journeying through an unforgiving landscape, Bishop Latour and his assistant, Father Vaillant, visit derelict towns and isolated homesteads to take the gospel to a beleaguered people. Of the two, Vaillant is the more courageous evangelist. Cather describes him as an unattractive looking man and tells us he has been given the nicknames "Whitey" and "Death-cheater" because of the ashen pallor of his face and his regular bouts of illness.

Toward the end of the book, Father Vaillant is sick again, and his bishop hints that it might be time for him to return to Rome and a more comfortable appointment. Vaillant entreats Latour not to dismiss him from his service in the southwestern territories, and in making his appeal, he tells Latour of the following experience:

> Down near Tuscon, a Pima Indian convert once asked me to go off into the
> desert with him, as he had something to show me. He took me into a place

so wild that a man less accustomed to these things might have mistrusted and feared for his life. We descended into a terrifying canyon of black rock, and there in the depths of a cave he showed me a golden chalice, vestments, and cruets, all the paraphernalia for celebrating Mass. His ancestors had hidden these sacred objects there when the mission was sacked by Apaches, he did not know how many generations ago. The secret had been handed down in his family, and I was the first priest who had ever come to restore to God his own. To me, that is the situation in a parable. The Faith, in that wild frontier, is like a buried treasure; they guard it, but they do not know how to use it to their soul's salvation. A word, a prayer, a service, is all that is needed to set free those souls in bondage.[1]

For Father Vaillant, the good news lay buried in the very soil to which he had been sent. Christianity was not a foreign religion there. The missionaries were not taking a new faith to the frontier. Rather, they were unearthing an old faith that had lain dormant, deep in the souls of the people. Vaillant continued his appeal, "I confess I am covetous of that mission. I desire to be the man who restores these lost children to God. It will be the greatest happiness of my life."[2]

In our exploration of the various shapes mission has taken over the centuries, we have arrived at our own stage of history. In this chapter I want to consider one of the shapes mission should take here in the post-Christian West at the beginning of the twenty-first century, and I find myself thinking about the persistent priest, Father Vaillant. I believe we too live in a culture where Christianity is not foreign but has been buried and is being forgotten. Christianity resonates with our culture, but many people don't know how, as Vaillant says, to use it for their soul's salvation. It needs missionaries to help *unearth* that treasure so that people who feel Christianity has no bearing on their lives can see its luster with new eyes.

This is not merely rhetoric. The decline in numbers of people in the US and Western Europe who identify as Christian shows no sign of slowing. The Pew Research Center's recent report into the future of religion in America shows that people are giving up on Christianity. In a 2020 study, Pew found that about 64 percent of Americans, including children, identified as Christian. People who identified as religiously unaffiliated, or religious "nones," accounted for 30 percent of the US population. But it was the rate of "switching" that concerned Pew. Switching is the term used to describe formerly Christian people changing their affiliation. The Center reports, "Depending on whether religious switching continues at recent rates, speeds up or stops entirely, the projections show Christians of all ages shrinking from 64% to between a little more than half (54%) and just above one-third (35%) of all Americans by 2070."[3]

In other words, the decline of Christianity in America isn't a contested matter. It's just a question of how rapid the decline will be.

In Western Europe, which has become one of the world's most secular regions, the majority of adults surveyed in another Pew Research Center report still consider themselves Christians, even if they seldom go to church. Pew's 2018 study *Being Christian in Western Europe* showed that:

> Non-practicing Christians (defined, for the purposes of this report, as people who identify as Christians, but attend church services no more than a few times per year) make up the biggest share of the population across the region. In every country except Italy, they are more numerous than church-attending Christians (those who go to religious services at least once a month). In the United Kingdom, for example, there are roughly three times as many non-practicing Christians (55%) as there are church-attending Christians (18%) defined this way.[4]

And here's an important point to note: the category of "non-practicing Christian" comprises a huge number of Europeans and Americans, and Pew's research showed there are a number of key differences between non-practicing Christians and those who identify as "nones." These include the following:

- Non-practicing Christians tend not to believe in the God described in the Bible, but they do trust in a higher power or spiritual force, unlike the "nones" who do not believe in such a supernatural power or force.
- Non-practicing Christians have a more positive view of churches and religious organizations than "nones."
- Non-practicing Christians are more likely than "nones" to say that their culture is superior to others and that it is necessary to have the country's ancestry to share the national identity.
- Non-practicing Christians are similar to "nones" in their support for legal abortion and same-sex marriage.

- Non-practicing Christians who are parents say they are bringing up their children as Christians. By contrast, the "nones" who are parents are raising their children with no religion.[5]

Remember, "non-practicing Christian" comprises a huge and growing percentage of people in the West. It can reasonably be suggested that they have buried the good news of the kingdom of God deep down in their collective unconscious. It somewhat shapes their outlook, values, and practices but needs someone to bring it to the surface, dust it off, and make it useful again.

But this can't look like a return to the old religious structures and practices that non-practicing Christians have abandoned. Today, people need to address challenges no one from the past ever needed to explore. These include things such as technological hubris, rampant mental health issues, deforestation, climate change, the costs of globalization, and an approach to politics that is increasingly polarized.

The tenth and final shape of mission is the work of unearthing the good news from the soil of post-Christendom. In contrast to the remissioning we examined in the previous chapter—where the goal was to reorient the church to new realities—unearthing is centered on bringing non-practicing Christians back to faith.

DUSTING OFF OUR RELATIONSHIP WITH POWER

From our quick historical tour of the various shapes of Christian mission, it is clear that the church has a fraught relationship with power. In fact, mission seems to flow more easily when the church has little temporal power. When the church does have such power, mission slows to a trickle. Perhaps that seems counterintuitive. It would seem more logical to assume that a wealthy, influential, powerful church would be more missionally effective than a less powerful one. And while it is true that Portuguese, Spanish, British, and American missionaries scattered throughout the world at the very time their countries of origin were at their wealthiest, the missionaries themselves were from fragile new groups. The Portuguese Jesuits were a young order, without the political influence they would later accrue. The British evangelicals were a marginal sect within Protestantism, as were the American revivalists. The seam of cross-cultural mission was often tapped at the fringe of the church.

It is interesting to note the way each of these groups grew to dominate the religious landscape in their respective countries, and the way their position of power fed their assumption that others should listen to them. In the twentieth century the fundamentalists, and later the conservative evangelicals, used that position to champion culture wars. Flush with power and influence, and craving more, movements like the Religious Right in the US attempted to coopt the legislative process to enforce a particular set of their Christian values on their societies. Non-practicing Christians and "nones" are allergic to this kind of hubris.

But what if, when we unearth the gospel in the West, we abandon the illusion that we are meant to win? What if the church in post-Christendom eschews any inclination to dominate or control the culture in which it finds itself? What if faithfulness becomes our metric rather than triumph?

Recently, I heard a peace-loving Muslim educator from Birmingham, England, speaking about his struggle to convince society that he and other Muslims are not trying to "take over" the education system and institute Sharia law in Britain. He was attempting to clear the reputations of a number of Muslim teachers who were unfairly fired when a fake letter was sent to the local council, which falsely portrayed them as part of a terror cell. Plagued by continual setbacks, he spoke of his frustration at the way the media and politicians continually depicted Muslim teachers. But he also made a surprising comment about his prospects of achieving justice: "I don't judge my success on whether I win or not. I judge it on whether I have been truly faithful to the cause."[6]

This is how someone who is used to being part of a religious minority thinks. Muslims make up just 4.4 percent of the UK population. Despite caricatures of English Muslims as radical extremists, the vast majority of them are law-abiding citizens seeking to live in peace in their community. They don't intend to conquer or control British society; they just seek to be "truly faithful" to their beliefs. The same can be said of Christians living in Islamic, Buddhist, or Hindu settings.

We similarly need to come to terms with the fact that Christians are a religious minority in the West, and we aren't supposed to prevail. Author and historian John Dickson refers to this as learning the "art of losing well."[7] Not denying that God urges us to be bold in speaking his truth to a world that often hates us, Dickson insists that we must also learn how to humbly accept society's verdict, even if it goes against us.

Dickson writes,

> Some Christian writers and leaders may well believe that the faithful are
> too "mousy" about their rights in a civil society. Sometimes I agree. Mostly,
> though, my greater concern is that a good part of the watching world
> believes the very opposite. For many today, Christians have a reputation
> for abusing power—claiming entitlements over society that are historical
> more than deserved. Today, it only takes a hint of the "bully" persona of
> the church to evoke all the evils of Christian history—the Crusades, the
> Inquisitions, and so on.[8]

The church's insistence that things be done our way isn't just met with accusations of bullying. People are also deeply skeptical that the church knows best anyway. History has taught society that when the church had temporal power it couldn't always be trusted to act in everyone's best interests. Dickson wisely says we should present our perspective as followers of Christ, arguing our case as compellingly as we can; but "if society rejects our case, we should not respond with an air of entitlement or demanding our rights. We should never be sore losers. No group in society should be better losers, more cheerful sufferers, than followers of the crucified Lord."[9]

This kind of humility should also extend to our sense of "ownership" over Western society. As I mentioned earlier, Christianity still resonates throughout the West, even if the real faith itself has been long buried—which gives some Christians the sense that Christianity has a privileged "preferred religion" status. However, this can come across as if we are saying that we invented Western culture and have some prior claim on how it should be conducted— for example, when some American Christians complain because Starbucks' Christmas cups don't have explicit Christian imagery on them;[10] or when Australian Christians insist that public schools host Easter parades.[11]

What if a freshly unearthed gospel rejected any sense of privilege or a striving after secular power? More than that, what if we expended whatever power and influence we do have in the interests of others? That's what we have seen throughout history. Whether it was the Celts, the Benedictines, the Moravians, or the abolitionists, they exercised whatever clout they had in the service of the poor and the lost, not for their own ends.

How far is the church in the West from this kind of humility and grace?

LIGHT OVERCOMES DARKNESS

In a world where politicians scream "America First," and their followers are fearful of being overrun by foreigners, the Border Church/La Iglesia Fronteriza (named in both English and Spanish) is a tiny beacon of hope.

Every Sunday since 2011, a beautiful congregation of Jesus-followers has met at the US-Mexico border, seeking the reign of God by breaking bread and worshiping Christ. Although one church, they are split into two congregations—one part meeting in Tijuana, the other in Friendship Park, San Diego. Between them stands a huge, rusted gate-like wall with cross-hatched metal cladding.

When the Border Church/La Iglesia Fronteriza first started meeting, the structure separating them was just a high fence with spaces big enough to pass the sacrament between. Today, each half of the congregation can only just make out the shadowy figures of their fellow parishioners through the wall. But still they meet.

They meet because this is what it means to remain faithful to the gospel. Even as the rhetoric about building bigger walls between the US and Mexico has ramped up in recent years, the members of Border Church/La Iglesia Fronteriza humbly, graciously continue to break bread together each week.

Near the end of the service, congregants press up against the wall and pray in English and in Spanish, the two sides calling to each other across the divide. They chant,

> God, here we stand and make our confession.
> Dios, aquí estamos y hacemos nuestra confesión.
> With our hands up against this wall we confess to you.
> Con nuestras manos en este muro te confesamos.[12]

They squeeze their pinky fingers through the holes in the cross-hatched cladding and wave to each other before turning away from the wall and toward each other to pass the sign of peace. Instead of a handshake, they touch their pinkies together.

This example of steadfast devotion to Christ and others stands in stark relief to a world that keeps building bigger walls. But rather than campaigning or marching or posting snarky memes about immigration policy, the Border Church/La Iglesia Fronteriza breaks bread and gives pinky waves. This little church—made up of deportees, refugees, tourists, and passersby—epitomizes Paul's words, "But God chose the foolish things of the world to shame the wise; God chose the weak things of the world to shame the strong" (1 Cor 1:27).

Our reading of history should fill us with a profound sense of confidence in God's sovereignty and grace. God is directing history to its true end, choreographing everything toward the restoration of all creation. And I believe every small act of faithfulness and love is used by God to that end. When we trust in this idea, we can be less concerned about obtaining the results we want and more content to be "truly faithful" to Christ. This involves seeing mission like water and recognizing that, at some times and in some places, it flows like a torrent and in others it slows to a trickle. Using a different metaphor (light, not water), Eric Costanzo, Daniel Yang, and Matthew Soerens express this same confidence in the coming kingdom when they say, "As the spool of time unwinds and history progresses, the characteristics, plans, and purposes of God's kingdom become clearer; it moves forward as light that is increasingly overwhelming darkness until all darkness has passed away and only light remains (Jn 1:5; 1 Jn 2:8; Rev 21)."[13]

Or as Jesus invites us to pray, "Your kingdom come, your will be done, on earth as it is in heaven" (Mt 6:10). Let us unearth this approach to our faith.

LEARNING FROM MARGINALIZED VOICES

Unearthing the gospel will not only involve cultivating a deeper sense of humility and grace, but it will also involve being willing to hear from voices previously marginalized by the Western church—women, people of color, and new immigrants. More than ever, we need to objectively examine Western culture with the help of those from other cultures.

Once, while speaking at a convention in Texas, my hosts informed me that their denomination was undergoing a huge leadership transition with all the "old guard" stepping aside to allow new leaders to take over. This was a matter of great excitement. The new team was to be inducted during the first session of the convention at which one of the other speakers, a Korean scholar, was scheduled to speak.

One by one, the new leaders were introduced and invited on stage as the emcee outlined their qualifications for their new portfolios. There was a lot of fanfare and frequent references to this group "leading our churches into the future."

Then the Korean scholar took the microphone.

He began by explaining how rapidly the Asian community was growing in the US—that it now made up about 7 percent of the nation's overall population, and that numbers were projected to surpass forty-six million by 2060.

He then let us know that Latinos accounted for 18 percent of the US population, or almost fifty-nine million people. And that the Black or African American percentage of the population was about 13 percent or forty-one million people. He even let us know that more than 50 percent of the American population was under forty and, in case we'd forgotten, that 50.7 percent were female.

Then, rather boldly, he pointed out that the new leadership team that had stood on the platform just minutes earlier was all male and nearly all white. None of them were Asian. They all looked like they were in their 40s or older. "So," he concluded, "I really don't think this is the team you need to lead you into the future." You could hear a pin drop.

The Korean speaker proceeded to explain that, if this denomination really did want to be led into the future, they needed to accept that the future is multi-ethnic and that young Americans expect to be led by women and people of color, not just older white men. To their credit, the convention delegates took this pretty well, at least from my observation. There appeared to be a general sense that he was right to call out the new leadership team as monocultural.

If the church is going to have anything to say in a globalized world, we must listen to the voices of those who have been marginalized or overlooked. This was Lesslie Newbigin's advice to the British churches in the 1980s. Coming back into a Western context after forty years in India, he was quick to signal how powerful and pervasive Western culture was, calling it the most powerful global force at work in the world today. But Newbigin was concerned not only with the extent of the influence of Western culture but also, as he saw it, that its influence was distinctly anti-Christian. In fact, he claimed that wherever Western culture "becomes the controlling doctrine for public life [it] drives religion into a smaller and smaller enclave."[14] Newbigin's most radical charge was that the church in the West lives in a state of syncretism with its culture. Westerners can't see it, he said, because they are as immersed in it as a fish is in water. To fully understand Western culture, and to unearth the gospel, requires help from voices outside that culture.

UNEARTHING A BROADER
UNDERSTANDING OF THE GOSPEL

For many non-Christians in the West, the buried good news isn't all that good, really. When asked what the gospel is, they'll often reply that it's a message about how to avoid going to hell when you die. Even a lot of Christians seem to think the gospel is essentially an explanation of the doctrine of atonement. Ask them what the good news is, and they'll tell you that Jesus died to atone for our sins so we can be forgiven by God and spend eternity with him. Although this is true, it's only part of the gospel. It's a message focused on freeing people from the existential burden of self-reflective guilt. It's a message our culture grew tired of and buried long ago.

Because many people today no longer feel a sense of guilt, Christians often feel the need to back up and first try to convince people to feel contrite about falling short of God's standard. Only then can they provide the news of Christ's sacrifice as the solution to their guilt. That's why so much preaching by evangelists in the twentieth century was characterized as guilt-inducement. Although he died before the turn of the century, D. L. Moody set the standard, using emotionally charged music and passionate preaching to convince people to repent and enjoy God's offer of forgiveness in Christ. He was followed by the flamboyant Billy Sunday and Aimee Semple McPherson, both of whom used every trick in the book to prick the consciences of their listeners. And the greatest evangelist of the twentieth century, Billy Graham, solidified this approach to the gospel through his extensive preaching of what we might call the "punitive gospel."

In his book, *The Suburban Captivity of the Church,* Tim Foster outlines this punitive understanding of the gospel this way:

- The Beginning: God created us to be perfect.
- The Problem: Human sin brings us under God's wrath.
- The Solution: Our sin and its consequences are transferred (imputed) to Jesus on the cross.
- The Future: There will be no condemnation for those who repent and believe.
- The Present: We must trust in the atoning death of Jesus. We live a holy life by the power of the Spirit. We wait, hope, and persevere.[15]

You might have seen this approach illustrated by the famous *Bridge to Life* tract,[16] showing God and humankind on two cliff edges, separated by an uncrossable gulf. Only the cross can span the divide and bring us into God's arms.

This presentation of the gospel is concerning for a number of reasons:

It only emphasizes individual sin, individual responsibility, and individual salvation. The approach doesn't take into account that systems and our contribution to them can be sinful. It also doesn't acknowledge that many people are as sinned against as they are sinners.

It assumes the onus is on us, the sinner. We have to make a decision to move toward God who, having sent his son to die for us, passively awaits us on the other side of the gulf.

It truncates the gospel to "Jesus came to die for us." By doing so, it ignores the significance of Jesus's ministry and the kingdom of God, something Jesus himself spends an inordinate amount of his ministry talking about and demonstrating.

Most of all, it holds to a strongly punitive understanding of God's wrath and how Jesus's death helps us avoid punishment.

This presentation of the gospel clearly found a receptive audience in the 1900s. Racked by two world wars, a global economic depression, and a Cold War that became hot in Korea, Vietnam, Czechoslovakia, and Hungry (and nearly in Cuba), twentieth-century people clearly carried a great burden of guilt. Humanity was broken, and people felt personally responsible for their part in it. When Billy Graham told them they could have their slates wiped clean, that all their sins could be forgiven, it was music to their ears.

But self-reflective guilt is a vanishing condition in the West today. People are more aware of being trapped in cycles of depression, or within social structures of injustice. They feel a loss of purpose and harbor fears about economic insecurity, broken relationships, and loneliness. They respond to a guilt-inducing message that they are sinners with a casual shrug of their shoulders and a wistful, "Meh." They know humankind is broken. They know *they* are broken. But, so what?

Depression, loneliness, lack of purpose, economic insecurity, racism, and misogyny are all conditions the gospel addresses. In the twenty-first century we need to learn how to proclaim a richer, more Jesus-oriented gospel, one that speaks to the felt needs of a new post-Enlightenment generation.

Our problem is there's no *Bridge to Life* booklet for that.

Returning to Tim Foster's work, although he rejects the punitive approach, he has developed an alternative that he calls the "telic gospel," from the Greek *telos*, meaning "purpose." For Foster, at its heart the gospel is about finding our true purpose in the fulfillment of God's good purposes for creation. In other words, embracing Christianity shouldn't simply be a punishment-avoidance strategy; it should be an invitation to live the good and beautiful life God intended for us from the beginning. Foster outlines the telic gospel using the same structure as he did to outline the punitive gospel. Here they are, side-by-side:

	The Punitive Gospel	The Telic Gospel
The Beginning	God created us to be perfect.	God created the world according to his good purposes.
The Problem	Human sin brings us under God's wrath.	Human sin opens the door for evil, thereby undermining God's purposes.
The Solution	Our sin and its consequences are transferred (imputed) to Jesus on the cross.	Jesus took our punishment. He conquers evil, brings forgiveness, and defeats death.
The Future	There will be no condemnation for those who repent and believe.	There will be a new social and political order according to God's purposes.
The Present	We must trust in the atoning death of Jesus. We live a holy life by the power of the Spirit. We wait, hope, and persevere.	The new order has begun with the resurrection of Jesus. We live in the light of the future in the power of the Spirit.[17]

According to Foster, the gospel that Jesus initiated and preached wasn't focused solely on the proclamation of individual salvation, self-preservation, and the avoidance of damnation. Jesus came preaching and demonstrating the kingdom of God.

New Testament scholar Scot McKnight puts it this way:

> The gospel is the story of the work of the triune God (Father, Son, and Spirit) to completely restore broken image-bearers (Gn. 1:26–27) in the context of the community of faith (Israel, Kingdom, and Church) through the life, death, and resurrection of Jesus Christ and the gift of the Pentecostal Spirit, to union with God and communion with others for the good of the world.[18]

In this way the gospel sounds like *good* news for modern people. It's more than "Jesus died for your sins." It's all about a new kingdom. In fact, the four canonical Gospels in our Bibles make this clear. Jesus' birth reveals him to be the rightful heir to the eternal throne promised to King David. His miracles point to the presence of God's kingdom and reveal it to be a place with no sickness or disease, no hunger, and no storms. Jesus' teaching lays down the demands of the kingdom, explaining its new ethic of love, and sounds an invitation for all to join.

Yes, his sacrificial death atones for our sins, and his resurrection establishes him as our King—the one whom God has appointed as the future judge of the world. But the gospel is the *whole* story of Jesus, not just his passion. And it doesn't just begin in the Gospel accounts. It is the story of the whole Bible, from beginning to end. It is all about the sovereign rule of the triune God, which must be accepted by us in faithful, grateful obedience and which shapes us into a redeemed society of persons who trust in God's present rule but hope for its final revelation, and who partner with God to fashion foretastes of that rule right now. That's a message worth digging up again.

So, what is the good and beautiful kingdom like? In their book *Kingdom Ethics*, David Gushee and Glen Stassen say that the book of Isaiah was the primary foundation of Jesus' teaching on the kingdom. They come to this conclusion because of the number of passages in Isaiah that specifically refer to the kingship of God and to his coming reign, and because of the number of times Jesus quotes Isaiah to make that very point about himself. There's little doubt that the Synoptic Gospel writers were profoundly aware of Isaiah's portrayal of the kingdom of God. Gushee and Stassen analyzed the Synoptic Gospels and Isaiah to distill what they termed "the seven marks of God's reign," which are:

1. deliverance/salvation;
2. justice;
3. peace;
4. healing;

5. restoration/rebuilding of community;

6. joy; and

7. the experience of God's presence.[19]

This is the gospel. Christ is king—as proved by his birth, life, miracles, teaching, death, and resurrection—and a relationship with him invites us into a world of deliverance, justice, peace, healing, community, joy, and the experience of God's presence. These are the very things we need to be sharing with this current generation.

To that end—and reminding us that we need to learn from marginalized voices—Robert Chao Romero points out that theologians of color can help us understand this broader version of the gospel. He writes,

> Brown theologians throughout the centuries ... have challenged this narrow and unbiblical view of the gospel and have proclaimed that Jesus came to save, redeem, and transform every aspect of our lives and the world. His salvation extends over all God's good creation, which has become twisted and corrupted as a consequence of sin. This includes everything distorted and broken in our world—whether personal, familial, social, or global. Nothing is left out. It includes our emotional brokenness and dysfunctional family relationships, but also poverty, racism, slavery, human trafficking, oppression of immigrants, warfare, lack of clean water, AIDS, gang violence, and lack of educational opportunity.[20]

UNEARTHING BIBLICAL HOLINESS

By the twentieth century, much of the rich holiness traditions of the Benedictines, the Anabaptists, and the Methodists had been boiled down to "Don't drink, don't have sex outside of marriage, and don't dance (because it could lead to having sex outside of marriage)." In more recent years, particularly in the US, holiness has been measured by an individual's political leanings and their stance on issues such as abortion and same-sex marriage. But these things are often veneers—having the appearance of godliness but serving only to cover up a range of secret sins.

What we have seen unfolding throughout the twenty-first century has been a great unveiling of those hidden sins, as people have used the power of social media to highlight their prevalence.

In the 1990s, we began hearing reports about the widespread sexual abuse of children by Catholic priests in Canada, the United States, Chile, Australia, Ireland, and across Europe. Then, in 2002, a now-famous investigation by *The Boston Globe* uncovered evidence that not only was the abuse rife across the Boston diocese but also that church leaders had covered up the crimes of others. Since then, various enquiries around the world have revealed unimaginably high numbers of cases and cover-ups. One study by the United States Conference of Catholic Bishops showed that close to five thousand Catholic priests and deacons in active ministry between 1950 and 2002 had been accused of sexual abuse by over ten thousand individuals.[21]

The Vatican says that from 2001 to 2010 they examined sex-abuse cases involving about three thousand priests, some of which dated back fifty years. But in 2017, Pope Francis acknowledged that the Vatican had a two-thousand-case backlog of sexual abuse allegations.[22]

In 2006, activist Tarana Burke first used the hashtag-slogan #MeToo to empower sexually assaulted people, especially young and vulnerable women, through finding strength in numbers. She and others began calling on sexually assaulted people to visibly show others that they too had been harassed and attacked, especially in the workplace. Then in 2017, American actress Alyssa Milano was shown a screenshot of a tweet, which read, "If all the women who have been sexually harassed or assaulted wrote 'Me too' as a status, we might give people a sense of the magnitude of the problem." Milano posted a reply, "If you've been sexually harassed or assaulted, write 'me too' as a reply to this tweet."[23] That's when things really blew up.

Whether it was in Hollywood, politics, sports, business, fashion, finance, or education, the #MeToo movement has highlighted the prevalence of sexual assault and harassment, resulting in the downfall of a number of famous male abusers. And the church has not been immune to this kind of scrutiny. The same year Alyssa Milano's tweet came out, Emily Joy and Hannah Paasch launched the hashtag #ChurchToo to highlight and stop sexual abuse within the church. The following year, about a hundred evangelical women launched #SilenceIsNotSpiritual, calling for radical change in the ways that allegations of sexual misconduct are dealt with in the church. Since then, the sexual misconduct of many high-profile Christian leaders has been uncovered.

This same method of rousing solidarity among victims has recently been used by those trammeled by the domineering and bullying tactics of a certain kind of (mainly) evangelical leader. We have seen multiple well-known Protestant pastors resign from their churches under the weight of a multitude of allegations of imperious, arrogant, and overbearing leadership. The great unearthing has continued.

As the fortunes of the church have declined in the West, some Christians have cried out for God to send a revival. But what if God's very response has been to expose the depth of corruption and abuse going on in the church? What if this great unveiling isn't the work of our enemies trying to discredit us, but the work of God unearthing the truth and purifying the church for the future? That would in fact be the very thing a holy God would do, wouldn't it?

I suspect this process, if taken seriously and positively, could be the catalyst for a renewed understanding of holiness—one that takes seriously the sins of injustice, inequity, avarice, and oppression as much as the sin of sexual immorality.

UNEARTHING OUR STEWARDSHIP OF CREATION

Another implication for an unearthed gospel is the need for us to think Christianly about climate change. A concern for the stewardship of creation has always been at the heart of biblical faith, but it was buried long ago. In the absence of the church addressing this challenge, such stewardship has been taken up by others: the contemporary environmental movement (which has its roots in the conservation movements of the nineteenth and early twentieth centuries) and the environmental justice movement and anti-nuclear campaign of the late twentieth century. These days, the effects of climate change are undeniable. Although some might have differing views about the degree to which these changes are human induced, the overwhelming majority of climate scientists—and the vast majority of young people across the world— have no doubt.

The Global Climate Strike began in Sweden in 2018 when (then) fifteen-year-old Greta Thunberg sat in front of the parliament building in Stockholm every day for three weeks to demand action on the climate crisis. The following year, similar strikes took place in 4,500 locations in 150 countries involving over six million people.[24]

In the US church—where anxieties about the ecology movement with its emphasis on Gaia theory[25] and links to New Age spiritualities have caused great reticence—the preferred term for climate activism is "creation care." But even a biblical call to steward the earth has had a mixed response in church circles. Some conservative evangelicals question why stewarding the earth is necessary, since Jesus is coming back anyway. But thoughtful consideration reveals how utilitarian that viewpoint is—essentially questioning the *usefulness* of stewarding the earth: if Jesus is coming back to take the faithful off to heaven and fry everything else, what is the *use* of us caring for the planet?

Even people who don't believe that Jesus will destroy the earth upon his return, often present ecological responsibility as a practical consideration. Students at the Global Climate Strike, for example, held signs about the future implications of doing nothing—"There is no Planet B," or "No nature = No future."[26] Many of the warnings about climate change are couched in terms of what will happen if we don't reduce CO_2 emissions—sea level rises, rampant bushfires, coral bleaching, and so forth. But what if creation care, or Christian environmentalism, wasn't just motivated by practical concerns, as important as they are? What if we were motivated by our *theology*—by our understanding of the nature and character of God?

Far from rubbing his hands in anticipation of obliterating the whole earth, the God we see in the Bible is intimately attached to creation. The psalmists write, "The earth is the LORD's, and everything in it, the world, and all who live in it" (Ps 24:1), and "For every animal of the forest is mine, and the cattle on a thousand hills. I know every bird in the mountains, and the insects in the fields are mine" (Ps 50:10–11). In fact, right throughout Scripture, God is portrayed as the earth's creator and owner (Job 38), its sustainer (Ps 147:8–9, 15–18; Heb 1:3), its director (Isa 40:15, 22–24), and its redeemer (Rom 8:20–22; 2 Cor 4:16–5:5).

God loves creation. And the earth reciprocates with praise and worship.

King David sings, "The heavens declare the glory of God; the skies proclaim the work of his hands. Day after day they pour forth speech; night after night they reveal knowledge. They have no speech, they use no words; no sound is heard from them. Yet their voice goes out into all the earth, their words to the ends of the world" (Ps 19:1–4).

Why bother stewarding the earth? Because God loves it. God is proud of it. It reflects God's glory and reveals God's creativity, grace, and power.

And whatever God loves, we should love too, right? That includes our rivers and coastlines, our rainforests, and coral reefs … and it must also include the people God loves—the poor, immigrants, refugees, widows, and orphans.

These are the very people most directly affected by the consequences of environmental degradation. It is the global poor who suffer most from malnutrition due to food shortages, higher rates of tropical disease, lung disease from pollution, and military conflicts over increasingly scarce natural resources.

Jesus told his disciples, "By this everyone will know that you are my disciples, if you love one another" (Jn 13:35). Stewarding the earth is an act of love—love for God, love for the things God loves, love for the people God loves. Even if a third of the planet's forest cover hadn't been flattened, even if half a million species weren't in danger of extinction, even if carbon pollution wasn't acidifying and warming the oceans, Christians would still be motivated to steward the earth because God has filled us with a love for all that he loves.

I don't believe God is planning to destroy the earth at the return of Christ. I believe the curse of human sin upon the earth will be lifted, the planet will be renewed, and heaven and earth will bleed into each other resulting in a whole new existence where love and justice are the norm. God never abandons the things he creates. He doesn't turn his back on Israel. He won't forsake the church. He won't desert the poor. And he won't discard creation. And therefore, neither should we.

All of that said, Christians need to be discerning about our stance. Some popular expressions of environmentalism have melded into a form of paganized worship of nature that denies the creator God. And, frankly, some messaging from the environmental movement can be shrill and impractical. Stewarding the creation will take a commitment to remaining well informed and balancing the needs of the poor with those of the planet.

KEEP DIGGING

In 2016, not far from the remote Ethiopian city of Aksum, a team of American archeologists were excavating in a rocky field. They were searching for relics of the ancient Aksumite kingdom—a trading empire that emerged in the first century AD and would go on to dominate much of eastern Africa and western Arabia. The region appeals to archaeologists because it is strewn with tall, carved Aksumite obelisks and it was also home to various pagan temples, dating back many centuries before the rise of Aksum.

As expected, the team found an assortment of relics, including a beautiful golden ring with the image of a bull's head, as well as nearly fifty cattle figurines—all evidence of Aksum's pagan history. But then a surprising artifact was unearthed. At first it looked like a simple stone pendant engraved with ancient Ethiopic words; but on closer inspection the archeologists discovered there was a cross carved into the top of the pendant. And the lettering was translated as "venerable." This might well have been a priestly ornament.

The only problem was that these items were dated to the fourth century, and Christianity wasn't believed to have spread to sub-Saharan Africa until much later.

But there were more surprising discoveries in store. Nearby, the team unearthed the corner of what would be revealed to be a huge building—18 meters (60 feet) long and 12 meters (40 feet) wide. There they came across a shocking inscription, asking "for Christ [to be] favorable to us."[27] It was a church! These discoveries not only changed what we understood about the history of Ethiopia but rewrote the story of the spread of Christianity into Africa.

Today, we too need to be patient excavators, unearthing an ancient story long since buried, bringing it to the light, and allowing it to change people's preconceptions or past understandings. The growing cohort of non-practicing Christians have some sense of this story, even if it's as C. S. Lewis described it, "the scent of a flower we have not found, the echo of a tune we have not heard, news from a country we have not visited."[28] Our task as excavators is to show how Jesus' life and message relates to things such as humility in the face of opposition; respect for the contributions of women, people of color, and new immigrants; an ethic that protects the poor and vulnerable; and a commitment to creation care. And so much more.

York Moore is a modern-day Billy Graham. The crowds he preaches to might not be as big, but Moore is continually on the road (or in the air), crisscrossing North America, preaching the gospel, and calling people to faith. Moore is a former national evangelist with InterVarsity USA, so his typical audiences are college students. When he speaks, he recounts the story of his dramatic conversion to Christianity, having grown up as an atheist and only coming to faith when he was a college student. The young adults who listen to him relate to his story, but they also find his way of sharing Christ fresh and contemporary. (He has more than four million likes on TikTok!)

But Moore does more than tell college students how to avoid going to hell when they die. He unearths the full gospel buried deep in the hearts of his audience, many of whom would be described as the non-practicing

Christians we looked at earlier. His preaching integrates social justice practices with the proclamation of the gospel. Indeed, he refers to himself as a justice evangelist and abolitionist. Under his influence, InterVarsity saw an increase in conversions for a decade, until the interruption of the COVID-19 pandemic. Moore writes, "While not all of InterVarsity's evangelistic strategies and practices revolve around a substantive integration of social justice and evangelism, this practical integration is a significant factor in the increased visibility, effectiveness, and relevance of one of America's oldest collegiate ministries. There is no doubt that America's collegiate environment is one where there is a substantial interest in global social justice."[29]

Recently, Moore arranged a series of InterVarsity events designed to raise money and awareness for International Justice Mission (IJM). At these events he would speak to college students on sex trafficking, forced labor, and the prostitution of children. His presentation combined his concern for actual slavery around the world with the spiritual slavery many young Americans sense. In his evangelistic appeal at these events, he concluded by calling people to give their lives to Jesus, saying,

> Tonight, the Christ who calls you is the Christ who has not only come to save the world from the hell to come, but also from the hell that is now ... Jesus has an answer for five-year-old Jyoti [a child-sex slave in Myanmar], and he has an answer for you here tonight as well. Whether our chains are physical or spiritual, Christ came to break the chains of slavery and tonight you can be free just as Jyoti is now free because of what Christ has done.[30]

I can vouch for this integrated approach to mission among college students. Some years ago, I spoke at an InterVarsity young leaders' event in Florida. Aside from the pre-planned seminars and workshops, the students made requests to the conference organizers to add new sessions, roundtables, and lunchtime meetings to discuss issues not considered by the planners but that were extremely important to them. These included what a Christian response should be to #MeToo and Black Lives Matter; how to think Christianly about the challenges raised by LGBTQI+ students; action on climate change; and navigating the complementarian-egalitarian debate. They even called out one of the mainstage speakers (not me!) when he used a slightly sexist allusion in one of his illustrations. I share this experience to reinforce York Moore's intuition that young Americans want a form of Christianity that broaches an integration of social justice and evangelism.

Contemporary missionaries need to get their hands dirty, doing the kind of cultural investigation we looked at in chapter eight as well as the substantive missiological work of unearthing a holistic gospel that glorifies Jesus, addresses contemporary issues, and brings healing to the brokenness of the human condition.

EPILOGUE

Where Will the Water Flow?

There are far, far better things ahead than any we leave behind.
C. S. LEWIS

In a crumbling chateau in the southern Czech town of Moravský Krumlov, you'll find an astonishing artistic achievement: the *Slav Epic*—a series of twenty huge paintings (the largest measuring over 6 by 8 meters [20 by 26 feet]) rendered by the Czech master Alphonse Mucha. Together, these canvases depict the history of the Slav people and their civilization. Each painting is teeming with detail, many with portraits of historical characters and dramatic war scenes. Observed as a whole, it is a staggering piece of work. Mucha conceived it as a monument for all the Slavic peoples, and he devoted the latter half of his artistic career to completing the work. It is truly a labor of love.

I once heard American preacher Jonny Ardavanis recall his visit to Moravský Krumlov, where he was surprised to come across an elderly Czech woman keenly examining just the bottom corner of the twentieth and final canvas. It struck him that this is how we often view life. We only focus on the events right in front of us and lose sight of the epic story that has unfolded up until this point. In fact, this is one of the reasons I've written this book.

But what if, well before Jonny Ardavanis had arrived at the chateau, that elderly woman had spent hours and hours examining all twenty canvases in close detail? What if he just happened to come across her as she was completing her inspection of the whole exhibition? She would be right to be focused on the bottom corner of the twentieth canvas, wouldn't she?

Well, that's where we find ourselves now. Having scrutinized our "canvases" (ten chapters looking at ten different shapes of mission in history), we have arrived at the bottom corner of the great epic that has been unfolding throughout history. I agree with Jonny Ardavanis, that if we fixate on our current age, we miss out on so much of what God is doing. But I hope you end this book feeling like you've inspected the whole exhibition, that your perspective is broad, and that you can see the bigger picture that is being painted by the Master Artist.

But it begs the question, where to from here? Can we predict what's in store for the church's mission based on what we've studied up to this point? That's like predicting where a river flows before you've navigated its full length.

In the 1984 film *Back to the Future*, the main protagonists Doc Brown and Marty McFly time-travel to 2015 where they discover a (then) future world of flying cars, hoverboards, and self-lacing shoes.[1] Despite getting a surprising number of predictions right, everyone focuses on that missing hoverboard. In fact, Liam Ryan's 2013 book about funny failed visions of the future from the past is titled *Dammit Science, Where's My Hoverboard?*[2]

Let's be honest, predicting the future is a tricky business.

It would be easy to dream up a future church located in the metaverse where we're all flying on unicorns over a 3D pasture, while the avatar of a kindly pastor (who looks like Doc Brown) guides us through various Bible stories that spring to life below us as we pray from on high. But what do I know?

Sure, I once co-wrote a book called *The Shaping of Things to Come*,[3] but I am neither a futurist nor the son of a futurist. I tend to agree with Robert Kiyosaki's maxim, "The best way to predict the future is to study the past or prognosticate."[4] And since I'm not great at prognosticating, I'll fall back to just studying the past. Which is what we've been doing throughout this book. We've explored the various cultural containers into which the mission of the church has been poured, and we've touched on what mission might look like in our current day and age.

Throughout this book, we have traveled far enough down this river together. We have learned some rowing skills. Our muscles have strained at the stream's various turns. We have become adept at reading the condition of this watercourse. We should now be able to anticipate something of what lies ahead.

REMEMBERING OUR IDENTITY

Whatever outward shapes our mission might take, the internal truth about our identity in Christ is indispensable. I hope you have been inspired by the many stories of women and men who were motivated by their identity as Christ-followers to do the most beautiful and selfless things in order to honor Christ and serve others. That is something we too must carry with us into the future. We are a company of fellow disciples, a redeemed society that has pledged allegiance to Christ our King. We're not simply social workers or cultural commentators. Nor are we a peculiar band of people committed to upholding some esoteric religious tradition. We are "good news" people—a quaint old phrase from the 1970s that means we are a story-formed community, and that story has everything to do with the King who has come and is still coming.

Like the many people whose lives we've examined in this book, we too must desire to see the gospel be reborn in every culture and community around the world. But we can only accomplish this by remembering our identity as Christ-followers and holding tightly to the truthfulness of the gospel story.

American professor Ed Stetzer says we need to know what to hold tightly in our right hand and what to hold loosely in our left. This is what some might call first-order and second-order issues. For Stetzer, we hold tightly to the authority of Scripture and a gospel focus, but we need to be gracious when we differ on issues that aren't core to the gospel. He writes,

> Even as we hold the left hand open, as men and women go into different cultures and contexts, we rejoice in the fact we have an unchanging gospel and an unchanging God. We must recognize that we will continue to be a church in the margins, sent and led by Jesus Christ, whose birth and crucifixion in the margins changed the world and continues to turn lives upside down.[5]

I hope as we move into the future that an awareness of what we hold in our right hand will be clear. With that in mind, I would like, very tentatively, to suggest a number of characteristics of the church of the future so that we can be prepared for the shapes mission might take.

THE FUTURE CHURCH WILL NOT BE WHITE

Gina Zurlo, the director of the Center for the Study of Global Christianity at Gordon-Conwell Theological Seminary, says, "The typical Christian today, globally, is a poor, young, uneducated woman in sub-Saharan Africa."[6] When put as starkly as that, it's a real wake-up call. We have been hearing for years now that Christianity is shifting to the Global South. The statistics keep bearing this out.

According to Zurlo's research, in 1900 only 18 percent of the world's Christians lived in Asia, Africa, Latin America, and Oceania. Today, those Christians make up 67 percent of the global church, and Zurlo predicts that by 2050 it will be 77 percent.[7] The largest concentration of Christians in the world is in Africa, where 27 percent of the world's Christians live. It is predicted that figure will be closer to 40 percent by 2050. By comparison, the United States and Canada were home to just 11 percent of all Christians in the world in 2020 and that number will likely drop to 8 percent by 2050. Furthermore, the median age of Christians in sub-Saharan Africa is just nineteen.[8]

And yet this reality is one that many people in the West struggle to come to terms with. Racist and ill-informed statements like the one we looked at in chapter eight—about the African church being a mile wide and an inch deep—betray the West's general superiority complex. In his book *The Next Christendom*, Philip Jenkins anticipated this very thing:

> As emerging Christianity becomes ever stranger to Northern eyes, it will acquire the same kind of bleak stereotypes that were in bygone years applied to Muslims. The Christian faith of the rising states, we will probably hear, is fanatical, super-stitious, demagogic: it is politically reactionary and sexually repressive.[9]

And yet this is the direction the water is flowing. African, Asian, Latin American, and Pasifika voices and practices will come to dominate the shape of global Christianity, and white Westerners will need to learn what it's like to be junior partners in that enterprise.

THE FUTURE CHURCH WILL BE DECLERICALIZED

In February 2023, an interesting religious phenomenon broke out at a university in Kentucky. Referred to as the Asbury Revival or Awakening, it was a student-led chapel service that ran nonstop for weeks, during which attendees felt the presence of God and responded in prayer, praise, confession, and renewed commitment. Thousands of people descended on the small town of Wilmore to attend the revival meetings, standing in line outside the college's main chapel, some to participate in what they believed was a move of God, others to simply see what was going on.

Inevitably, an event as popular as the Asbury Revival attracted its share of famous Christians, well-known preachers, and church influencers wanting to be part of what God was doing. But the students weren't impressed. They made clear the event was to remain student led. But more than that, the chapel meetings weren't controlled by a small group of nominated student leaders, but by anyone who felt led by the Spirit.

When Laura Levens, a professor from nearby Baptist Seminary of Kentucky attended, she reported, "When I asked who was in charge, I was told, 'No one is.'"[10]

This perfectly illustrates what has been written about the spirituality of Millennials.[11] The Asbury phenomenon was a revival without obvious leadership—a long way from the evangelicalism of their parents who were so enamored with celebrity preachers and leaders.

This gels with Lesslie Newbigin's prediction that the church of the future would need to rely less and less on a professional model of leadership.[12] Even the most clerical denominations, such as the Roman Catholic Church, realize their reliance on credentialed officeholders has run its course.[13] Indeed, across the Western world and in nearly every denomination, the recruitment of candidates for ordained leadership has hit a wall. But before we bemoan this fact, we should recall that the church's mission has always been conducted by passionate, selfless, loving people, committed to alerting others to the universal reign of God through Christ. As we've seen, the kingdom has been advanced throughout history by domestic servants, wounded soldiers, doctors, artists, photographers, freed slaves, bootmakers, and bricklayers.

During the social upheavals of the 1960s, German Jesuit priest and theologian Karl Rahner said, "The church in the future will be one built from below by basic communities as a result of free initiative and association. We should make every effort not to hold up this development, but to promote it and direct it on the right lines."[14]

I take him to mean the church needs to become more democratized—a radical stance for a Jesuit priest to make in the 1960s. But while we Protestants might feel freer of the hierarchical bureaucracy that has burdened our Catholic friends, we too need to be open to more participation by the laity, by people of color, and by women.

This of course is not only a religious trend. Across the world right now, "unqualified" visionaries are leading major initiatives. The movement for climate change mitigation isn't driven by an eminent climate scientist but by twenty-year-old Greta Thunberg. Her calls for stronger action on climate change have been taken up by students and young people across the globe.

In 2012, Malala Yousafzai was only fifteen when she was shot in the head by Taliban gunmen for the "crime" of advocating for the education of girls in Pakistan. Surviving her injuries, Yousafzai has become a global advocate for women's and children's rights, establishing the not-for-profit Malala Fund, which offers education and training to girls aged fourteen to eighteen. Her mantra is "books, not bullets," as she addresses world leaders on the need to fight terrorism and violence with education and understanding.

In 2017, a seven-year-old Syrian girl named Bana Alabed became the voice of the siege of Aleppo by using Twitter to document the airstrikes, destruction, hunger, and displacement she and her family were experiencing. Her heart-breaking tweets about her fear of dying with her family and her longing for peace led to increased awareness of the situation in Syria.

Even more recently, unnamed women have been at the forefront of escalating protests in Iran, sparked by the death in custody of Mahsa Amini—a woman detained and killed by "morality police" for not wearing her hijab tightly enough.

I share these stories only to show that grassroots movements don't need to be led by so-called experts or people of great influence. Similarly, this trend will impact the church, and new missional movements will emerge that are not led by archbishops or cardinals but by ordinary spirit-led missionaries.

Examples of this include the microchurch and dinner church movements.[15] Both initiatives seek to generate godly lay leaders to launch new congregations that either meet around tables or are focused on a particular need or demographic. Another example is the Korean church, which has grown from person-to-person, family-to-family, and community-to-community. Because the early Korean church couldn't rely on foreign clergy, they developed as a lay-led movement. Lay people became passionate about sharing their faith with others, because they themselves became Christians by someone sharing their faith with them. This is how Korean Catholic priest Paul Kim Bo Rok explains it:

> In the parish we are two priests and four sisters, but the real work of mission and religious instruction is done by the laity, both in the eight courses of catechesis and in the very active ecclesial movements ... Each year, we celebrate two or three rites of collective baptism of adults: each time the baptized are 200, 300, or even more ... Deeper formation in the faith is given after baptism and is the task of the [lay] ecclesial movements. Becoming Christian means entering into a group that draws you in deeply, gives you norms of behavior and effort, gives you prayers to say every day. When one enters the church one accepts everything. This is the Korean spirit: either you accept and commit yourself, or you don't accept and go away.[16]

THE FUTURE CHURCH WILL BE CULTURALLY LITERATE

As we explored in chapters eight and ten, the church will need to continue the work of reading culture and contextualizing the gospel in fresh ways. We need scouts—women and men willing to seek the Lord for discernment into how they can best practice biblically faithful ministry in their cultures and contexts. In 1 Chronicles 12, we read about the thousands of warriors who flocked to David's side to join him in his quest to become the king over all Israel. Among that number were two hundred chiefs and all their relatives from the tribe of Issachar. They were "men who understood the times and knew what Israel should do" (1 Chr 12:32). Similarly, we need women and men who read the signs of the times and know the best course to take.

For too long, some Christians have had an anxious approach to culture, trying to assess whether certain societal trends or particular cultural artifacts are "safe" for Christian consumption. But theologian Kevin Vanhoozer proposes we become more adept at reading culture confidently and Christianly. He says,

> How should Christians interpret culture? [My proposal] advocates reading cultural texts on their own terms and in light of the biblical text. The goal of such reading is the understanding of faith: discerning the meaning of cultural texts and trends in light of the gospel of Jesus Christ.[17]

This is the very work to which contextualizers are committed. The goal is genuine understanding with a posture of openness—a posture many anxious church leaders find difficult. But in an increasingly secular West, we need guides.

Vanhoozer offers a number of reasons why we need to get better at reading culture. First, it is his view that "cultural illiteracy is harmful to our spiritual health."[18] The church needs to know what cultural trends are forming our spirit. As Vanhoozer says, "It helps to be able to name the powers and principalities that vie for the control of one's mind, soul, heart, and strength."[19]

Second, he says reading culture allows us "to be sure that the scripts [we] preform in everyday life are in accordance with the Scriptures—the story of what God is doing in Jesus Christ through the Spirit to give meaning and life to the world—rather than some other story."[20] And third, we need to become culturally literate "because we need to know where we are in the drama of redemption. The world is our stage, but culture is the setting for our next scene."[21]

I would add two more reasons. We need to be equipped to understand culture so that we can read its underlying philosophy, to be able to discern what we can affirm and what we need to resist. But also, open engagement with culture helps us to love our neighbors. It shows our willingness to listen, attend to, and take seriously the things they engage with and enjoy. As Trevin Wax of the North American Missionary Board says,

> Almost every cultural phenomenon has aspects that can be affirmed by Scripture, as well as aspects that are idolatrous distortions of the truth. To only focus on what can be affirmed is to dull the prophetic edge of the gospel's hard truth. To only focus on what should be challenged is to fail to show how the culture's longings are answered in Jesus. Above all, participate in the activities around you, understand what resonates with people to connect with them as Jesus did, and live out an exemplary Christian life.[22]

THE FUTURE CHURCH WILL BE DEVOTED TO HOLINESS, JUSTICE, AND EVANGELISM

Earlier I referred to the Asbury Revival as an example of declericalized leadership, but it is also an example of the renewed interest in integrating holiness, justice, and evangelism. The student-led meetings at Asbury's chapel didn't only invite people to a revived personal experience of God's grace; they also sought to revive the attendees' commitments to acceptance and inclusion. Laura Levens reported that prayer requests were posted on boards in the chapel.

> People prayed for the sick, for the salvation of Kentucky and other regions of the world, against spiritual warfare. They prayed over trauma, body issues, broken relationships, inclusion of marginalized students. There are hints of struggle with purity culture and body image on the boards. There is outright prayer over the harms committed by the church. I learned that a few days earlier, a student wrote a prayer for acceptance of the sacred worth of queer students that was anonymously and harshly rubbed out, only to be rewritten on the board by someone else later in the night.[23]

In her book, *The Mystic Way of Evangelism*, Elaine Heath makes a compelling case for the reintegration of holiness, justice-seeking, and evangelism. Drawing on the example of the early Christian mystics, she reminds us that holiness is not a form of rule-keeping or cultural withdrawal but rather it is a gift of God. Heath writes,

> To be holy is to be set aside exclusively for God's purposes ... We are not set aside and made holy for our own pursuits; we are now in partnership with God in God's mission ... The holiness of God's people provides both hope and agency in the transformation of the world.[24]

Heath reminds us that perhaps the greatest exemplars of holiness—the Christian mystics—were also exceptional evangelists. We saw the same thing when we studied the German pietists in an earlier chapter. True holiness, not legalism or false piety, propels God's people into the world around them. It fills us with God's love for our neighbor. Heath continues,

> Evangelism is intrinsically relational, the outcome of love of neighbor, for to love our neighbor is to share the love of God holistically. The proper context for evangelism is authentic Christian community, where the expression of loving community is the greatest apologetic for the gospel.

Holiness—being given to God and God's mission in this world—is a way of life that is expressly concerned with evangelism.[25]

As ever, the church of the future must be a holy church, and our holiness demands of us that we love our neighbors *holistically*, as servants. This involves speaking about the gospel of Christ, sharing the story and the ideas that shape our understanding of God's love for us. But it also requires that we demonstrate what the good news of the kingdom looks like in real terms, right here, right now. That in turn means we must be willing to make a stand on justice and freedom, for human dignity, even if it is to our own detriment. Whether it was St. Francis aligning himself with the poor, or Ntsikana working for nonviolence in southern Africa, or Alice Harris documenting atrocities in the Congo, or Mary Slessor rescuing abandoned babies in the Niger, we have encountered myriad ways that our forebears have undertaken this work.

But we live this way precisely because we find this vision rooted in the story of our King Jesus. As biblical scholar Esau McCauley writes,

> Kingship in the Bible is linked to justice. We see this in the royal psalms (Ps 72:1–4). According to the psalmist, the king—who reflects God's own justice—is on the side of the poor and disinherited. Jesus' kingly sonship is inseparable from God's justice because Israel's king cares for the poor.[26]

The gift of holiness insists we engage in both justice and evangelism, in both deed and word. As Newbigin says,

> I do not think the idea of "Christian presence" can replace evangelism in the life of the church. Jesus was not only himself the good news, but he was also himself the evangelist. His deeds were interpreted by words ... The words interpreted the deeds and the deeds authenticated the words.[27]

THE FUTURE CHURCH WILL BE MORAL BUT NOT MORALIZING

We must walk the fine line between morality and moralizing. So many people in our culture think Christians no longer have the moral authority to lecture them on how to live their lives. And I agree. There have been too many cases of child sexual abuse, moral failure by leaders, pastors with jets, complicity with the oppression of Indigenous peoples and minorities, and plain old garden-variety hypocrisy to set ourselves up as judges of other people's behavior. We need to recover the good and beautiful life revealed in Christ and to live out our alternate morality boldly and unambiguously, but without the moralizing.

Throughout this book we've encountered some true paragons of virtue—from German pietists such as Nikolaus von Zinzendorf and the Moravians, to the abolitionists and moral crusaders such as William Wilberforce and Earl Shaftesbury. Their campaigns weren't focused on telling others how to live. They were either beacons of an alternate ethic or they were campaigning on behalf of the silent powerless. We can learn a thing or two from these people. They practiced their morality thoughtfully and intentionally.

In an age when ethics are practiced on the Internet via memes and hot takes, and those we disagree with are routinely canceled, we need to do the hard work of researching what moral principles inform any particular issue, exploring competing principles when they arise, and determining which we find most compelling. It isn't always easy to discern how questions of human morality should be answered both in the light of the Christian message and of our contemporary world, especially when new issues emerge. We need to remain adept at seeing and appreciating alternative points of view in such a way that we can learn from others and live in peace with those who disagree with us.

But most importantly, we need to ask how we can authentically, honestly, fairly, and compassionately act on our convictions.

THE FUTURE CHURCH WILL BE SPIRITUALLY RICH

From the Benedictines and the Celts to the German pietists and the Moravians, from the British evangelicals and abolitionists to the Pentecostals, great missionary movements have emerged from dynamic, worshiping communities of faith and not merely from innovation or new methods and techniques. Likewise, the church of tomorrow will need to see how indebted the missionary enterprise is to a rich Christian spirituality.

If many of us are honest, though, we might admit that our current churches are somewhat lifeless spiritually. Someone recently quipped that most evangelical worship is like a Coldplay concert followed by a TED talk. Even mainline churches can be dominated to some extent by legalism and a pervasive spiritual mediocrity. But the church needs to strive for the mystery, joy, and freedom that birthed so many of the missionary movements we have looked at.

Secularism has stripped many people of the experience of ritual and religious tradition and left Western society utterly disenchanted. Rock star Nick Cave, who unexpectedly lost both of his young sons in recent years, has spoken about the lack of rituals that allow for a spiritual or metaphysical response to death and grief. Although not a Christian, he recently recounted how he attended an All-Souls Day service at his local church in England. Also called The Commemoration of All the Faithful Departed, this is a time of prayer and remembrance for those we have loved and who are no longer with us. Cave explained how incredibly moving it was to hear the names of all those connected with the church who had died that year, as they were solemnly read out ... for over thirty minutes. It affected him in a way that no secular funeral or wake had done.[28]

In his recent book *Faith, Hope and Carnage*, Cave discusses the spiritual-not-religious designation many people use these days, writing, "The word 'spirituality' is a little amorphous for my taste. It can mean almost anything, whereas the word 'religious' is just more specific ... Religion is spirituality with rigor, I guess, and, yes, it makes demands on us."[29]

I think churches in the future need to recognize the enormous contribution we can make to a disenchanted world. Not with a Coldplay concert and a TED talk, but as a repository of spiritual wisdom and deep religious practice—the kind that makes demands on us. Lesslie Newbigin considered this to be part of the church's priestly role in modern society, claiming that the church worships God on behalf of the whole world, just as Israel's priests offered sacrifices on behalf of the whole nation. Newbigin explains it this way:

> Indeed true Christian worship is an offering on behalf of the whole of mankind. The church as a whole is called to be God's holy priesthood for all of the human family ... This means, for example, that in our worship we should try to offer up to God all that is best in the art and music and thought of the world around us. All of it belongs to God, and all of it should be offered to God in our solemn acts of worship.[30]

In saying this I'm not suggesting traditional liturgy is the only way to express our spirituality. The African church shows us how a huge range of liturgical styles—from the traditional Anglican and Catholic churches to the Ethiopian Church movement to Pentecostalism—can shape a spiritually rich community devoted to mission, if it is Spirit-led and filled with joy and freedom.

THE FUTURE CHURCH WILL BE LOCAL AND CONNECTED

Parish Collective is a network that connects people to be the church in the neighborhood. Their founders, Tim Soerens and Paul Sparks, say their purpose is to subvert what may be the two most fragmenting forces of our day: the myth of the individual and living above place. The corrosive effects of individualism are well known, but the phrase "living above place" refers to our tendency to develop structures in our cities that insulate us from the causes and effects that are present in our lives. For example, we buy food at a grocery store without any awareness of who grew that food or where or how it was transported to that store; and we are oblivious to the effects of gentrification and changes in the built environment. Soerens, Sparks, and Dwight Friesen write,

> What happens when a society lives above place for generations? Over the course of time, whole populations can develop a cocooned way of life, unaware of how their lives really affect each other and the world at large.[31]

This combination of individualism and living above place leads to social ills like homogeneity and consumerism. And this in turn affects the church. We "shop" for churches that meet our individual preferences and desires, driving by a dozen local churches if a distant one meets our family's needs. But the Parish Collective team say, "If we don't learn to be the church in our everyday lives, we lose our power to collectively confront injustices, we ignore the gifts of our neighbors and we perpetuate the systems that keep us apart."[32]

Parish Collective's slogan—"rooted and connected"—expresses the belief that neighborhood-based churches need to be rooted deeply in the collective life of their neighbors, as well as being connected broadly to other, similar churches across the country, for support, encouragement, and ideas.

Earlier, we noted that the majority of the world's Christians will soon be living in Asia, Africa, Latin America, and Oceania, where individualism and living above place are not the great problems they are in the West. This is one of the things we need to learn from the Christians in those parts of the world. Many non-Western cultures are collectivist and highly localized. The well-known African proverb attests to this: "If you want to go fast, go alone; if you want to go far, go together." Many African churches are serving their neighborhoods selflessly and at great cost. They are doing more than most American churches do for their neighbors, despite having significantly fewer resources.

In the West, big regional megachurches, offering many programs and services, will probably continue to appeal to some. However, I think an increasing number of people will seek out local churches that are deeply rooted in the neighborhood, trusting God to weave new relationships and projects for the common good. As Majora Carter and Tim Soerens write,

It's never been more important to foster unity between all the diverse followers of Christ within our local contexts. Joining God's renewal within the broken systems of our world, we seek to reconcile fractured relationships and celebrate differences by collaborating across cultural barriers and learning to live in solidarity with those in need. If ever there was going to be a robust movement of unity in the 21st century church it will likely be lay-led, local, and in the neighborhood. When unity and trust grows between us, it is amazing how we can work together and build peace for the common good.[33]

THE FUTURE CHURCH WILL BE HYBRID AND INTERCONNECTED

Given what has been said above about the richness and beauty of Christian liturgy and worship and the need to be rooted in the neighborhood, perhaps it seems contradictory to also talk of streamed church services and hybrid digital experiences. Though it may be wise to approach some of these expressions with caution, if we really think mission is shaped like water then we can't avoid the fact that, in our time in history, we are seeing a seismic shift in human interaction brought on by the digital revolution. Today, new technologies promise to change human society as never before, and, as our historical survey showed, those involved in Christian mission have often been quick to adopt new technologies for the purpose of spreading the gospel. In our digital age, church leaders have rapidly engaged with the use of websites and social media platforms to share Christ. This will only increase in the days ahead, and we can only hope it will also deepen.

Paul Sparks and Sunia Gibbs from the Parish Collective point out how important it is for highly localized parish communities to connect across the country and around the world. They write,

> This is the most interconnected moment the world has ever experienced. While this reveals Divine diversity, the dominant stories of our time often unravel local cultures and diminish our differences, producing false homogeny and erasure. We must produce an alternative by reimagining our connections. As we intentionally build relationships across contexts, we are seeking a spacious gospel that illuminates and confronts our biases, convinces us of generous inclusion, and honors the unique way the Good News manifests itself in places different from our own. The practice of linking across parishes exposes our inequities, expands our creativity, and weaves together a church across time and place that can manifest the multi-faceted beauty of God.[34]

While this need for interconnectedness has always been important, its urgency has accelerated in the last few years. The world has recently faced an interesting confluence of streams—the arrival of a global pandemic and the emergence of information technologies that have made remote interfacing more possible than ever. Churches around the world complied with government lockdowns to help stop the spread of the COVID-19 virus, forcing them to discover and use digital solutions so they could continue to operate. Although the end of lockdowns in most countries has relieved the situation, churches, schools, seminaries, and other organizations won't ever be quite the same. The age of "hybridity" has arrived.

At first glance it might seem as though localism is threatened by the digital age. Won't too much time on screens contribute to living above place, the very thing we are seeking to avoid? Well, yes and no. An overuse of screens can indeed draw us out of meaningful engagement with our neighbors, but if used correctly, digital technologies can be the very means of developing global movements of neighborhood mission.

Canadian pastor Carey Nieuwhof recently wrote a popular article titled "3 Things That Will Be True About Growing Churches In the Future." In it he argues for the importance of hybrid church, while expressing an awareness of the grave limitations posed by the digital space.[35] The three things Nieuwhof mentions are:

Digital ministry will be about genuine connection. Nieuwhof writes, "Right now, many churches are using digital ministry for content distribution via YouTube and social, but in its fullest form, digital ministry is about people. Ultimately, the goal of digital content is not consumption, it's connection and community. The goal is not the number of followers, views, minutes watched, likes, comments (as significant as they might be). Content alone doesn't lead to engagement. Community and connection do."[36]

An experience of God will replace information about *God.* Nieuwhof is conscious of how limited the screen is for conveying serious ideas. He says, "People are hungry for true community, deeper experiences, and authentic transcendence. Which is why churches that are growing are focusing more and more on creating experiences that engage more than just the head on a Sunday but also engage the heart and relationship."[37]

Future churches will go to people, rather than expect people to come to them. Nieuwhof makes the obvious point about the convenience of access made possible in the digital space. More people can connect with a church, even if they never enter the church's physical building.

Another proponent of hybrid church is British Methodist pastor, Pete Philips. Writing on this issue he says,

> Hybrid offers a place to include people—to include disabled people, to include unwell people, to include the housebound, to include those who have fears stopping them coming into a strange place with "strange" people, to include those who work or rest when we worship on a specific timetable. Hybrid Church offers a new opportunity to include more people in the body of Christ.[38]

None of this answers the question about whether there will be hoverboards in the future. But I trust our exploration of the various shapes mission has taken throughout history has filled you with the hope that, whatever cultural trends and forces reshape mission, both today and the future, we are in safe hands. God continues to direct history, unfurling "God's Dream Society on earth, spreading out from the land of Israel to encompass the whole world."[39]

As Winston Churchill once remarked, "The future is unknowable, but the past should give us hope."[40]

BIBLIOGRAPHY

CHRISTIAN HISTORY

Allen, Roland. *The Spontaneous Expansion of the Church: And the Causes Which Hinder It*. Grand Rapids: Eerdmans, 1962.

Apess, William. *On Our Own Ground: The Complete Writings of William Apess, a Pequot*. Edited by Barry O'Connell. https://english.hku.hk/staff/kjohnson/PDF/engl6a_kj_apess_lookingglass.pdf.

Bayliss, Richard. *Provincial Cilicia and the Archaeology of Temple Conversion*. Oxford: Archaeopress, 2004.

Bruce, F. F. *The Spreading Flame: The Rise and Progress of Christianity from Its First Beginnings to the Conversion of the English*. Exeter: Paternoster Press, 1964.

Calvin, John. *Institutes of the Christian Religion*. Edited by John T. McNeill. Translated by Ford Lewis Battles. Philadelphia: Westminster Press, 1960.

Carr, E. H. *What is History?* Middlesex: Penguin Books, 1964.

Chadwick, Owen. *The Reformation*. London: Penguin Books, 1965.

Cowan, James. *The New Zealand Wars: A History of the Maori Campaigns and the Pioneering Period*, vol. 2. Auckland: W. A. G. Skinner, 1923.

D'Aubigne, Jean Henri Merle. *History of the Reformation in the Sixteenth Century*, vol. 1. Glasgow: William Collins, 1845.

Dickson, John. *Bullies and Saints: An Honest Look at the Good and Evil of Christian History*. Grand Rapids: Zondervan, 2021.

Dugmore, Clifford William. *The Journal of Ecclesiastical History*. United Kingdom: Cambridge University Press, 2003.

Edwards, David L. *Christianity: The First Two Thousand Years*. London: Cassell, 1997.

Fahs, Sophia Lyon. *Uganda's White Man of Work: A Story of Alexander M. Mackay*. New York: Young People's Missionary Movement, 1907.

Fielder, Klaus. *The Story of Faith Missions: From Hudson Taylor to Present Day Africa*. Oxford: Regnum Books, 1994.

Foster, John. *After the Apostles: Missionary Preaching of the First Three Centuries*. Sydney: ANZEA Publishers, 1972.

Hodgkins, Christopher. *Reforming Empire: Protestant Colonialism and Conscience in British Literature*. Columbia, MI: University of Missouri Press, 2022.

Holland, Tom. *Dominion: The Making of the Western Mind*. London: Little, Brown, 2019.

Hutton, J. E. *A History of the Moravian Church*. Charleston: Bibliolife, 2016.

Isichei, Elizabeth. *A History of Christianity in Africa: From Antiquity to Present*. Lawrenceville, NJ: Africa World Press, 1995.

Jeal, Tim. *Livingstone*. New Haven: Yale University Press, 2013.

Kane, J. Herbert. *A Concise History of the Christian World Mission: A Panoramic View of Missions from Pentecost to the Present*. Grand Rapids: Baker Book House, 1978.

Kenny, Robert. *The Lamb Enters the Dreaming: Nathanael Pepper and the Ruptured World*. Carlton North, AU: Scribe, 2007.

Kipling, Rudyard. "The White Man's Burden: The United States & The Philippine Islands, 1899." The Kipling Society. https://www.kiplingsociety.co.uk/poem/poems_burden.htm.

Latourette, Kenneth Scott. *A History of the Expansion of Christianity: The First Five Centuries, Volume I*. Grand Rapids: Zondervan, 1970.

——. *A History of the Expansion of Christianity: The Thousand Years of Uncertainty 500–1500 AD, Volume II*. Grand Rapids: Zondervan, 1970.

——. *The Great Century: The Americas, Australasia, and Africa*. Grand Rapids: Zondervan, 1970.

——. *The Thousand Years of Uncertainty: 500 A. D. to 1500 A. D.* Grand Rapids: Zondervan, 1970.

Lehane, Brendan. *Early Celtic Christianity*. London: Constable, 1996.

Lindsay, Andrew J. *The Life, Teaching, and Legacy of Martin Luther*. Grand Rapids: WestBow Press, 2013.

Lipner, Julius. *Brahmabandhab Upadhyay: The Life and Thought of a Revolutionary*. Delhi: Oxford University Press India, 1999.

Livingstone, W. P. *Mary Slessor of Calabar: Pioneer Missionary*. London: Hodder & Stoughton, 2013.

MacCulloch, Diarmaid. *A History of Christianity: The First Three Thousand Years*. London: Penguin, 2009.

——. *Reformation: Europe's House Divided 1490–1700*. London: Penguin, 2003.

McGrath, Alister. "C. S. Lewis." In *A Cloud of Witnesses: Ten Great Christian Thinkers*. Downers Grove: InterVarsity Press, 1990.

Meyendorff, John. *Living Tradition: Orthodox Witness in the Contemporary World*. Crestwood, NY: St. Vladimir's Seminary Press, 1978.

Morris, J. Brent. *Oberlin, Hotbed of Abolitionism: College, Community, and the Fight for Freedom and Equality in Antebellum America*. Beaufort: University of South Carolina Press, 2014.

Moss, Candida. *The Myth of Persecution: How Early Christians Invented a Story of Martyrdom*. New York: Harper Collins, 2013.

Neill, Stephen. *Twentieth Century Christianity: A Survey of Modern Religious Trends by Leading Churchmen*. London: Collins, 1962.

———. *A History of Christian Missions*. Middlesex: Penguin, 1966.

Noll, Mark. *The Rise of Evangelicalism: The Age of Edwards, Whitefield and the Wesleys*. Downers Grove: InterVarsity Press, 2003.

Perry, Arthur Latham. *Williamstown and Williams College: A History*. Charleston, SC: Nabu Press, 2011.

"Saint Boniface." *Academic Dictionaries and Encyclopedias*. Accessed May 3, 2022. https://en-academic.com/dic.nsf/enwiki/17279.

"Saint Columbanus, Abbot of Luxeuil and Bobbio (543–615)." Catholic Answers. Accessed April 6, 2022. https://www.catholic.com/encyclopedia/columbanus-saint.

Singmaster, Elsie. *Martin Luther: The Story of His Life*. Boston: Houghton Mifflin, 1917.

Smither, Edward. *Christian Mission: A Concise Global History*. Bellingham: Lexham Press, 2019.

Southern, R. W. *Western Society and the Church in the Middle Ages*. London: Penguin, 1970.

"Spirituality Matters 2017: June 1ˢᵗ–June 7ᵗʰ." Oblates of St. Francis de Sales. June 1, 2017. https://www.oblates.org/spirituality-matters-feed/spirituality-matters-2017-june-1st-june-7ᵗʰ.

Stiller, Brian C. *From Jerusalem to Timbuktu: A World Tour of the Spread of Christianity*. Downers Grove: InterVarsity Press, 2018.

Templin, J. A. *Ideology on a Frontier: The Theological Foundation of Afrikaner Nationalism, 1652–1910*. Westport, CT: Greenwood, 1984.

Trapnell, Judson. *Bede Griffiths: A Life in Dialogue*. Albany: State University of New York, 2001.

Wesley, John. *The Journal of John Wesley*. Chicago: Moody Press, 1974.

Woodbridge, John D., and Frank A. James III. *Church History, Volume 2: The Pre-Reformation to the Present Day*. Grand Rapids: Zondervan, 2013.

CULTURAL STUDIES

Lebedoff, David. *The Same Man: George Orwell and Evelyn Waugh in Love and War*. New York: Random House, 2008.

McIntyre, Alasdair. *After Virtue: A Study in Moral Virtue*. Notre Dame, IN: University of Notre Dame Press, 2007.

Ong, Walter. *Orality and Literacy: The Technologizing of the World*. New York: Methuen & Co., 1982.

Ryan, Liam. *Dammit Science, Where's My Hoverboard?: Hilarious Visions of the Future from the Past*. London: Hardie Grant Books, 2013.

FICTIONAL WORKS

Achebe, Chinua. *Things Fall Apart*. London: Penguin Publishing Group, 1994.

Cather, Willa. *Death Comes for the Archbishop*. London: Folio Society, 2008.

Hardy, Thomas. "Christmas 1924." *Winter Words in Various Moods and Metres.* New York City: MacMillan, 1928.

Kingsolver, Barbara. *The Poisonwood Bible.* New York: Harper Perennial, 1999.

Shakespeare, William. *Macbeth.* Edited by George Hunter. London: Penguin Press, 2015.

Tsiolkas, Christos. *Damascus.* Sydney: Allen & Unwin, 2019.

Zemeckis, Robert, dir. *Back to the Future.* 1985; Universal City, CA: Amblin Entertainment.

GENERAL HISTORY

Churchill, Winston. *A History of the English-Speaking Peoples: The Great Democracies,* vol. 4. London: Dodd Mead & Co., 1958.

Wall, Joseph Frazier. *Andrew Carnegie.* Oxford: Oxford University Press, 1970.

MISSION STUDIES

Adams, Graham. *Holy Anarchy: Dismantling Domination, Embodying Community, Loving Strangeness.* London: SCM Press, 2022.

Andrews, Dave. *People of Compassion.* Eugene, OR: Wipf & Stock, 2008.

Boyd, Gregory A. *Benefit of the Doubt: Breaking the Idol of Certainty.* Grand Rapids: Baker Books, 2013.

Calfee, Rodney, Caleb Crider, Larry E. McCrary, Wade Stephens, and Zach Bradley. *Tradecraft Workbook: For the Church on Mission.* Louisville: Upstream Collective, 2017.

Cave, Nick, and Seán O'Hagan. *Faith, Hope and Carnage.* Melbourne: Text Publishing, 2022.

Corbett, Steve, and Brian Fikkert. *When Helping Hurts: How to Alleviate Poverty Without Hurting the Poor… and Yourself.* Chicago: Moody Publishers, 2012.

Costanzo, Eric, Daniel Yang, and Matthew Soerens. *Inalienable: How Marginalized Kingdom Voices Can Help Save the American Church.* Grand Rapids: InterVarsity Press, 2022.

D-Davidson, Vee J. *Transforming Communication: Progressing from Cross-Cultural to Intercultural Communication of Christ.* Grand Rapids: Zondervan, 2022.

Dickson, John. *The Best Kept Secret of Christian Mission: Promoting the Gospel with More than Our Lips.* Grand Rapids: Zondervan, 2010.

Dinner Church. Accessed April 4, 2023. https://dinnerchurch.com.

Dreher, Rod. *The Benedict Option: A Strategy for Christians in a Post-Christian Nation.* New York: Penguin Random House, 2017.

Foster, Tim. *The Suburban Captivity of the Church: Contextualising the Gospel for Post-Christian Australia.* Melbourne: Acorn Press, 2014.

Frost, Michael, and Alan Hirsch. *The Shaping of Things to Come: Innovation and Mission for the 21st-Century Church,* rev. ed. Grand Rapids, MI: Baker Books, 2013.

Gampiot, Aurélien Mokoko. *Kimbanguism: An African Understanding of the Bible.* University Park, PA: Penn State University Press, 2017.

Garrison, David. *A Wind in the House of Islam: How God is Drawing Muslims Around the World to Faith in Jesus Christ.* Monument: WIGTake Publishers, 2014.

Glasser, Arthur F. "Timeless Lessons from the Western Missionary Penetration of China." In *Missiology*, vol. 1, 1973.

Guder, Darrell, ed. *Missional Church: A Vision for the Sending of the Church in North America.* Grand Rapids: Eerdmans, 1998.

———. *The Incarnation and the Church's Witness.* Eugene, OR: Wipf & Stock, 2005.

Gushee, David, and Glen Stassen. *Kingdom Ethics: Following Jesus in Contemporary Context.* Grand Rapids: William B. Eerdmans Publishing Company, 2016.

Hammond, Kim, and Darren Cronshaw. *Sentness: Six Postures of Missional Christians.* Downers Grove: InterVarsity Press, 2014.

Heath, Elaine. *The Mystic Way of Evangelism: A Contemplative Vision for Christian Outreach.* Grand Rapids: Baker Books, 2017.

Hiebert, Paul G. *The Gospel in Human Contexts: Anthropological Explorations for Contemporary Missions.* Grand Rapids: Baker Books, 2009.

Hill, Graham, ed. *Servantship: Sixteen Servants on the Four Movements of Radical Servantship.* Eugene, OR: Wipf & Stock, 2013.

Hunter, George. *The Celtic Way of Evangelism: How Christianity Can Reach the West … AGAIN.* Nashville: Abingdon Press, 2010.

Jenkins, Philip. *The Next Christendom: The Coming of Global Christianity.* Oxford: Oxford University Press, 2011.

Jones, E. Stanley. *The Christ of the Indian Road.* New York: Abingdon Press, 1925.

———. *A Song of Ascents: A Spiritual Autobiography.* Nashville: Abingdon Press, 1968.

Katongole, Emmanuel M. *African Theology Today.* Eugene, OR: Wipf & Stock, 2002.

Keller, Timothy. *Counterfeit Gods: The Empty Promises of Money, Sex, and Power, and the Only Hope That Matters.* New York: Penguin, 2009.

Kraft, Charles H., ed. *Appropriate Christianity.* Pasadena: William Carey Library, 2005.

Kullberg, Kelly Monroe, and Lael Arrington. *Faith and Culture: A Guide to a Culture Shaped by Faith.* Grand Rapids: Zondervan, 2011.

Love, Rick. *Glocal: Following Jesus in the 21st Century.* Eugene, OR: Wipf & Stock, 2017.

McCaulley, Esau. *Reading While Black: African American Biblical Interpretation as an Exercise in Hope.* Grand Rapids: InterVarsity Press, 2020.

McKnight, Scot. *One.Life: Jesus Calls, We Follow.* Grand Rapids: Zondervan, 2010.

Morrison, J. H. *The Missionary Heroes of Africa: Tales from Early Modern Missions.* New York: George H. Doran Company, 1922.

Murray, Stuart. *Post-Christendom: Church and Mission in a Strange New World.* Eugene: Cascade Books, 2018.

Neill, Stephen. *Call to Mission.* Philadelphia: Fortress Press, 1970.

Newbigin, Lesslie. *The Good Shepherd: Meditations on Christian Ministry in Today's World.* Madras: Christian Literature Society, 1977.

——. *Foolishness to the Greeks: The Gospel and Western Culture.* Grand Rapids: Eerdmans, 1986.

——. *Unfinished Agenda: An Updated Autobiography.* Eugene, OR: Wipf & Stock, 1993.

——. *The Open Secret: An Introduction to the Theology of Mission.* Grand Rapids: Eerdmans, 1995.

Padilla, Rene. *Mission Between the Times: Essays on the Kingdom.* Carlisle: Langham Monographs, 2010.

Pao, David W., and Richard R. Cook, ed. *After Imperialism: Christian Identity in China and the Global Evangelical Movement.* Cambridge: Lutterworth Press, 2012.

Romero, Robert Chao. *Brown Church: Five Centuries of Latina/o Social Justice, Theology, and Identity.* Grand Rapids: InterVarsity Press, 2020.

Sanders, Brian. *Microchurches: A Smaller Way.* Independently published, 2019.

Schmidlin, Joseph. *Catholic Mission History.* Techny, IL: Divine Word Mission Press, 1933.

Sparks, Paul, Tim Soerens, and Dwight J. Friesen. *The New Parish: How Neighborhood Churches are Transforming Mission, Discipleship and Community.* Downers Grove: InterVarsity Press, 2014.

Vanhoozer, Kevin, Charles A. Anderson, and Michael J. Sleasman, eds. *Everyday Theology: How to Read Cultural Texts and Interpret Trends.* Grand Rapids: Baker Books, 2007.

Volf, Miroslav. *Exclusion and Embrace: A Theological Exploration of Identity, Otherness, and Reconciliation.* Nashville: Abingdon Press, 2019.

Wainwright, Geoffrey. *Lesslie Newbigin: A Theological Life.* Oxford: Oxford University Press, 2000.

Warren, Max. *I Believe in the Great Commission.* Grand Rapids: Eerdmans Publishing Company, 1976.

Westmeier, Karl-Wilhelm. *The Evacuation of Shekomeko and the Early Moravian Missions to Native North Americans.* New York: Edwin Mellen Press, 1994.

Yancey, Philip. *What's So Amazing About Grace?* Grand Rapids: Zondervan, 1997.

JOURNALS AND ONLINE ARTICLES

"About OMS and the 24-7 Prayer." Order of the Mustard Seed. Accessed August 30, 2022. https://www.orderofthemustardseed.com/about/oms-and-24-7-prayer/.

"Alice Seely Harris Archive." Antislavery Usable Past. Accessed March 31, 2023. http://antislavery.nottingham.ac.uk/solr-search?facet=collection%3A%22Alice+Seeley+Harris+Archive%22.

Anderson, Gerald H. "Jones E. Stanley (1884–1973): American Methodist missionary to India, global evangelist, and author." BU School of Theology. https://www.bu.edu/missiology/missionary-biography/i-k/jones-e-stanley-1884-1973.

"Australian School Principal Says 'No Easter Parade.'" *CBN News,* January 15, 2023. https://www2.cbn.com/news/world/australian-school-principal-says-no-easter-parade.

Baker, Nick. "The Baptist pastor using Twitch and Fortnite to spread the faith." *ABC News,* March 27, 2021. https://www.abc.net.au/news/2021-03-27/the-baptist-pastor-who-s-spreading-the-faith-with-fortnite/100026318.

Bawden, Anna. "Save the Children claims most 'orphans' have living parent." *The Guardian*, November 24, 2009. https://amp.theguardian.com/society/2009/nov/24/save-the-children-orphans-report.

Beckner, W. Benjamin. "Eugène Casalis and the French Mission to Basutoland (1833-1856)." First Fruits Papers. Wilmore, KY: First Fruits Press, 2013.

"BedBible.com Reports on 2022 Worldwide Sex Trafficking Statistics." *GlobeNewswire*, February 9, 2022. https://www.globenewswire.com/news-release/2022/02/09/2382047/0/en/BedBible-com-Reports-on2022-Worldwide-Sex-Trafficking-Statistics.html.

"Being Christian in Western Europe." Pew Research Center, May 29, 2018. https://www.pewresearch.org/religion/2018/05/29/being-christian-in-western-europe/.

Bible Society. Accessed April 10, 2023. https://www.biblesociety.org.uk.

Bouma, Jeremy. "What's the Value of Studying Church History? An Excerpt from 'Church History, vol 2' Explains." Zondervan Academic, August 15, 2013. https://zondervanacademic.com/blog/whats-the-value-of-studying-church-history-an-excerpt-from-church-history-vol-2-from-pre-reformation.

"Bruce Lee, a symbol of Hong Kong revolt." *The Business Standard*. July 24, 2019. https://www.tbsnews.net/international/bruce-lee-symbol-hong-kong-revolt.

Burgess, Richard. "Bringing Back the Gospel: Reverse Mission among Nigerian Pentecostals in Britain." *Journal of Religion in Europe*, 4, 3 (2011): 429–449.

Burns, Peter. "How To Be Like Water." *Mind Cafe. Medium*, February 2, 2022. https://medium.com/mind-cafe/how-to-be-like-water-208e849698e0.

Calhoun, David B. "Mary Slessor 'Mother of All the Peoples.'" The C. S. Lewis Institute, December 4, 2010. https://www.cslewisinstitute.org/resources/mother-of-all-the-peoples/.

Carter, Majora, and Tim Soerens. "Sign 4." Parish Collective. Accessed December 12, 2022. https://www.parishcollective.org/5signs.

Challies, Tim. "The Rio Olympics and Calvin's Mission." *Challies*, August 9, 2016. https://www.challies.com/articles/the-rio-olympics-and-calvin%E2%80%99s-mission/.

Cheng-Tozun, Dorcas. "What Majority-World Missions Really Looks Like." *Christianity Today*, August 26, 2019. https://www.christianitytoday.com/ct/2019/august-web-only/what-majority-world-missions-really-looks-like.html.

Cochran, Joey. "Studying Great Evangelicals' Lives Made Me Less Ambitious." *Christianity Today*, February 17, 2022. https://www.christianitytoday.com/ct/2022/february-web-only/evangelical-controversy-abuse-scandal-less-ambitious.html.

"COVID-19 Seen Worsening Overall Trend in Human Trafficking." United Nations, February 2, 2022. https://www.unodc.org/unodc/frontpage/2021/February/share-of-children-among-trafficking-victims-increases—boys-five-times-covid-19-seen-worsening-overall-trend-in-human-trafficking—says-unodc-report.html.

Dall, Nick. "In the Name of the Father, the Son and Simon Kimbangu." *OZY*, September 4, 2019.

De Souza, T. R. "The Goa Inquisition.' ACTA INDICA. Accessed April 16, 2022. https://ishwarsharan.com/features/the-goa-inquisition-t-r-de-souza/.

Diamant, Jeff. "The countries with the 10 largest Christian populations and the 10 largest Muslim populations." Pew Research Center, April 1, 2019. https://www.pewresearch.org/fact-tank/2019/04/01/the-countries-with-the-10-largest-christian-populations-and-the-10-largest-muslim-populations/.

Dickson, John. "The Art of Losing Well." *Eternity News*, May 1, 2015, https://www.eternitynews.com.au/opinion/the-art-of-losing-well/.

Dilley, Andrea Palpant. "The Surprising Discovery About Those Colonialist, Proselytizing Missionaries." *Christianity Today*, January 8, 2014, https://www.christianitytoday.com/ct/2014/january-february/world-missionaries-made.html.

Dulles, Avery. "What Distinguishes the Jesuits?" *America the Jesuit Review*, January 15, 2007. https://www.americamagazine.org/faith/2007/01/15/what-distinguishes-jesuits.

"E. Stanley Jones." Asbury University. Accessed February 3, 2023. https://www.asbury.edu/academics/resources/library/archives/biographies/e-stanley-jones.

"Facts and Figures About Orphanage Tourism." ReThink Orphanages. Accessed March 30, 2023. https://rethinkorphanages.org/problem-orphanages/facts-and-figures-about-orphanage-tourism.

Freston, Paul. "Reverse Mission: A Discourse In Search Of Reality?" *PentecoStudies*, Vol. 9, No. 2 (2010): 153–174.

"Gaia Hypothesis." Environment and Ecology. Accessed April 4, 2023. http://environment-ecology.com/gaia/70-gaia-hypothesis.html#Controversial_concepts.

Galli, Mark. "The Man Who Wouldn't Give Up." *Christian History Institute*, 36 (1992). https://christianhistoryinstitute.org/magazine/article/man-who-would-not-give-up.

Giangravé, Claire. "Clergy shortage grows to more than 3k Catholics for every priest, Vatican data shows." *Religion News Service*, October 16, 2020. https://religionnews.com/2020/10/16/a-clergy-shortage-there-are-now-more-than-14k-catholics-for-every-priest-vatican-data-shows/.

Hadley, Mark, dir. *Undeceptions*. Episode 75, "Global Christianity." Aired August 1, 2022, podcast. https://undeceptions.com/podcast/global-christianity/?fbclid=IwAR1OdHfyLvWIt3CADjfeuT9WInakSJb2PuVNIjlsd5J0JIc8_W2wPOV99ak.

Healey, Joseph Graham. "When it Comes to Nurturing Faith, Smaller is Often Better." *America, the Jesuit Review*, May 24, 2016. https://www.americamagazine.org/issue/when-smaller-better.

Healy, Hazel. "10 Steps to World Peace." *New Internationalist*, September 18, 2018. https://newint.org/features/2018/09/18/10-steps-world-peace.

Heidler, Jeanne T. and David S. Heidler. "Manifest Destiny." *Britannica*. Accessed February 3, 2023. https://www.britannica.com/event/Manifest-Destiny.

Hiebert, Paul G. "Critical Contextualization." *International Bulletin of Mission Research* 11, no. 3 (1987): 104.

Hill, Graham Joseph. "Learning from World Christianity." Global Church Project, December 29, 2015, https://grahamjosephhill.com/post-1/.

Hodder, Edwin. "The Life and Work of the Seventh Earl of Shaftesbury." Accessed September 1, 2022. https://www.ebooksread.com/authors-eng/edwin-hodder/the-life-and-work-of-the-seventh-earl-of-shaftesbury—by-edwin-hodder-ala/page-32-the-life-and-work-of-the-seventh-earl-of-shaftesbury—by-edwin-hodder-ala.shtml.

"Home Page." Back to Jerusalem. Accessed April 4, 2023. https://backtojerusalem.com.

Keenan, Danny. "Story: Te Whiti-o-Rongomai II, Erueti." *Dictionary of New Zealand Biography*, first published in 1993, updated November 2012. https://teara.govt.nz/en/biographies/2t34/te-whiti-o-rongomai-iii-erueti.

Kim, Sebastian. "Shalom as the Dual Approach of Peacemaking and Justice-Seeking: The Case of South Korea." Fuller Studio. Accessed August 22, 2022. https://fullerstudio.fuller.edu/shalom-as-the-dual-approach-of-peacemaking-and-justice-seeking-the-case-of-south-korea/.

Kiyosaki, Robert. "Future Tense." Rich Dad, December 2007. https://www.richdad.com/future-tense.

Ladner, Keri. "The quiet rise of Christian dominionism." *The Christian Century*, September 22, 2022. https://www.christiancentury.org/article/features/quiet-rise-christian-dominionism.

Lausanne Movement. "Lausanne Occasional Paper 55: Diasporas and International Students: The New People Next Door. Accessed May 4, 2021. https://lausanne.org/content/lop/diasporas-and-international-students-the-new-people-next-door-lop-55.

Lausanne Movement. "The Cape Town Commitment: A Confession of Faith and a Call to Action." 2011. Accessed August 22, 2022. https://lausanne.org/content/ctc/ctcommitment.

"Leopold II: King of Belgium." *Britannica*. Accessed March 31, 2023. https://www.britannica.com/biography/Leopold-II-king-of-Belgium.

Levens, Laura. "What I witnessed this week at the Asbury revival." *Baptist Global News*, February 16, 2023. https://baptistnews.com/article/what-i-witnessed-this-week-at-the-asbury-revival/.

"Liberation Theology: Roman Catholicism." *Britannica*. Accessed March 31, 2023. https://www.britannica.com/topic/liberation-theology.

Lifewords. Accessed April 10, 2023. https://www.lifewords.global.

Little, John. "Count Zinzendorf (1700–1755)." *Evangelical Times*, July 1, 2000. https://www.evangelical-times.org/count-zinzendorf/.

Loyola, St. Ignatius. "Formula of the Institute of Society of Jesus." Society of Ignatians, July 21, 1550. Accessed April 3, 2023, https://societyofignatians.com/why-2/the-why-of-all-the-saints/the-why-of-all-ignatian-heroes-2/.

Mack, David. "Christians Upset Over Starbucks Cups Are Trolling Baristas." *BuzzFeed News*, November 9, 2015. https://www.buzzfeednews.com/article/davidmack/a-very-starbucks-christmas.

Magister, Sandro. "South Korea, the Asian Tiger of the Church." Chiesa, April 18, 2012. http://chiesa.espresso.repubblica.it/articolo/1350223bdc4.html?eng=y.

"Modeling the Future of Religion in America." Pew Research Center, September 13, 2022. https://www.pewresearch.org/religion/2022/09/13/modeling-the-future-of-religion-in-america/.

Moore, R. York. "Gospelizing the Social: Why Social Justice & Evangelism Work Together." Missio Nexus, April 1, 2013. https://missionexus.org/gospelizing-the-social-why-social-justice-evangelism-work-together/.

"Moravian Moment #167—Moravian Revival: A Modern Pentecost – Part 1." The Moravian Church, May 23, 2010. https://moravians.net/en/about-us/34-moravian-moments/274-moravian-moment-167.

Newbigin, Lesslie. "Evangelism in the City." Reformed Review, 41 (1987).

———. "Gospel and Culture—But Which Culture?" Missionalia, 17, 3 (1989).

Newman, Caroline. "Why Millennials are Leaving Religion but Embracing Spirituality." University of Virginia, December 14, 2015. https://news.virginia.edu/content/qa-why-millennials-are-leaving-religion-embracing-spirituality.

Newton, John. "Dependence upon God—The Sense of Sin—Doubts, Jan. 1776." The Reformed Reader. Accessed February 3, 2023. http://www.reformedreader.org/rbb/newton/letter19.htm.

———. "Thoughts Upon the African Slave Trade, 1788." Accessed February 3, 2023. https://trisagionseraph.tripod.com/Texts/African.html.

Nieuwhof, Carey. "3 Things That Will Be Tue About Growing Churches In the Future." Carey Nieuwhof. Accessed February 3, 2023. https://careynieuwhof.com/3-things-that-will-be-true-about-growing-churches-in-the-future/.

Ntabeni, Mphuthumi. "Ntsikana, the first Xhosa Christian." Southern Cross, January 14, 2014. https://www.scross.co.za/2014/01/ntsikana-the-first-xhosa-christian/.

de Oliveira, Sandro G. "Global South Reverse Mission in Europe: An Examination of the Limiting Factors and Prospects." Global Missiology, 18, 3 (July 2021). http://ojs.globalmissiology.org/index.php/english/article/view/2506.

"Oration of Frederick Douglass." American Missionary 39, no. 6 (June 1885): 164.

"Our Latest Work." Our World in Data. Accessed April 10, 2023. https://ourworldindata.org/blog.

Parker, Michael. "Mobilizing a Generation for Missions." Christianity Today, August 6, 2009. http://www.christianitytoday.com/history/2009/august/mobilizing-generation-for-missions.html.

Phillips, Pete. "What is Hybrid Church?" Premier Digital, May 5, 2021. https://www.premierdigital.info/post/what-is-hybrid-church.

Pohran, Nadya. "Both Truly Christian and Truly Indian: A 20th century example of Indianized Christianity in the visions of E. Stanley Jones." Nidān 4, no. 2 (2019): 79.

Quiggle, Gregg. "Giant with Clay Feet." Worthwhile Theology Magazine. Moody Center, December 2020. https://moodycenter.org/wp-content/uploads/2020/12/worthwhile-theology-magazine.pdf.

Quinn, Annalisa. "A church draws families together across the US-Mexico border. A wall pushes them further apart." Boston Globe, November 4, 2022. https://apps.

bostonglobe.com/special-projects/2022/10/road-trip-america/boder-church-service-tijuana.

Reed, Brian, and Hamza Syed. *The Trojan Horse Affair*. Performed by Brian Reed and Hamza Syed. 2022, New York: Serial Productions/New York Times. Podcast. https://podcasts.apple.com/us/podcast/the-trojan-horse-affair/id1606918193.

Roser, Max. "The world is awful. The world is much better. The world can be much better." Our World in Data, July 20, 2022. https://ourworldindata.org/much-better-awful-can-be-better.

Šerić, Matija. "Global Poverty: A Disease Affecting More Than a Billion People." *Eurasia Review*, January 31, 2023. https://www.eurasiareview.com/31012023-global-poverty-a-disease-affecting-more-than-a-billion-people-oped/.

Sharma, Ruchira. "'People get bored quickly': how UK teens turned to social media for their news." *The Guardian*, July 24, 2022. https://www.theguardian.com/society/2022/jul/24/people-get-bored-quickly-how-uk-teens-turned-to-social-media-for-their-news.

Smalley, William A. "Cultural Implications of an Indigenous Church." *Missiology: An International Review*, os-5, 2 (1958).

Sparks, Paul, and Sunia Gibbs. "Sign 5." Parish Collective. Accessed December 12, 2022. https://www.parishcollective.org/5signs.

Stetzer, Ed. "Insights from Keller on Contextualizing." Church Leaders, February 22, 2022. https://churchleaders.com/voices/417490-insights-from-keller-on-contextualizing.html.

———. "Ten Things We Must Do to Prepare for the Future of the Church." *Church Growth Magazine*. Accessed April 27, 2023. https://churchgrowthmagazine.com/ten-things-we-must-do-to-prepare-for-the-future-of-the-church/.

"The Amazing Journey of 24-7 Prayer." *Renewal Journal*, September 28, 2019, https://renewaljournal.com/2019/09/18/the-amazing-journey-of-24-7-prayer/.

"The Bridge to Life." Navigators. Accessed April 13, 2023. https://www.navigators.org/resource/the-bridge-to-life.

The Gideons International. Accessed April 10, 2023. https://www.gideons.org.

The Nature and Scope of Sexual Abuse of Minors by Catholic Priests and Deacons in the United States, 1950–2002 (PDF). John Jay School of Criminal Justice, 2004, https://www.usccb.org/sites/default/files/issues-and-action/child-and-youth-protection/upload/The-Nature-and-Scope-of-Sexual-Abuse-of-Minors-by-Catholic-Priests-and-Deacons-in-the-United-States-1950-2002.pdf.

"The Population of Poverty USA." Poverty USA. Accessed February 3, 2023. https://www.povertyusa.org/facts.

The Pour Over. Accessed April 10, 2023. https://www.thepourover.org.

"'The Queen of Okoyong': The legacy of Mary Slessor." *BBC News*, January 2, 2015. https://www.bbc.co.uk/news/uk-scotland-tayside-central-30577100.

"The Rule of Benedict." The Order of Saint Benedict. Accessed April 3, 2023. http://www.
    archive.osb.org/rb/text/toc.html#toc.
The World Bank. "Sharp, Long-lasting Slowdown to Hit Developing Countries
    Hard." Press Release, January 10, 2023. https://www.worldbank.org/en/news/
    press-release/2023/01/10/global-economic-prospects.
"This man is dangerous." On an Overgrown Path, July 30, 2008. https://www.
    overgrownpath.com/2008/07/this-man-is-dangerous.html.
Thompson, Clive. "Clive Thompson on the New Literacy." Wired, August 24, 2009. https://
    www.wired.com/2009/08/st-thompson-7/#ixzz0hb7Y4fLi.
Travis, John. "The C-1 to C-6 Spectrum." Evangelical Missions Quarterly, 34, 4 (October 1988).
"Vision." Parish Collective. Accessed December 12, 2022. https://www.parishcollective.
    org/vision.
Wax, Trevin. "From Stephen Colbert to Taylor Swift: 4 Reasons I Write Cultural Commentary."
    The Gospel Coalition, January 14, 2016. https://www.thegospelcoalition.org/blogs/
    trevin-wax/from-stephen-colbert-to-taylor-swift-4-reasons-i-write-cultural-commentary/.
Welby, Justin. "Archbishop Welby on the first black Anglican bishop." Anglican Communion
    News Service, June 30, 2014. https://www.anglicannews.org/news/2014/06/
    archbishop-welby-on-the-first-black-anglican-bishop.aspx.
"What Are the Spiritual Exercises?" Ignatian Spirituality and Loyola Press. Accessed April 3,
    2023. https://www.ignatianspirituality.com/ignatian-prayer/the-spiritual-exercises/
    what-are-the-spiritual-exercises.
"What Charles Dickens Saw in Rome." Rome in the Footsteps of an XVIIIth Century Traveller.
    Accessed April 12, 2022. https://www.romeartlover.it/Dickens.html.
"William Apess Leads the Bloodless Mashpee Revolt of 1833." New England Historical
    Society. Accessed November 16, 2022. https://www.newenglandhistoricalsociety.
    com/william-apess-leads-the-bloodless-mashpee-revolt-1833/.
Zurlo, Gina A., Todd M. Johnson, and Peter F. Crossing. "World Christianity and Mission 2020:
    Ongoing Shift to the Global South." International Bulletin of Mission Research 44 (2020): 12.
Zurlo, Gina. "Why the future of the world's largest religion is female—and African."
    Religion News Service, March 24, 2022. https://religionnews.com/2022/03/24/
    why-the-future-of-the-worlds-largest-religion-is-female-and-african/.
Zylstra, Sarah Eekhoff. "Made in China: The Next Mass Missionary Movement."
    Christianity Today, January 1, 2016. https://www.christianitytoday.com/ct/2016/
    january-february/made-in-china-next-mass-missionary-movement.html.

HISTORICAL WORKS/CLASSICS

Aristides. Apology of Aristides. New Advent. Accessed March 25, 2022. https://www.
    newadvent.org/fathers/1012.htm.
Cicero, Marcus Tullius. Orator ad M. Brutum. Charleston, SC: BiblioBazaar, 2009.
Clement I. Clementine Homilies. Charleston, SC: Nabu Press, 2010.

Eusebius. *Ecclesiastical History*. New Advent. Accessed March 25, 2022. https://www.newadvent.org/fathers/2501.htm.

Lactantius. *On the Anger of God*. New Advent. Accessed March 18, 2022. https://www.newadvent.org/fathers/0703.htm.

Martyr, St. Justin. *The First Apology*. New Advent, 5. Accessed March 20, 2022. https://www.newadvent.org/fathers/0126.htm.

Octavius. *Octavius*. New Advent. Accessed March 25, 2022. https://www.newadvent.org/fathers/0410.htm.

Tatian. *Address to the Greeks*. New Advent. Accessed March 20, 2022. https://www.newadvent.org/fathers/0202.htm.

Tertullian. *Apology*. New Advent. Accessed March 25, 2022. https://www.newadvent.org/fathers/0301.htm.

The Epistle of Mathetes to Diognetus. New Advent. Accessed March 25, 2022. https://www.newadvent.org/fathers/0101.htm.

NOTES

PROLOGUE: THE SHAPE OF WATER

1   The word *besar* is used in Is 40:9, 41:27, 52:7, 61:1.

2   Lesslie Newbigin, "Evangelism in the City," *Reformed Review 41*, Autumn 1987, 5.

3   E. H. Carr, *What is History?* (Middlesex, UK: Penguin Books, 1964), 44.

4   Edward Smither, *Christian Mission: A Concise Global History* (Bellingham, WA: Lexham Press, 2019), xvi.

5   Cicero, *Orator ad M. Brutum* (Charleston, SC: BiblioBazaar, 2009), chapter XXXIV, section 120 (46 BC).

6   Stephen Neill, *Call to Mission* (Philadelphia: Fortress Press, 1970), 24.

7   John Woodbridge and Frank James III, *Church History, Volume 2: The Pre-Reformation to the Present Day* (Grand Rapids: Zondervan, 2013), excerpted in Jeremy Bouma, "What's the Value of Studying Church History? An Excerpt from 'Church History, vol 2' Explains," *Zondervan Academic*, August 15, 2013, https://zondervanacademic.com/blog/whats-the-value-of-studying-church-history-an-excerpt-from-church-history-vol-2-from-pre-reformation.

8   Peter Burns, "How To Be Like Water," *Mind Café*, February 1, 2022, https://medium.com/mind-cafe/how-to-be-like-water-208e849698e0.

9   "Bruce Lee, a symbol of Hong Kong revolt," *The Business Standard*, July 24, 2019, https://www.tbsnews.net/international/bruce-lee-symbol-hong-kong-revolt.

10 Arthur Latham Perry, *Williamstown and Williams College: A History* (Charleston, SC: Nabu Press, 2011), 359.

11 For the record, they were Samuel J. Mills, James Richards, Francis LeBaron Robbins, Harvey Loomis, and Byram Green.

12 Joey Cochrane, "Studying Great Evangelicals' Lives Made Me Less Ambitious," *Christianity Today*, February 17, 2022, https://www.christianitytoday.com/ct/2022/february-web-only/evangelical-controversy-abuse-scandal-less-ambitious.html.

13 Ibid.

1. THE FIRST SHAPE: GOD SLAYING

1   Christos Tsiolkas, *Damascus* (Sydney: Allen & Unwin, 2019), 87–88.

2   Kim Hammond and Darren Cronshaw, *Sentness: Six Postures of Missional Christians* (Downers Grove: InterVarsity Press, 2014).

3   Quoted in John Foster, *After the Apostles: Missionary Preaching of the First Three Centuries* (Sydney: ANZEA Publishers, 1972), 26–27.

4   *Clementine Homilies* (Charleston, SC: Nabu Press, 2010), I.9–10.

5   Ibid.

6   Kenneth Scott Latourette, *A History of the Expansion of Christianity: The First Five Centuries, Volume I* (Grand Rapids: Zondervan, 1970), 187.

7   Lactantius, *On the Anger of God*, New Advent, 2, https://www.newadvent.org/fathers/0703.htm (accessed March 18, 2022).

8   Latourette, *The First Five Centuries*, 187.

9   Minucius Felix puts this argument on the lip of his friend Octavius in a document also titled *Octavius*. Quoted in Foster, *After the Apostles*, 58–59.

10 St. Justin Martyr, *The First Apology*, New Advent, 5, https://www7000000000.newadvent.org/fathers/0126.htm (accessed March 20, 2022).

11 The following points follow Foster, *After the Apostles*, 72ff.

12 See Acts 2:16–21 (Peter quoting Joel), Acts 2:25–28 (Peter quoting Psalms), Acts 3:12–26 (Peter quoting Deuteronomy), Acts 13:16–41 (Paul quoting Psalms), Acts 15:13–21 (James quoting Amos), and Acts 26:2–23 (Paul quoting "the prophets and Moses"). In the sermons he directed to Gentile audiences, Paul tended to appeal more to natural revelation than to Scripture.

13 Foster, *After the Apostles*, 80.

14 *The Epistle of Mathetes to Diognetus*, 7, New Advent, https://www.newadvent.org/fathers/0101.htm (accessed March 25, 2022).

15 Foster, *After the Apostles*, 80–81.

16 Ibid.

17 Tatian, *Address to the Greeks*, 29, New Advent, https://www.newadvent.org/fathers/0202.htm (accessed March 20, 2022).

18 Gregory, *Address to Origen*, quoted in Foster, 88.

19 John Dickson, *The Best Kept Secret of Christian Mission: Promoting the Gospel with More Than Our Lips* (Grand Rapids: Zondervan, 2010), 93.

20 Aristides, *Apology of Aristides*, New Advent, 15–16, https://www.newadvent.org/fathers/1012.htm (accessed March 25, 2022).

21 Tertullian, *Apology*, 37, 40, New Advent, https://www.newadvent.org/fathers/0301.htm (accessed March 25, 2022).

22 Ibid.

23 Octavius, *Octavius*, New Advent, https://www.newadvent.org/fathers/0410.htm (accessed March 25, 2022).

24 Candida Moss, *The Myth of Persecution: How Early Christians Invented a Story of Martyrdom* (New York: Harper Collins, 2013), 186.

25 Tom Holland, *Dominion: The Making of the Western Mind* (London: Little, Brown, 2019), 93–94.

26 Eusebius, *Ecclesiastical History* V. 42, *New Advent*, https://www.newadvent.org/fathers/2501.htm (accessed March 25, 2022).

27 Holland, *Dominion*, 93.

28 John Calvin, *Institutes of the Christian Religion*, ed. John T. McNeill; trans. Ford Lewis Battles; 2 vols.; LCC (Philadelphia: Westminster Press, 1960), I.11.8.

29 Timothy Keller, *Counterfeit Gods: The Empty Promises of Money, Sex, and Power, and the Only Hope That Matters* (New York: Penguin, 2009), xvii.

30 Gregory A. Boyd, *Benefit of the Doubt: Breaking the Idol of Certainty* (Grand Rapids: Baker, 2013), 64.

31 Keller, *Counterfeit Gods*, xviii.

32 Quoted in Ed Stetzer, "Insights from Keller on Contextualizing," *Church Leaders*, February 22, 2022, https://churchleaders.com/voices/417490-insights-from-keller-on-contextualizing.html.

2. THE SECOND SHAPE: PEACEMAKING

1 "Saint Boniface," *Academic Dictionaries and Encyclopedias*, https://en-academic.com/dic.nsf/enwiki/17279 (accessed May 3, 2022).

2 Richard Bayliss, *Provincial Cilicia and the Archaeology of Temple Conversion* (Oxford: Archaeopress, 2004), 39.

3 The term "Celtic" refers to the language and culture groups of Indo-European areas, including Ireland, Scotland, Wales, the Isle of Man, Cornwall, and Brittany. Later in the chapter, other, more specific, descriptors will be used to describe these missionaries.

4 Sebastian Kim, "Shalom as the Dual Approach of Peacemaking and Justice-Seeking: The Case of South Korea," *Fuller Studio*, https://fullerstudio.fuller.edu/shalom-as-the-dual-approach-of-peacemaking-and-justice-seeking-the-case-of-south-korea/ (accessed August 22, 2022).

5 Lausanne Movement, *The Cape Town Commitment: A Confession of Faith and a Call to Action* (2011), https://lausanne.org/content/ctc/ctcommitment (accessed August 22, 2022).

6 John Dickson, *Bullies and Saints: An Honest Look at the Good and Evil of Christian History* (Grand Rapids: Zondervan, 2021), 144.

7 F. F. Bruce, *The Spreading Flame: The Rise and Progress of Christianity from Its First Beginnings to Eighth-Century England* (Exeter, UK: Paternoster Press, 1964), 374. You can read the whole of Patrick's *Confessio* in English here: https://www.confessio.ie/etexts/confessio_english#.

8 Ibid.

9   George Hunter, *The Celtic Way of Evangelism: How Christianity Can Reach the West …
    Again* (Nashville: Abingdon Press, 2010), 19–20.

10 Diarmaid MacCulloch, *A History of Christianity: The First Three Thousand Years*
    (London: Penguin, 2009), 333.

11 "Saint Columbanus, Abbot of Luxeuil and Bobbio (543–615)," Catholic Answers,
    https://www.catholic.com/encyclopedia/columbanus-saint (accessed April 6, 2022).

12 Smither, *Christian Mission*, 28.

13 "Spirituality Matters 2017: June 1st–June 7ᵗʰ," *Oblates of St. Francis de Sales*, June 1,
    2017, https://www.oblates.org/spirituality-matters-feed/spirituality-matters-2017-
    june-1st-june-7th.

14 Hunter, *The Celtic Way of Evangelism*, 21.

15 Ibid., 22.

16 Ibid.

17 MacCulloch, *A History of Christianity*, 343.

18 Ibid.

19 Brendan Lehane, *Early Celtic Christianity* (London: Constable, 1996), 209.

20 MacCulloch, *A History of Christianity*, 344.

21 World Bank Press Release, "Sharp, Long-lasting Slowdown to Hit Developing
    Countries Hard," January 10, 2023, https://www.worldbank.org/en/news/
    press-release/2023/01/10/global-economic-prospects.

22 Matija Šerić, "Global Poverty: A Disease Affecting More Than a Billion
    People," *Eurasia Review*, January 31, 2023, https://www.eurasiareview.
    com/31012023-global-poverty-a-disease-affecting-more-than-a-billion-people-oped/.

23 William Shakespeare, *Macbeth*, ed. George Hunter (London: Penguin Press, 2015),
    5.5. 25–27.

24 Hazel Healy, "10 Steps to World Peace," *New Internationalist*, September 18, 2018,
    https://newint.org/features/2018/09/18/10-steps-world-peace.

3. THE THIRD SHAPE: FLAME BEARING

1   Bruce, *The Spreading Flame*, 161.

2   Ibid., 418.

3   R. W. Southern, *Western Society and the Church in the Middle Ages* (London: Penguin,
    1970), 60.

4   Quoted in Philip Yancey, *What's So Amazing About Grace?* (Grand Rapids: Zondervan,
    1997), 82.

5   The full Rule can be accessed at the Order of Saint Benedict website: http://www.
    archive.osb.org/rb/text/toc.html#toc (accessed April 3, 2023).

6   Notwithstanding Bernard's enthusiastic preaching of the Second Crusade and his
    involvement in encouraging war against the Slavic tribes in the east. See Kenneth

Scott Latourette, *A History of the Expansion of Christianity, 500–1500 AD, Volume II, The Thousand Years of Uncertainty 500–1500 AD* (Grand Rapids: Zondervan, 1970), 193.

7   "What Are the Spiritual Exercises?" Ignatian Spirituality and Loyola Press, https:// www.ignatianspirituality.com/ignatian-prayer/the-spiritual-exercises/what-are-the-spiritual-exercises/ (accessed April 3, 2023).

8   Ibid.

9   Stephen Neill, *A History of Christian Missions* (Middlesex UK: Penguin, 1966), 148.

10   MacCulloch, *A History of Christianity*, 705.

11   Owen Chadwick, *The Reformation* (London: Penguin, 1965), 335.

12   St. Ignatius Loyola, "Formula of the Institute of Society of Jesus," July 21, 1550, cited by the Society of Ignatians in "The Only Why: St. Ignatius' Bottom Line," https:// societyofignatians.com/why-2/the-why-of-all-the-saints/the-why-of-all-ignatian-heroes-2/ (accessed April 3, 2023).

13   Avery Dulles, "What Distinguishes the Jesuits?" *America the Jesuit Review*, January 15, 2007, https://www.americamagazine.org/faith/2007/01/15/ what-distinguishes-jesuits.

14   Diarmaid MacCulloch, *Reformation: Europe's House Divided 1490–1700* (London: Penguin, 2003), 645.

15   Rod Dreher, *The Benedict Option: A Strategy for Christians in a Post-Christian Nation* (New York: Penguin Random House, 2017), 19.

16   Alasdair McIntyre, *After Virtue: A Study in Moral Virtue* (Notre Dame, IN: University of Notre Dame Press, 2007), 245.

17   All this information and more can be found at Our World in Data, https:// ourworldindata.org/blog (accessed April 10, 2023).

18   Holland, *Dominion*, 514–517.

19   See United Nations, "COVID-19 Seen Worsening Overall Trend in Human Trafficking," February 2, 2022, https://www.unodc.org/unodc/frontpage/2021/February/share-of-children-among-trafficking-victims-increases–boys-five-times-covid-19-seen-worsening-overall-trend-in-human-trafficking–says-unodc-report.html.

20   GlobeNewswire, "BedBible.com Reports on 2022 Worldwide Sex Trafficking Statistics," February 9, 2022, https://www.globenewswire.com/ news-release/2022/02/09/2382047/0/en/BedBible-com-Reports-on2022-Worldwide-Sex-Trafficking-Statistics.html.

21   Poverty USA, "The Population of Poverty USA," https://www.povertyusa.org/facts (accessed February 3, 2023).

22   Max Roser, "The world is awful. The world is much better. The world can be much better," Our World in Data, July 20, 2022, https://ourworldindata.org/ much-better-awful-can-be-better.

4. THE FOURTH SHAPE: SPIRIT SEEKING

1   Quoted in John Meyendorff, *Living Tradition: Orthodox Witness in the Contemporary World* (Crestwood, NY: St Vladimir's Seminary Press, 1978), 173.

2   Elsie Singmaster, *Martin Luther: The Story of His Life* (Boston: Houghton Mifflin, 1917), 35.

3   Andrew J. Lindsay, *The Life, Teaching, and Legacy of Martin Luther* (Grand Rapids: WestBow Press, 2013), 12.

4   Quoted in "What Charles Dickens Saw in Rome," Rome in the Footsteps of an XVIIIth Century Traveller, https://www.romeartlover.it/Dickens.html (accessed April 12, 2022).

5   Quoted in Jean Henri Merle D'Aubigne, *History of the Reformation in the Sixteenth Century,* Vol I (Glasgow: Collins, 1845), 148.

6   Joseph Schmidlin, *Catholic Mission History* (Techny, IL: Divine Word Mission Press, 1933), 259.

7   Herbert J. Kane, *A Concise History of the Christian World Mission: A Panoramic View of Missions from Pentecost to the Present* (Grand Rapids: Baker Book House, 1978), 75.

8   Tim Challies, "The Rio Olympics and Calvin's Mission," Challies, August 9, 2016, https://www.challies.com/articles/the-rio-olympics-and-calvin%E2%80%99s-mission/.

9   Kane, *Concise History of the Christian World Mission,* 76.

10   Ibid.

11   John Little, "Count Zinzendorf (1700–1755)," *Evangelical Times,* July 1, 2000, https://www.evangelical-times.org/count-zinzendorf/.

12   In the previous chapter, I spoke of the early Jesuits as a great missionary movement; but, as with all long-lasting global organizations, it is difficult to sustain the core values of a movement. In subsequent generations Jesuits did both honorable and dishonorable things. Their relentless persecution of the Hussites and Moravians (and others they supposed to be enemies of the papacy) was brutal. And in chapter five, we will see some reprehensible behavior by Jesuit missionaries around Goa and in the Bay of Bengal in India.

13   David L. Edwards, *Christianity: The First Two Thousand Years* (London: Cassell, 1997), 394.

14   Quoted in "Moravian Moment # 167—Moravian Revival: A Modern Pentecost – Part 1," The Moravian Church, May 23, 2010, https://moravians.net/en/about-us/34-moravian-moments/274-moravian-moment-167.

15   MacCulloch, *Reformation,* 700.

16   John Wesley, *The Journal of John Wesley* (Chicago: Moody Press, 1974), 35.

17   Ibid., 35–36.

18   Ibid., 36.

19   J. E. Hutton, *A History of the Moravian Church: The Moravians—Founding the Early Protestant Church as The Bohemian Bretheren, and the Christian Revival in 18th Century Germany* (Charleston, SC: Bibliolife, 2016), 194.

20 From Herman Melville's *White-Jacket,* quoted in Christopher Hodgkins, *Reforming Empire: Protestant Colonialism and Conscience in British Literature* (Columbia, MI: University of Missouri Press, 2022), 245.

21 Karl-Wilhelm Westmeier, *The Evacuation of Shekomeko and the Early Moravian Missions to Native North Americans* (New York: Edwin Mellen Press, 1994), 425.

22 Mark A. Noll, *The Rise of Evangelicalism: The Age of Edwards, Whitefield and the Wesleys* (Downers Grove: InterVarsity Press, 2010), 162.

23 See "About OMS and 24-7 Prayer," Order of the Mustard Seed, https://www.orderofthemustardseed.com/about/oms-and-24-7-prayer/ (accessed August 30, 2022).

24 See Order of the Mustard Seed, https://www.orderofthemustardseed.com (accessed August 30, 2022).

25 "The Amazing Journey of 24-7 Prayer," *Renewal Journal,* September 28, 2019, https://renewaljournal.com/2019/09/18/the-amazing-journey-of-24-7-prayer/.

5. THE FIFTH SHAPE: WORDSMITHING

1 Sophia Lyon Fahs, *Uganda's White Man of Work: A Story of Alexander M. Mackay* (New York: YPMM, 1907), 5.

2 £5,000 would equate to almost $132,000 today.

3 Quoted in J. H. Morrison, *The Missionary Heroes of Africa: Tales from Early Modern Missions* (New York: George H Doran Company, 1922), 176.

4 Dictionary.com, s.v. "Enlightenment."

5 Kane, *A Concise History of the Christian World Mission,* 96.

6 Quoted in Arthur F Glasser, "Timeless Lessons from the Western Missionary Penetration of China," *Missiology,* Vol. 1, 1973, 462.

7 MacCulloch, *A History of Christianity,* 874.

8 Quoted in Andrea Palpant Dilley, "The Surprising Discovery About Those Colonialist, Proselytizing Missionaries," *Christianity Today,* January 8, 2014, https://www.christianitytoday.com/ct/2014/january-february/world-missionaries-made.html.

9 Quoted in David Lebedoff, *The Same Man: George Orwell and Evelyn Waugh in Love and War* (New York: Random House, 2008), 6.

10 Edwin Hodder, "The Life and Work of the Seventh Earl of Shaftesbury," https://www.ebooksread.com/authors-eng/edwin-hodder/the-life-and-work-of-the-seventh-earl-of-shaftesbury-by-edwin-hodder-ala/page-32-the-life-and-work-of-the-seventh-earl-of-shaftesbury-by-edwin-hodder-ala.shtml (accessed September 1, 2022).

11 Rudyard Kipling, *The White Man's Burden* (1899).

12 See Jeanne T. Heidler and David S. Heidler, "Manifest Destiny," Britannica, for more information, https://www.britannica.com/event/Manifest-Destiny (accessed February 3, 2023).

13 T. R. De Souza, "The Goa Inquisition," ACTA INDICA, https://ishwarsharan.com/features/the-goa-inquisition-t-r-de-souza/ (accessed April 16, 2022).

14 Dilley, "The Surprising Discovery About Those Colonialist, Proselytizing Missionaries."

15 Ibid.

16 Walter Ong, *Orality and Literacy: The Technologizing of the World* (New York: Methuen & Co, 1982), 129.

17 Ruchira Sharma, "'People get bored quickly': how UK teens turned to social media for their news," *The Guardian*, July 24, 2022, https://www.theguardian.com/society/2022/jul/24/people-get-bored-quickly-how-uk-teens-turned-to-social-media-for-their-news.

18 Quoted in Clive Thompson, "Clive Thompson on the New Literacy," *Wired*, August 24, 2009, https://www.wired.com/2009/08/st-thompson-7/#ixzz0hb7Y4fLi.

19 Ibid.

20 Ong, *Orality and Literacy*, 70.

21 https://www.gideons.org (accessed April 10, 2023).

22 https://www.biblesociety.org.uk (accessed April 10, 2023).

23 https://www.lifewords.global (accessed April 10, 2023).

24 https://www.thepourover.org (accessed April 10, 2023).

25 https://www.pastorskar.com (accessed April 10, 2023).

26 Nick Baker, "The Baptist pastor using Twitch and Fortnite to spread the faith," *ABC News*, March 27, 2021, https://www.abc.net.au/news/2021-03-27/the-baptist-pastor-who-s-spreading-the-faith-with-fortnite/100026318.

6. THE SIXTH SHAPE: FREEDOM FIGHTING

1 Quoted in Emmanuel M. Katongole, *African Theology Today* (Eugene, OR: Wipf & Stock, 2002), 122–123.

2 "Leopold II: King of Belgium," https://www.britannica.com/biography/Leopold-II-king-of-Belgium (accessed March 31, 2023).

3 See "Alice Seely Harris Archive," Antislavery Usable Past, http://antislavery.nottingham.ac.uk/solr-search?facet=collection%3A%22Alice+Seeley+Harris+Archive%22 (accessed March 31, 2023).

4 Klaus Fielder, *The Story of Faith Missions: From Hudson Taylor to Present Day Africa* (Oxford: Regnum Books, 1994), 245.

5 MacCulloch, *A History of Christianity*, 870.

6 John Newton, "Dependence upon God—The Sense of Sin—Doubts, Jan 1776," *The Reformed Reader*, http://www.reformedreader.org/rbb/newton/letter19.htm (accessed February 3, 2023).

7 John Newton, "Thoughts Upon the African Slave Trade, 1788," https://trisagionseraph.tripod.com/Texts/African.html (accessed February 3, 2023).

8 Tim Jeal, *Livingstone* (New Haven: Yale University Press, 2013), 296.

9   "'The Queen of Okoyong': The legacy of Mary Slessor," *BBC News*, January 2, 2015, https://www.bbc.co.uk/news/uk-scotland-tayside-central-30577100.

10 Chinua Achebe, *Things Fall Apart* (London: Penguin, 1994), 125.

11 Ibid., 61.

12 W. P. Livingstone, *Mary Slessor of Calabar: Pioneer Missionary* (London: Hodder & Stoughton, 2013), 157.

13 See, for example, David B. Calhoun "Mary Slessor 'Mother of All the Peoples,'" *Knowing & Doing: C. S. Lewis Institute*, December 4, 2010, https://www.cslewisinstitute.org/resources/mother-of-all-the-peoples/.

14 See, for example, "Facts and Figures About Orphanage Tourism," ReThink Orphanages, https://rethinkorphanages.org/problem-orphanages/facts-and-figures-about-orphanage-tourism (accessed March 30, 2023).

15 Anna Bawden, "Save the Children claims most 'orphans' have living parent," *The Guardian*, November 24, 2009, https://amp.theguardian.com/society/2009/nov/24/save-the-children-orphans-report.

16 "Oration of Frederick Douglass," *American Missionary* 39, no. 6 (June 1885): 164.

17 Gregg Quiggle, "Giant with Clay Feet," *Worthwhile Theology Magazine*, Moody Center, December 2020, https://moodycenter.org/wp-content/uploads/2020/12/worthwhile-theology-magazine.pdf, 16.

18 J. Brent Morris, *Oberlin, Hotbed of Abolitionism: College, Community, and the Fight for Freedom and Equality in Antebellum America* (Beaufort: University of South Carolina Press, 2014), 3.

19 J. A. Templin, *Ideology on a Frontier: The Theological Foundation of Afrikaner Nationalism, 1652–1910* (Westport, CT: Greenwood, 1984), 8–9.

20 See "Liberation Theology: Roman Catholicism," Britannica, https://www.britannica.com/topic/liberation-theology (accessed March 31, 2023).

21 George McCall Theale, *Basuto Record: Copies of Official Documents of Various Kinds from 1833 to 1868*, quoted in W. Benjamin Beckner, "Eugène Casalis and the French Mission to Basutoland (1833–1856)," *First Fruits Papers* (Wilmore, KY: First Fruits Press, 2013), 205.

22 Beckner, "Eugène Casalis and the French Mission to Basutoland (1833–1856)," 194.

23 Max Warren, *I Believe in the Great Commission* (Grand Rapids: Eerdmans Publishing Company, 1976), 110.

24 See Lesslie Newbigin, *The Open Secret: An Introduction the Theology of Mission* (Grand Rapids: Eerdmans, 1995), 110, 113.

25 Steve Corbett and Brian Fikkert, *When Helping Hurts: How to Alleviate Poverty Without Hurting the Poor … and Yourself* (Chicago: Moody Publishers, 2012), 61–62.

26 Ibid.

27 Darrell Guder, *The Incarnation and the Church's Witness* (Eugene, OR: Wipf & Stock, 2005), xii-xiii.

7. THE SEVENTH SHAPE: UNSHACKLING

1   Justin Welby, "Archbishop Welby on the first black Anglican bishop," *Anglican Communion News Service*, June 30, 2014, https://www.anglicannews.org/news/2014/06/archbishop-welby-on-the-first-black-anglican-bishop.aspx.

2   David Garrison, *A Wind in the House of Islam: How God is Drawing Muslims Around the World to Faith in Jesus Christ* (Monument, CO: WIGTake Publishers, 2014), 244.

3   William A. Smalley, "Cultural Implications of an Indigenous Church: A Practical Anthropology," (1958), 55.

4   Roland Allen, *The Spontaneous Expansion of the Church: And the Causes Which Hinder It* (Grand Rapids: Eerdmans, 1962), 42.

5   Quoted in Brian C. Stiller, *From Jerusalem to Timbuktu: A World Tour of the Spread of Christianity* (Downers Grove: InterVarsity Press, 2018), 80.

6   Elizabeth Isichei, *A History of Christianity in Africa: From Antiquity to the Present* (New Jersey: Africa World Press, 1995), 101.

7   Mphuthumi Ntabeni, "Ntsikana, the first Xhosa Christian," *The Southern Cross*, January 14, 2014, updated October 10, 2016, https://www.scross.co.za/2014/01/ntsikana-the-first-xhosa-christian/.

8   Ibid.

9   Ibid.

10 Ibid.

11 Stiller, *From Jerusalem to Timbuktu*, 78.

12 Danny Keenan, "Story: Te Whiti-o-Rongomai III, Erueti," *Dictionary of New Zealand Biography*, first published in 1993, updated November 2012, https://teara.govt.nz/en/biographies/2t34/te-whiti-o-rongomai-iii-erueti.

13 Ibid.

14 Quoted in Dave Andrews, *People of Compassion* (Eugene, OR: Wipf & Stock, 2008), 56.

15 James Cowan, *The New Zealand Wars: A History of the Maori Campaigns and the Pioneering Period*, Vol. 2 (Auckland: W. A. G. Skinner, government printer, 1923), 505.

16 "Te Whiti," *New Zealand History*, https://nzhistory.govt.nz/people/erueti-te-whiti-o-rongomai-iii, updated December 12, 2019.

17 Quoted in "William Apess Leads the Bloodless Mashpee Revolt of 1833," New England Historical Society, https://www.newenglandhistoricalsociety.com/william-apess-leads-the-bloodless-mashpee-revolt-1833/ (accessed November 16, 2022).

18 Ibid.

19 Ibid.

20 William Apess, *On Our Own Ground: The Complete Writings of William Apess, a Pequot*, ed. Barry O'Connell, https://english.hku.hk/staff/kjohnson/PDF/engl6a_kj_apess_lookingglass.pdf. 1.

21 Ibid.

22 Kenneth Scott Latourette, *The Great Century: The Americas, Australasia, and Africa* (Grand Rapids: Zondervan, 1970), 203.

23 Graham Adams, *Holy Anarchy: Dismantling Domination, Embodying Community, Loving Strangeness* (London: SCM Press, 2022), 121.

8. THE EIGHT SHAPE: CONTEXTUALIZING

1   Robert Kenny, *The Lamb Enters the Dreaming: Nathanael Pepper and the Ruptured World* (Carlton North, AU: Scribe, 2007).

2   Barbara Kingsolver, *The Poisonwood Bible* (New York: HarperPerennial, 1999), 276.

3   Quoted in David W. Pao and Richard R. Cook, *After Imperialism: Christian Identity in China and the Global Evangelical Movement* (Cambridge: Lutterworth Press, 2012), 15.

4   René Padilla, *Mission Between the Times: Essays on the Kingdom* (Carlisle, UK: Langham Monographs, 2010), 113.

5   Stetzer, "Insights From Keller on Contextualizing."

6   Michael Parker, "Mobilizing a Generation for Missions," *Christianity Today*, August 6, 2009, http://www.christianitytoday.com/history/2009/august/mobilizing-generation-for-missions.html.

7   Ibid.

8   "E.StanleyJones", AsburyUniversity, Biographies, https://www.asbury.edu/academics/resources/library/archives/biographies/e-stanley-jones (accessed February 3, 2023).

9   Rick Love, *Glocal: Following Jesus in the 21st Century* (Eugene, OR: Wipf & Stock, 2017), 38–39.

10 E. Stanley Jones, *The Christ of the Indian Road* (New York: Abingdon Press, 1925), 212.

11 Jones's ashram movement shouldn't be confused with a Catholic version founded by the seventeenth-century Italian Jesuit priest Roberto de Nobili, a Christian missionary who adopted the various forms of a Hindu *sannyāsi*. That movement embraces Vedanta and the teachings of the East, attempting to combine them with the Christian faith. As we'll see later, Jones's movement was more distinctly Christian, adopting mainly the outward appearance of ashram practice rather than Eastern teachings.

12 Charles Van Engen, "Toward a Contextually Appropriate Methodology in Mission Theology," in Charles Kraft, *Appropriate Christianity* (Pasadena: William Carey Library, 2005), 194.

13 Quoted in Vee J. D-Davidson, *Transforming Communication: Progressing from Cross-Cultural to Intercultural Communication of Christ* (Grand Rapids: Zondervan, 2022), 212.

14 Julius Lipner, *Brahmabandhab Upadhyay: The Life and Thought of a Revolutionary* (Delhi: Oxford University Press India, 1999), 209.

15 Judson Trapnell, *Bede Griffiths: A Life in Dialogue* (Albany: State University of New York, 2001), 193.

16 "This man is dangerous," On an Overgrown Path, July 30, 2008, https://www. overgrownpath.com/2008/07/this-man-is-dangerous.html.

17 E Stanley Jones, *A Song of Ascents: A Spiritual Autobiography* (Nashville: Abingdon Press, 1968), 220–221.

18 Ibid., 22.

19 Nadya Pohran, "Both Truly Christian and Truly Indian: A 20th century example of Indianized Christianity in the visions of E. Stanley Jones," *Nidān*, Volume 4, No. 2, December 2019, 73.

20 John Travis, "The C-1 to C-6 Spectrum," *Evangelical Missions Quarterly* 34:4 (October 1998), 408.

21 Gerald H. Anderson, "Jones, E. Stanley (1884-1973): American Methodist missionary to India, global evangelist, and author," BU School of Theology, reprinted from Gerald H. Anderson, *Biographical Dictionary of Christian Missions* (New York: Macmillan Reference USA, 1998), https://www.bu.edu/missiology/missionary-biography/i-k/jones-e-stanley-1884-1973 (accessed April 26, 2023).

22 Nick Dall, "In the Name of the Father, the Son and Simon Kimbangu," *OZY*, September 4, 2019, https://web.archive.org/web/20191104151419/https://www.ozy.com/flashback/in-the-name-of-the-father-the-son-and-simon-kimbangu/96261/.

23 MacCulloch, *A History of Christianity*, 964–965. MacCulloch's quotation regarding "the prophets of Satan, missionaries, the Belgian government" was attributed to Kimbangu after his death. See MacCulloch's footnote 101 on p. 965.

24 Aurélien Mokoko Gampiot, *Kimbanguism: An African Understanding of the Bible* (University Park, PA: Penn State University Press, 2017), vi.

25 Dall, "In the Name of the Father, the Son and Simon Kimbangu."

26 Stephen Neill, *Twentieth Century Christianity* (London: Collins, 1962), 243.

27 Kingsolver, *The Poisonwood Bible*, 276.

28 Quoted in Paul G. Hiebert, *The Gospel in Human Contexts: Anthropological Explorations for Contemporary Missions* (Grand Rapids: Baker Books, 2009), 26.

29 This list is summarized from Rodney Calfee, Caleb Crider, Larry McCrary, et al., *Tradecraft Workbook* (Louisville: Upstream Collective, 2017), chapter four.

30 Paul G. Hiebert, "Critical Contextualization," *International Bulletin of Mission Research*, Volume 11, Issue 3, 1987, 104.

31 Ibid.

32 Stetzer, "Insights from Keller on Contextualizing."

9. THE NINTH SHAPE: REMISSIONING

1 Andrew Carnegie, *The Autobiography of Andrew Carnegie and His Essay The Gospel of Wealth* (Mineola, NY: Dover Publications, 2014), 249.

2 Joseph Frazier Wall, *Andrew Carnegie* (Oxford: Oxford University Press, 1970), 1013.

3   Thomas Hardy, "Christmas 1924," *Winter Words in Various Moods and Metres* (New York City: MacMillan, 1928).

4   Quoted in Miroslav Volf, *Exclusion and Embrace* (Nashville: Abingdon Press, 2019), 279.

5   Stuart Murray, *Post-Christendom: Church and Mission in a Strange New World* (Eugene, OR: Cascade Books, 2018), 132.

6   Clifford William Dugmore, *The Journal of Ecclesiastical History* (United Kingdom: Cambridge University Press, 2003), 184.

7   Murray, *Post-Christendom*, 150.

8   Darrell L. Guder (ed.), *Missional Church: A Vision for the Sending of the Church in North America* (Grand Rapids: Eerdmans, 1998), 7.

9   Lesslie Newbigin, *Unfinished Agenda* (Eugene, OR: Wipf & Stock, 1993), 90.

10 Ibid., 106.

11 Lesslie Newbigin, *The Open Secret: An Introduction the Theology of Mission* (Grand Rapids: Eerdmans, 1995), 29.

12 Lesslie Newbigin, *Foolishness to the Greeks* (Grand Rapids: Eerdmans, 1986), 1.

13 Ibid., 79.

14 Ibid., 143.

15 Geoffrey Wainwright, *Lesslie Newbigin: A Theological Life* (Oxford: Oxford University Press, 2000), 383.

16 Summarized from Newbigin, *Foolishness to the Greeks*.

17 Guder, *Missional Church*, 6.

18 Ibid., 4.

19 Ibid., 11–12.

20 Gina A. Zurlo, Todd M. Johnson, and Peter F. Crossing, "World Christianity and Mission 2020: Ongoing Shift to the Global South," *International Bulletin of Mission Research*, 2020, Vol. 44, 12.

21 Graham Joseph Hill, "Learning from Majority World, Indigenous, & Diaspora Christians," Graham Hill/Global Church Project, December 29, 2015, https://grahamjosephhill.com/post-1/.

22 Smither, *Christian Mission*, 184.

23 Sarah Eekhoff Zylstra, "Made in China: The Next Mass Missionary Movement," *Christianity Today*, January 1, 2016, https://www.christianitytoday.com/ct/2016/january-february/made-in-china-next-mass-missionary-movement.html.

24 See https://backtojerusalem.com (accessed April 4, 2023).

25 Zylstra, "Made in China: The Next Mass Missionary Movement."

26 Jeff Diamant, "The countries with the 10 largest Christian populations and the 10 largest Muslim populations," Pew Research Center, April 1, 2019, https://www.pewresearch.org/fact-tank/2019/04/01/the-countries-with-the-10-largest-christian-populations-and-the-10-largest-muslim-populations/.

27 Sandro G. de Oliveira, "Global South Reverse Mission in Europe: An Examination of the Limiting Factors and Prospects," *Global Missiology*, Vol. 18, No. 3 (July 2021), http://ojs.globalmissiology.org/index.php/english/article/view/2506.

28 Quoting Paul Freston in "Reverse Mission: A Discourse In Search Of Reality?" *PentecoStudies*, Vol. 9, No. 2 (2010): 153–74. Available online at https://doi.org/10.1558/ptcs.v9.i2.8948 (accessed June 28, 2021).

29 Quoting Richard Burgess, "Bringing Back the Gospel: Reverse Mission among Nigerian Pentecostals in Britain," *Journal of Religion in Europe 4* (3), 2011: 429–49. Available online at https://doi.org/10.1163/187489211X593499.

30 Oliveira, "Global South Reverse Mission in Europe."

31 Ibid.

32 Ibid.

33 Ibid.

34 Ibid.

35 Ibid.

36 Dorcas Cheng-Tozun, "What Majority-World Missions Really Looks Like," *Christianity Today*, August 26, 2019, https://www.christianitytoday.com/ct/2019/august-web-only/what-majority-world-missions-really-looks-like.html.

37 Oliveira, "Global South Reverse Mission in Europe."

38 Lausanne Committee for World Evangelization, *Lausanne Occasional Paper 55: Diasporas and International Students: The New People Next Door*, 2004, https://lausanne.org/content/lop/diasporas-and-international-students-the-new-people-next-door-lop-55 (accessed May 4, 2021).

39 Quoted in Graham Hill, *Servantship: Sixteen Servants on the Four Movements of Radical Servantship* (Eugene, OR: Wipf & Stock, 2013), 89.

40 See, for example, Keri Ladner, "The quiet rise of Christian dominionism," *The Christian Century*, September 22, 2022, https://www.christiancentury.org/article/features/quiet-rise-christian-dominionism.

10. THE TENTH SHAPE: UNEARTHING

1 Willa Cather, *Death Comes for the Archbishop* (London: Folio Society, 2008), 154.

2 Ibid.

3 Pew Research Center, "Modeling the Future of Religion in America," September 13, 2022, https://www.pewresearch.org/religion/2022/09/13/modeling-the-future-of-religion-in-america/.

4 Pew Research Center, "Being Christian in Western Europe," May 29, 2018, https://www.pewresearch.org/religion/2018/05/29/being-christian-in-western-europe/.

5 Summarized from "Being Christian in Western Europe."

6 Brian Reed and Hamza Syed, "The Trojan Horse Affair," February 2022 in *Serial*, produced by Serial Productions/New York Times, podcast, https://podcasts.apple.com/us/podcast/the-trojan-horse-affair/id1606918193.

7   John Dickson, "The Art of Losing Well," *Eternity News*, May 1, 2015, https://www. eternitynews.com.au/opinion/the-art-of-losing-well/.

8   Ibid.

9   Ibid.

10 David Mack, "Christians Upset Over Starbucks Cups Are Trolling Baristas," *BuzzFeed News*, November 9, 2015, https://www.buzzfeednews.com/article/ davidmack/a-very-starbucks-christmas.

11 "Australian School Principal Says 'No Easter Parade,'" CBN News, *Christian Broadcasting Network*, January 15, 2023, https://www2.cbn.com/news/world/ australian-school-principal-says-no-easter-parade.

12 Annalisa Quinn, "A church draws families together across the US-Mexico border. A wall pushes them further apart," *Boston Globe*, November 4, 2022, https://apps.bostonglobe. com/special-projects/2022/10/road-trip-america/boder-church-service-tijuana.

13 Eric Costanzo, Daniel Yang, and Matthew Soerens, *Inalienable: How Marginalized Kingdom Voices Can Help Save the American Church* (Downers Gove: InterVarsity Press, 2022), 29.

14 Lesslie Newbigin, "Gospel and Culture—But Which Culture?" *Missionalia*, 17, 3 (1989): 213.

15 Tim Foster, *The Suburban Captivity of the Church* (Melbourne: Acorn, 2014), 22.

16 *The Bridge to Life*, Navigators, https://www.navigators.org/resource/the-bridge-to-life/ (accessed April 13, 2023).

17 Foster, *The Suburban Captivity of the Church*, 22.

18 Scot McKnight, "The Small and Big Gospel," in Kelly Monroe Kullberg and Lael Arrington, *Faith and Culture: A Guide to a Culture Shaped by Faith* (Grand Rapids: Zondervan, 2011), 273.

19 David Gushee and Glen Stassen, *Kingdom Ethics: Following Jesus in Contemporary Context* (Grand Rapids: William B. Eerdmans Publishing Company, 2016), 33–37.

20 Robert Chao Romero, *Brown Church: Five Centuries of Latina/o Social Justice, Theology, and Identity* (Downers Grove: InterVarsity Press, 2020), 12.

21 *The Nature and Scope of Sexual Abuse of Minors by Catholic Priests and Deacons in the United States*, 1950–2002 (PDF), John Jay School of Criminal Justice, 2004, https:// www.usccb.org/sites/default/files/issues-and-action/child-and-youth-protection/ upload/The-Nature-and-Scope-of-Sexual-Abuse-of-Minors-by-Catholic-Priests-and-Deacons-in-the-United-States-1950-2002.pdf (accessed April 30, 2023).

22 Ibid.

23 @Alyssa_Milano, Twitter, October 15, 2017, https://twitter.com/Alyssa_Milano/ status/919659438700670976.

24 Vanora Bennett, "2019, the year the world woke up to climate change," European Bank for Reconstruction and Development, November 27, 2019, https://www.ebrd.com/ news/2019/2019-the-year-the-world-woke-up-to-climate-change.html.

25 Gaia theory is a controversial view on environmentalism that states that the earth and all living creatures evolve as a single, coevolutionary process. First proposed in the

1960s by James Lovelock, Gaia theory is named for the primordial Greek goddess of the earth. For more information, see "Gaia Hypothesis," Environment and Ecology, http://environment-ecology.com/gaia/70-gaia-hypothesis.html#Controversial_ concepts (accessed April 4, 2023).

26 Associated Press, "Climate protestors rally as Europe votes on parliament," *New York Post*, May 24, 2019, https://nypost.com/2019/05/24/climate-protesters-rally-as-europe-votes-on-parliament/.

27 Leah MarieAnn Klett, "1,700-year-old Christian church uncovered in Ethiopia sheds new light on spread of Christianity," *The Christian Post*, December 31, 2019, https://www.christianpost.com/news/1700-year-old-christian-church-uncovered-in-ethiopia-sheds-new-light-on-spread-of-christianity.html.

28 C. S. Lewis, in Alister McGrath, *A Cloud of Witnesses: Ten Great Christian Thinkers* (Downers Grove: InterVarsity Press, 1990), 127.

29 R. York Moore, "Gospelizing the Social: Why Social Justice & Evangelism Work Together," *Missio Nexus*, April 1, 2013, https://missionexus.org/gospelizing-the-social-why-social-justice-evangelism-work-together/.

30 Ibid.

EPILOGUE: WHERE WILL THE WATER FLOW?

1 *Back to the Future*, directed by Robert Zemeckis (1985; Universal City, CA: Amblin Entertainment).

2 Liam Ryan, *Dammit Science, Where's My Hoverboard?* (London: Hardie Grant Books, 2013).

3 Michael Frost and Alan Hirsch, *The Shaping of Things to Come: Innovation and Mission for the 21st-Century Church* rev. ed. (Grand Rapids: Baker Books, 2013).

4 Robert Kiyosaki, "Future Tense," Rich Dad, December 2007, https://www.richdad.com/future-tense.

5 Ed Stetzer, "Ten Things We Must Do to Prepare for the Future of the Church," *Church Growth Magazine*, https://churchgrowthmagazine.com/ten-things-we-must-do-to-prepare-for-the-future-of-the-church/ (accessed April 27, 2023).

6 Gina Zurlo, "Global Christianity," *Undeceptions*, episode 75, podcast, https://undeceptions.com/podcast/global-christianity/?fbclid=IwAR1OdHfyLvWIt3CADjf euT9WInakSJb2PuVNIjlsd5J0JIc8_W2wPOV99ak.

7 Gina Zurlo, "Why the future of the world's largest religion is female—and African", *Religion News Service*, March 24, 2022, https://religionnews.com/2022/03/24/why-the-future-of-the-worlds-largest-religion-is-female-and-african/.

8 Ibid.

9 Philip Jenkins, *The Next Christendom: The Coming of Global Christianity* (Oxford: Oxford University Press, 2003), 199.

10 Laura Levens, "What I witnessed this week at the Asbury revival," *Baptist Global News*, February 16, 2023, https://baptistnews.com/article/what-i-witnessed-this-week-at-the-asbury-revival.

11 See, for example, Caroline Newman, "Why Millennials are Leaving Religion but Embracing Spirituality," University of Virginia, December 14, 2015, https://news.virginia.edu/content/qa-why-millennials-are-leaving-religion-embracing-spirituality.

12 See page 175 of this book.

13 Claire Giangravé, "Clergy shortage grows to more than 3k Catholics for every priest, Vatican data shows," *Religion News Service*, October 16, 2020, https://religionnews.com/2020/10/16/a-clergy-shortage-there-are-now-more-than-14k-catholics-for-every-priest-vatican-data-shows/.

14 Joseph Graham Healey, "When it comes to nurturing faith, smaller is often better," *America, the Jesuit Review*, May 24, 2016, https://www.americamagazine.org/issue/when-smaller-better.

15 See, for example, Brian Sanders, *Microchurches: A Smaller Way* (Independently Published, 2019); and https://dinnerchurch.com (accessed April 4, 2023).

16 Sandro Magister, "South Korea, the Asian Tiger of the Church," April 18, 2012, http://chiesa.espresso.repubblica.it/articolo/1350223bdc4.html?eng=y.

17 Kevin Vanhoozer, *Everyday Theology: How to Read Cultural Texts and Interpret Trends* (Grand Rapids: Baker Books, 2007), 44.

18 Ibid., 34.

19 Ibid.

20 Ibid.

21 Ibid.

22 Tevin Wax, "From Stephen Colbert to Taylor Swift: 4 Reasons I Write Cultural Commentary," The Gospel Coalition, January 14, 2016, https://www.thegospelcoalition.org/blogs/trevin-wax/from-stephen-colbert-to-taylor-swift-4-reasons-i-write-cultural-commentary/.

23 Levens, "What I witnessed this week at the Asbury revival."

24 Elaine Heath, *The Mystic Way of Evangelism: A Contemplative Vision for Christian Outreach* (Grand Rapids: Baker Books, 2017), 4.

25 Ibid.

26 Esau McCaulley, *Reading While Black: African American Biblical Interpretation as an Exercise in Hope* (Downers Grove: InterVarsity Press, 2020), 90.

27 Lesslie Newbigin, *The Good Shepherd: Meditations on Christian Ministry in Today's World* (Madras: Christian Literature Society, 1977), 62.

28 Kate Mossman, "How Family Tragedies Give Nick Cave an Awful Authenticity," *The Australian Financial Review*, December 2, 2022, https://www.afr.com/life-and-luxury/arts-and-culture/how-family-tragedies-give-nick-cave-an-awful-authenticity-20221129-p5c29o.

29   Nick Cave and Seán O'Hagan, *Faith, Hope and Carnage* (Melbourne: Text Publishing, 2022).

30   Newbigin, *The Good Shepherd*, 30.

31   Paul Sparks, Tim Soerens, and Dwight J. Friesen, *The New Parish: How Neighborhoods are Transforming Mission, Discipleship, and Community* (Downers Grove: InterVarsity Press, 2014), 24.

32   https://www.parishcollective.org/vision (accessed December 12, 2022).

33   Majora Carter and Tim Soerens, "Sign 4," https://www.parishcollective.org/5signs (accessed December 12, 2022).

34   Paul Sparks and Sunia Gibbs, "Sign 5," https://www.parishcollective.org/5signs (accessed December 12, 2022).

35   Carey Nieuwhof, "3 Things That Will Be True About Growing Churches In the Future," https://careynieuwhof.com/3-things-that-will-be-true-about-growing-churches-in-the-future/ (accessed February 3, 2023).

36   Ibid.

37   Ibid.

38   Pete Phillips, "What is Hybrid Church?" *Premier Digital*, May 5, 2021, https://www.premierdigital.info/post/what-is-hybrid-church.

39   Scot McKnight, *One Life: Jesus Calls, We Follow* (Grand Rapids: Zondervan, 2010), 31.

40   Winston Churchill, A *History of the English-Speaking Peoples IV* (London: Dodd Mead & Co., 1958), 387.

Made in the USA
Columbia, SC
03 November 2023

25447206R00167